The Sociology of

An Introductory Reader

Edited by
Eric Butterworth and David Weir

The Sociology of Modern Britain

An Introductory Reader

 Fontana/Collins

First published in Fontana 1970
Reprinted with corrections August 1970
Third impression November 1970
Fourth impression June 1971

Printed in Great Britain
For the Publishers Wm. Collins Sons & Co Ltd
14 St. James's Place, London, SW1
By Richard Clay (The Chaucer Press) Ltd
Bungay, Suffolk

Contents

4 Work

5 Class

6 Power

7 Values

Introduction

The main purpose of this book is to introduce students to the study of their own society. Sociology provides a frame of reference, an approach, which allows us to make some sense of our society even where it would be impossible to consider more than a fraction of the mass of material which is being produced about it.

An increasing number of people are taking courses on 'British society' which have a bearing on their training or reflect their concern to understand social processes, and social functions which affect them. For many, given the reading available, this may reflect a heavy diet of factual material (the number of households, rate of divorce, circulation of newspapers and the like) which becomes largely concerned with what is rather than with how or why. It tends to lose out on sociological perspective and relevance. For a smaller number the diet is excessively rich in the esoteric ramifications of fashionable theories, and this presents problems of a different nature.

It is our view that the two diets mentioned are equally unsatisfactory for the student who is a beginner. He may have had no previous intensive contact with the social sciences. However he has lived in this society, or one similar to it, all his life. Our decision to compile the book arose from our experience in teaching a wide range of students, most of whom were adults, in University Extra-Mural and internal settings, on professional courses of many kinds, and in other educational institutions. We recognized a number of factors which made the courses on this theme less satisfactory than they might have been. Our book is an attempt to remedy some of these deficiencies.

In the first place the teacher has to begin where the student happens to be, with a particular experience of life and a system of beliefs and attitudes which help him to explain that experience. He has already views about his society, although they may be misinformed or based on untenable assumptions about how things happen. He requires in this situation, it seems to us, material which allows him to examine some of the preconceptions he has. As Walter Lippmann, the American writer, has said: 'For the most part we do not first see, and then define, we define first and then see. We are told about the world before we see it. We imagine most things before we experience them. And these preconceptions, unless education has made us acutely aware, govern deeply the whole process of perception.'

This is an *introductory* Reader. Had we been trying to meet the needs of University students near the end of their courses our selection would have been quite different in a number of respects. An attempt has been made to introduce a range of topics and approaches, with a balance between what is descriptive and what is analytical and conceptual. One chapter, on values, has been provided specifically to offer opportunities for the discussion of many of the areas of study where preconceptions which reveal much about the social attitudes and 'political' stance of the student are most likely to be found. Everyone has views about what is happening to the family, our educational system, the Welfare State, and the 'Condition of Britain' question, and in some courses it may be desirable for the teacher to start from here.

Every chapter has an introductory section which is designed to pose some of the important questions which arise in the particular context of our Readings without providing a detailed commentary on all the relevant sociological concepts and issues. To some extent these arise in Readings, but the book can be used most profitably in conjunction with one of the text-books in current use. The Textbook Reference section at the end contains detailed page references to the most relevant themes that any of the courses for which we are catering will wish to cover, irrespective of whether we have specific Readings on all of them.

The Readings follow the introductory section in each

chapter. Because of the audience it was felt unnecessary to reproduce the detailed footnotes and references many of them contained. As far as possible references in the text to authors or books have either been included in the Further Reading at the end of the relevant chapter or omitted altogether. The common practice of numbering tables according to their place in the particular Reading rather than the numbers to be found in the work from which they are taken has been followed.

As far as further reading is concerned, we concentrate on books which are reasonably easy to obtain. Many are in paperback, and using our source-book it would be possible to obtain a wide range of material quite cheaply. In the Further Reading at the end of this section suggestions are made for two kinds of books: one is of reference material, on Modern Britain, containing a great deal of information on aspects of the social structure, though not necessarily informed by a specifically sociological standpoint, and the other of general introductory material to the study of society or the sociological viewpoint.

Several criteria have guided us in the course of our selection of Readings. Readability is one of these, and although there are varying degrees of difficulty represented it is hoped that the most difficult can be tackled successfully with the help of the references provided. The variations in the level of the Readings, and the different approaches to be found in them, are not fortuitous: they are designed to pose questions from which every student must start. Some are deliberately short, lending themselves to class discussion; others may be more properly studied independently. The authors have used most of the Readings for teaching purposes over a period of several years. In some cases the Readings deal with similar material from different points of view, and this is a deliberate policy to make links between themes which cut across the boundaries of chapters, and reinforce, for example, the sense of interrelationships between social institutions and an awareness of the cumulative consequences of social change.

In our experience of introductory courses, much original and relevant work never finds its way to the student body, even though it may be mentioned in the reading lists. University libraries may have only single copies of a journal containing an article recommended to many students. The problems are much worse in other educational settings. Often these may be compounded by the teaching of the subject by teachers not themselves trained in it who feel equally in need of a frame of reference. Systematic teaching demands this. Too often, perhaps, subjects may be introduced to students as a series of disconnected episodes of merely intrinsic interest. We have chosen work which is not on the whole readily available to the student, often from journals and books to which he is unlikely to have access. We have avoided choosing from paperbacks which are cheap though in one or two cases books have reappeared in paperback after our original selection was made. Some comparative material on the United States and Britain has been introduced, as has material by Americans about Britain.

There are many personal elements which arise in making a choice of Readings and we have tried to be explicit about some of them, but our focus throughout has been upon the specific needs and requirements of the students taking introductory courses, largely in non-University settings. The audience we have aimed at covers a wide range. There are members of the general public whose interest in the nature of their society may have been stimulated by television programmes, colour supplements and the like. These may or may not move on to adult classes, or courses of study, such as those provided by the Open University Extra-Mural Departments, by the W.E.A., and by local authorities. Many students at Colleges of Education, Technical Colleges and Colleges of Further Education undertake general introductory courses in Sociology, much of the content of which relates to Britain, and this is beginning to develop in the sixth forms of some schools. Professional or pre-professional courses of training, in-service and refresher courses for such groups as hospital administrators, nurses and social workers, are more and more common. As the amount of this provision in the social sciences increases, the problems of teaching it and gaining access to relevant material become, if anything, greater than they have been before.

It is hoped that this source-book of Readings will go some way to meeting some of the needs of students and teachers involved in the kinds of courses we have mentioned. Its value will depend on the extent to which it is used, and we would welcome comments and criticisms from those teaching or studying in this field.

We should like to thank the many colleagues, friends and students with whom we discussed the book. Barbara Hutchinson dealt efficiently with numerous administrative problems; she also typed large parts of the manuscript, as did Eileen Lee. Our wives Ann Butterworth and Mary Weir deserve a special debt of gratitude for their tolerance of all the collaborative meetings between us.

Acknowledgements to authors, editors and publishers are included in the headings to the readings. We should like to point out that the readings are in most cases extracted from or shortened versions of the originals.

Eric Butterworth and David Weir

October, 1969

Further Reading and Reference

Modern Britain

J. A. BANKS (ed.): *Studies in British Society*, London, Routledge and Kegan Paul, 1969.

† A. CARR SAUNDERS, D. C. JONES AND C. A. MOSER: *A Survey of Social Conditions in England and Wales*, Oxford University Press, 1958.

* R. K. KELSALL: *Population*, London, Longmans, 1968.

D. C. MARSH: *The Changing Structure of England and Wales, 1871–1961*, London, Routledge and Kegan Paul, 1965.

† A. T. WELFORD et al. (eds.): *Society*, London, Routledge and Kegan Paul, 1962.

Introduction to Sociology

* P. BERGER: *Invitation to Sociology*, London, Penguin Books, 1966.

* E. CHINOY: *Sociological Perspective*, New York, Random House, 17th imp., 1967.

C. WRIGHT MILLS: *The Sociological Imagination*, New York, Oxford University Press, 1959 and London, Penguin Books, 1970.

* Available in paperback
† Reference

Chapter One **Family**

The word family means many things to different people. It is usual to think of it as composed of husband, wife and their children. This is the *nuclear* family which is the normal household unit in Britain. Members of this family are usually biologically related, though this is not invariably the case: the institution of adoption provides the same legal basis as for any other family. There are differences in the way the term nuclear family is used: in most cases it refers to parents and children living together but sometimes it is used to describe members of a nuclear family wherever they might happen to be.

Most people are members of two families during their lives. The first is the family of *origin* (or orientation) in which our earliest experiences take place. The second is the family of *marriage* (or procreation) in which we play the roles of parents. The functions of the family involve on the one hand internal processes, the ways in which the family operates as a system of relationships and on the other those which relate to the wider society.

In common with other advanced industrial societies of the West the nuclear family is the primary unit but the extended family can still remain important. This term refers to a grouping which is wider than the nuclear family but involves those related by marriage or kinship. The studies of Bethnal Green by Young and Willmott and Townsend referred to in Further Reading, provide interesting evidence for the continuing vitality of one kind of extended family. Among some immigrant groups to Britain, for example Pakistanis and Indians, the norm remains the joint family based on the authority, for certain defined purposes, of the head of this three-generation grouping, but in practice more and more begin to live in modified forms of the nuclear family, possibly with certain relatives present in the household unit. The definition of household used in the ten-yearly census is: 'one person living alone or a group of persons living together, partaking of meals prepared together and benefiting from a common housekeeping'.

It is important to see social institutions such as the family not in monolithic terms but as changing rapidly in certain ways. Advertising portrays the image of what Dr. Leach in his 1967 Reith Lectures on the family and marriage referred to as 'the cereal packet norm'—the family which includes young children. The first Reading arises from research undertaken by Rosser and Harris in the Swansea area which demonstrates that this period takes up less than half of the normal cycle of family life. In future this stage of procreation (phase II) will take up a smaller proportion of the family cycle because of changes which result from earlier ages of marriage, fewer children born within a shorter period, and greater expectation of life. As Rosser and Harris point out each phase of the cycle has its characteristic patterns of household composition, family behaviour and social participation in the life of the community.

The work of Elizabeth Bott from which the second Reading is taken arose from her intensive study of twenty families in London reflecting different structures and forms of organization. As she points out, all three of the types of organization she discusses were found in all families but the relative amounts varied considerably. She relates the type of organization which predominates in a family to the external social relationships of its members. One implication from her work is that if the family moves from the area where husband and wife have connected social networks and segregated roles to perform to another where they are on their own as a nuclear family this is likely to have consequences for their roles and their way of life. The move from Bethnal Green to Greenleigh in Young and Willmott's *Family and Kinship* illustrates this from a rather different point of view.

The relationships which develop within the family are influenced by the experience and expectations of its members and the kind of work, for example, which its adult members undertake. Tunstall, on the Hull fisherman, shows how much the husband's job influences relationships between members of his family and how attitudes to pay shaped within the family carry over to labour-management relationships. The next Reading, about dock-work in the Port of Manchester, shows how a system involving irregular hours had a bearing on the high regard of the docker for family life and an attitude and knowledge of his children far more intimate than that achieved by the fisherman. De-casualization of dock-work will obviously change this situation in a number of respects.

Another example of the close-knit comradeship of a group which, like the fishermen, arises from their contact not only in the work-situation but also in the neighbourhood and in their leisure activities is to be found in the study of Featherstone, a mining district in Yorkshire, featured in the Reading in Chapter IV by Dennis, Henriques and Slaughter. A contrast with these working-class situations is provided in part of the Reading by Hubert later in this chapter when she discusses the independence, before marriage, of the middle-class girl.

The thesis put forward by Dennis in the third Reading about relationships is that the family is the only social institution in an increasingly specialized society in which people are perceived and valued as whole persons, and marriage the only place where the individual can expect esteem and love. The emphasis upon this and upon sociability helps to account for the increasing popularity of marriage even when the divorce rates are rising. It is suggested that romantic love becomes the only valid basis for marriage, unlike the situation which prevails among minorities from Asia living in Britain where marriage is to be viewed as an alliance between families of roughly equivalent social status. A dynastic view of marriage among 'top people' is part of the subject-matter of the Reading by Lupton and Wilson in Chapter VI.

The discussion of romantic love is taken further by Little. He shows how the link between love and marriage which is now taken for granted is the product of historical circumstances and what functions this has in delimiting the area of responsibility for the individual more successfully than is possible in societies whose kinship patterns reflect much more detailed and wide-ranging obligations to a wider range of kinsfolk.

A substantial number of people do not experience a 'normal' family situation, either as children or adults, for a variety of reasons. The Reading by Illsley and Thompson shows the varieties of experience and structure which may be collected together under the unsatisfactory blanket term 'broken homes'. Among the factors which have to be taken into account are how the home was broken, the ages of the children, and the diversity of their subsequent upbringing. Some effects were social and others economic or psychological. One of the findings of the authors on this evidence from Aberdeen is that the conditions were least favourable as a whole for children who were illegitimate, those brought up in institutions, and children of separated and divorced parents.

Among the broken homes were those which were a consequence of the death of a parent. The next Reading is concerned with the loss of a husband for widows with young children and the consequences for them in terms not only of economic position but also of their social situation. Marris provides a sensitive and perceptive view of the condition of widowhood that can be compared with other forms of singleness, whether voluntary or enforced. His sample was drawn from those areas of London mentioned in connection with the books by Young and Willmott. He concludes that the adjustment to widowhood is more a concern to achieve an independent status rather than remarriage or other forms of companionship available to the widow.

Kinship and the wider bonds of family are seen in two contrasting settings. Loudon deals with an area in the Vale of Glamorgan and the way in which shared kinship connections and gossip provide a social cement for the established, setting them off from newcomers who are unaware of kinship links. His reference to 'affines' (the spouse and other relatives in law) raises the question of the terminology of kinship. This is covered in Turner's *Family and Kinship in Modern Britain* referred to in Further Reading. Although it has been assumed that kinship among the middle class is less important than among working-class groups there is evidence to suggest that despite the fact that kinship may involve different things for the middle classes it remains important. Hubert suggests that frequency of contact, for instance, cannot, among the middle class, be taken in isolation as the criterion of a close relationship. In her sample from Highgate in London it was not possible to assume that ties of affection were unimportant even where contact was infrequent. The interchange of daily services played little part in the lives of those interviewed.

The impact of the wider society is felt in all kinds of ways. There are more opportunities for women to go out to work, and for a variety of reasons including greater levels of aspiration and economic hardship the patterns of family life change to meet these new requirements. In some areas, such as the centres of the textile industry in Lancashire and Yorkshire, and the Potteries, there has been a long tradition of women working but elsewhere this has developed more recently. Those women wishing to work full-time face many difficulties. The inevitable compromise between what women would like to do and what is practicable or necessary may lead to unfortunate features of the family situation where a number of adverse factors are combined. There is a lack of provision of nursery accommodation, for example, for women who have to work full-time either because they have no husband living with them or because the husband is an invalid. Arising out of the Reading by Yudkin and Holme are many questions about attitudes towards the mothers of children of school age working and also about the role of women in society. The study by Myrdal and Klein of *Women's Two Roles* discusses the latter issue, with a wealth of comparative material. The relevance of many of these questions to social policy is apparent.

A rather different view of the cycle of family life from that contained in the reading by Rosser and Harris is to be found in the contribution by Abrams. He is concerned in particular with the stages of the life cycle, especially as these relate to the economic position of the family. He discusses the way in which increased leisure affects the sort of goods and services provided and suggests that consumption displaces birth, education and occupation as the basis of social class differences. This can be contrasted with some of the Readings in Chapter V which emphasize different points of view. At the same time the question of how far consumption has displaced or influenced class position is one it is worthwhile to pursue.

Finally the Reading from Hole and Attenburrow looks at the affluence of the present day as this is reflected in consumer expenditure. Contrasts between Britain and the United States emerge and some factual basis is provided for our consideration of social changes which affect expenditure on the home.

Family Structure 1
C. Rosser and C. C. Harris

Reprinted with permission from C. Rosser and C. C. Harris: *The Family and Social Change*, London, Routledge and Kegan Paul, 1965, pp. 164–7.

So far we have been examining the composition of the households in which our subjects lived at the time of our survey. For purposes of analysis and exposition, we have classified these into a series of 'household types', following the categories used by Young and Willmott in their study of Bethnal Green. The result is an essentially static, 'snap-shot' view of Swansea at a particular point in time. We must now emphasize the somewhat obvious, but neglected, point that from the point of view of individual families these are not separate 'household types' but phases in a continuous cycle of development. Domestic groups are 'born' at marriage, expand with births, reach a sort of climax as the period of procreation is passed and as the children grow to maturity, and decline as the children marry and 'leave the nest' to found elementary families (and separate domestic groups) of their own. The original domestic group finally disintegrates with the death of one or both of the original partners. This is the normal and universal familial process. With each phase of the cycle, the composition of the domestic group alters—as children are born, or as they leave home on marriage (or bring in their spouses to form composite households). This natural and continuous rhythm of the successive generations must obviously underlie any discussion either of household composition or of family relationships external to the individual household. Here in this endless process are the essential dynamics of family life. It is of course a continuous process within each individual family, though it can without great difficulty be divided into a series of arbitrary but recognizable phases, much as can the life-span of a particular individual. As there are 'seven ages of man', so there seem to be four ages of the family. In the table, we show the phases into which we have divided this continuous and repetitive cycle of growth and decline, together with the numbers and proportions of the persons in our Swansea sample who fell by our definitions into each phase (taking married persons only of course, since marriage is the starting point of the cycle):

Table 1. The Family Cycle

Family Phase	Definition	Numbers in our Sample	Percentage of total
Phase I: Home-Making	From marriage to the birth of the first child	297	17
Phase II: Procreation	From the birth of first child to the marriage of the first child	808	47
Phase III: Dispersion	From the marriage of the first child to the marriage of the last child	262	16
Phase IV: Final	From marriage of last child to death of original partners	358	20
Total		1,725	100

We have taken these particular beginning and ending points for the four phases because they can be easily identified for the persons in our sample, and because of course they do represent clear and distinct milestones in the progress of an individual family through this typical cycle. In the average case, with marriage about the age of 23, the first phase lasts about two years, the second about twenty-three years (since it is from the birth to marriage of the first child). The length of the final two phases depends on the number of children born and on the facts of longevity. There have been dramatic changes in this average and normal family cycle over the last half-century or so with the striking decline in family size and the marked improvement in life-expectancies. And it is useful in order to clarify and emphasize these changes, particularly those in family size, to divide Phase II which we have called the Phase of Procreation into two sub-phases—'child-bearing' during which births are actually occurring, and 'child-rearing' in which the children born are growing to maturity. It is the very great shortening of the actual period of child-bearing, comparing say the present generation of women with that of their grandmothers, which has produced the most marked change in this family cycle.

Each age or phase has its characteristic pattern of household composition, of family behaviour, and of social participation in the life of the community of which the family concerned is a component. The dominant social characteristic of the first phase is that it is a period of very considerable adjustments and re-arrangements in relationships, particularly with the sudden arrival on the scene of a new set of relatives—the in-laws. Our survey revealed that the majority of marriages begin with the newly-married couple living temporarily with relatives, more often than not in the home of the bride's parents. Hence characteristically this first phase of the family cycle is often spent wholly or partly in a composite household. In the second phase of the cycle, the characteristic domestic group for the larger part of this period consists of parents and dependent children, though towards the end of this phase it is not uncommon for a composite household covering three generations to be again formed with an elderly parent or parents from either the wife's or the husband's side (more usually the former) coming to live with the family.

The Phase of Dispersion begins with the marriage of the first child and continues until all the children are married. As the children marry and leave home, the domestic group goes through a period of declining size, though commonly the size of the group may expand temporarily as one or other of the married children starts off marriage by bringing the spouse into the parental household. The partial rupture of relationships characteristic of this phase may thus be softened by the formation of a temporary composite household. When all the children have in fact married, even if they have not all left home, the family concerned has entered the last phase of the cycle—and in most cases the original couple find themselves on their own once more.

This, briefly expressed, is of course a model of the life-cycle covering the normal or typical case. There are, it scarcely needs to be emphasized, numerous variations in practice on this general model of the four ages of the family. Some persons never marry and thus never enter on this cycle. Others marry but never have any children and are thus permanently halted as it were in the first phase. In other cases the cycle is abnormal through the death of one or both partners early in the marriage, or through 'broken homes' produced by separations or divorces (though these latter accounted for only 1.5 per cent of the cases in our sample). In yet others, one or more of the children may never marry and remain permanently in the parental home—the case for example of the spinster daughter living with and caring for her elderly father and mother, or of the bachelor son maintaining the home for his widowed mother. In some cases the couple concerned may have well above the 'normal' number of children which will affect in their case the length of the two final phases. These many variations are, however, minority instances. In the vast majority of cases the process that we have outlined above does in fact represent the pattern of family development over the succeeding generations.

Family Structure 2
E. Bott

Reprinted with permission from E. Bott: *Family and Social Network*, London, Tavistock Publications, 1957, pp. 52–61.

The organization of familial activities can be classified in many ways. I find it useful to speak of 'complementary', 'independent', and 'joint' organization. In complementary organization, the activities of husband and wife are different and separate but fitted together to form a whole. In independent organization, activities are carried out separately by husband and wife without reference to each other, in so far as this is possible. In joint organization, activities are carried out by husband and wife together, or the same activity is carried out by either partner at different times.

All three types of organization were found in all families. In fact, familial tasks could not be carried out if this were not so. But the relative amounts of each type of organization varied from one family to another. The phrase *segregated conjugal role-relationship* is here used for a relationship in which complementary and independent types of organization predominate. Husband and wife have a clear differentiation of tasks and a considerable number of separate interests and activities. They have a clearly defined division of labour into male tasks and female tasks. They expect to have different leisure pursuits, and the husband has his friends outside the home and the wife has hers. The phrase *joint conjugal role-relationship* is here used for a relationship in which joint organization is relatively predominant. Husband and wife expect to carry out many activities together with a minimum of task differentiation and separation of interests. They not only plan the affairs of the family together but also exchange many household tasks and spend much of their leisure time together.

Among the research couples, there were some general resemblances in the type of organization characteristically followed in a particular type of activity but, within these broad limits, there was a great deal of variation. Thus in all families there was a basic division of labour, by which the husband was primarily responsible for supporting the family financially and the wife was primarily responsible for housework and childcare; each partner made his own differentiated but complementary contribution to the welfare of the family as a whole. But within this general division of labour, there was considerable variation of detail. Some wives worked, others did not. Some families had a very flexible division of labour in housework and childcare by which many tasks were shared or interchangeable, whereas other families had a much stricter division into the wife's tasks and the husband's tasks.

Similarly, there were some activities, such as making important decisions that would affect the whole family, that tended to be carried out jointly by husband and wife. But here too there was considerable variation. Some husbands and wives placed great emphasis on joint decision, whereas others hardly mentioned it. Couples who stressed the importance of joint decisions also had many shared and interchangeable tasks in housework and childcare.

In activities such as recreation, including here entertaining and visiting people as well as hobbies, reading, going to the cinema, concerts, and so forth, there was so much variation that it is impossible to say that one form of organization was consistently dominant in all families.

The research couples made it clear that there had been important changes in their degree of conjugal segregation during their married life. In the first phase, before they had children, all couples had had far more joint activities, especially in the form of shared recreation outside the home. After their children were born the activities of all couples had become more sharply differentiated and they had had to cut down on joint external recreation. Data from the group discussions with wives in the third phase, when the children were adolescent and leaving home, suggest that most husbands and wives do not return to the extensive joint organization of the first phase even when the necessity for differentiation produced by the presence of young children is no longer great.

But the differences in degree of segregation of conjugal roles among the research families cannot be attributed to differences in phase of development, because all the families were in more or less the same phase. Early in the research, it seemed likely that these differences were related in some way or another to forces in the social environment of the families. In first attempts to explore these forces an effort was made to explain conjugal segregation in terms of social class. This attempt was not very successful. The husbands who had the most segregated role-relationships with their wives had manual occupations, and the husbands who had the most joint role-relationships with their wives were professional or semi-professional people; but there were several working-class families that had relatively little segregation, and there were professional families in which segregation was considerable. Having a working-class occupation is a necessary but not a sufficient cause of the most marked degree of conjugal segregation. An attempt was also made to relate degree of segregation to the type of local area in which the family lived, since the data suggested that the families with most segregation lived in homogeneous areas of low population turnover, whereas the families with predominantly joint role-relationships lived in heterogeneous areas of high population turnover. Once again, however, there were several exceptions.

Because I could not understand the relationship between conjugal segregation, social class, and neighbourhood composition, I put social class and neighbourhood composition to one side for the time being and turned to look more closely at the immediate environment of the families, that is, at their actual external relationships with friends, neighbours, relatives, clubs, shops, places of work, and so forth. This approach proved more fruitful.

First it appeared that the external social relationships of all families assumed the form of a network rather than the form of an organized group. In an organized group, the component individuals make up a larger social whole with common aims, interdependent roles, and a distinctive subculture. In network formation, on the other hand, only some, not all, of the component individuals have social relationships with one another.

For example, supposing that a family, X, maintains relationships with friends, neighbours, and relatives who may be designated as A, B, C, D, E, F . . . N, one will find that some but not all of these external persons know one another. They do not form an organized group in the sense defined above. B might know A and C but none of the others; D might know F without knowing A, B, or E. Furthermore, all of these persons will have friends, neighbours, and relatives of their own who are not known by family X. In a network the component external units do not make up a larger social whole; they are not surrounded by a common boundary.

Second, although all the research families belonged to networks rather than to groups, there was considerable variation in the 'connectedness' of their networks. By connectedness, I mean the extent to which the people known by a family know and meet one another independently of the family. I use the word 'close-knit' to describe a network in which there are many relationships among the component units, and the word 'loose-knit' to describe a network in which there are few such relationships. Strictly speaking, 'close-knit' should read 'close-knit relative to the networks of the other research families,' and 'loose-knit' should read 'loose-knit relative to the networks of the other research families.' The shorter terms are used to simplify the language, but it should be remembered that they are shorthand expressions of relative degrees of connectedness and that they are not intended to be conceived as polar opposites.

A qualitative examination of the research data suggests that the degree of segregation of conjugal roles is related to the degree of connectedness in the total network of the family. Those families that had a high degree of segregation in the role-relationship of husband and wife had a close-knit network; many of their friends, neighbours, and relatives knew one another. Families that had a relatively joint role-relationship between husband and wife had a loose-knit network; few of their relatives, neighbours, and friends knew one another. There were many degrees of variation between these two extremes. On the basis of our data. I should therefore like to put forward the following hypothesis: the degree of segregation in the role-relationship of husband and wife varies directly with the connectedness of the family's social network. The more connected the network, the greater the degree of segregation between the roles of husband and wife. The less connected the network, the smaller the degree of segregation between the roles of husband and wife.

At first sight this seems to be an odd relationship, for it is hard to see why the social relationship of other people with one another should affect the relationship of husband and wife. What seems to happen is this. When many of the people a person knows interact with one another—that is, when the person's network is close-knit—the members of his network tend to reach consensus on norms and they exert consistent informal pressure on one another to conform to the norms, to keep in touch with one another, and, if need be, to help one another. If both husband and wife come to marriage with such close-knit networks, and if conditions are such that the previous pattern of relationships is continued, the marriage will be super-imposed on these pre-existing relationships, and both spouses will continue to be drawn into activities with people outside their own elementary family (family of pro-creation). Each will get some emotional satisfaction from these external relationships and will be likely to demand correspondingly less of the spouse. Rigid segregation of con-jugal roles will be possible because each spouse can get help from people outside.

But when most of the people a person knows do not interact with one another, that is, when his network is loose-knit, more variation on norms is likely to develop in the network, and social control and mutual assistance will be more fragmented and less consistent. If husband and wife come to marriage with such loose-knit networks or if conditions are such that their networks become loose-knit after marriage, they must seek in each other some of the emotional satisfactions and help with familial tasks that couples in close-knit networks can get from outsiders. Joint organization becomes more necessary for the success of the family as an enterprise.

Relationships 1
J. Tunstall

Reprinted with permission from J. Tunstall: *The Fisherman*, London, MacGibbon & Kee, 1962, pp. 160–5.

For three-quarters of her days the fisherman's wife is apart from her husband. Her main preoccupation is usually children and she is likely to have a slightly larger family than those of other working-class women. For instance, in sixty fishing families where the husband was in his thirties, the average number of children was over three—and many of the wives would, of course, later have more children.

While he is at sea the fisherman arranges for a regular weekly amount of money to be sent to his wife. The man can choose any amount he likes but any fisherman who allots his wife less than the whole of his basic wage is likely to become an object of derision to his mates. Many men allot their wives as much as £10 a week. In addition, husbands tend to buy substantial items like furniture and children's clothing.

A fisherman's wife, therefore, tends to be slightly better off than her neighbour—particularly since she does not have to feed her husband for a large part of the time. That she has comparatively more money than her neighbours, and probably more children, both contribute to the fact that few fishermen's wives go out to work.

The fishermen themselves are invariably against their wives working. When ashore, a fisherman likes to have all his meals cooked by his wife, and since his turn-round time between trips is more often than not in the middle of the week, this alone prevents his wife going out to work. But even in the fish processing houses, which are often willing to let women come and go very casually, and would not object to a woman taking three days off every three weeks, few fishermen's wives are found at work. Fishermen often think it is an insult to their capacity, or perhaps to their status as men, if their wives go out to work. What is the point of his sacrifice, his willingness to go fishing and to accept its hardships in order to get money, if his wife then decides to go out to work as well? Fishermen say quite frankly that they are jealous of their wives going out and meeting men—which would of course happen at work. Similarly, most fishermen while at sea discourage their wives from going out in the evenings. They are often critical too of the extent to which their wives visit their own mothers. But they accept mothers-in-law at worst as a necessary evil.

When her husband is at sea the wife needs understanding, companionship, help with her children, and a chance of escaping sometimes from what is otherwise the prison of her home. In the majority of cases these needs are satisfied by her mother. It seems to be usually only when the mother is dead, or does not live in Hull, or herself goes out to work, that the woman has to turn to a sister, perhaps, or a neighbour. When the woman's own family begin to grow up—especially when her eldest daughter is old enough to help in the house and to become a female gossip-partner—she may see less of her mother; although fishermen's wives are far from neglectful when their mother's help in domestic tasks is no longer required. Without exception, every fisherman's wife I interviewed, who had at least two children under ten years of age, and a mother alive in Hull, saw the mother regularly.

The fisherman's wife organizes her life around the task of bringing up her children—and this inevitably becomes in many ways more important than her other main task of looking after her husband during the ninety days or so each year when he is ashore.

The fisherman remains something of a stranger to his children. Men at sea talk a good deal about their 'bairns' but the attitude seems disinterested and more like that of an uncle than a father. Some men try to compensate for their absence by giving lavish presents to their children. One fisherman, complaining he was seldom home, said: 'The wife told me not long ago that my little daughter asked, "Mummy, who's that man who comes to stay with us?"'

During the last decade fishermen made up about 2½% of the working men of Hull and East Riding, but accounted for about 5% of the divorces. This is hardly surprising in view of the strains inevitably imposed on the fisherman's marriage.

In many cases, it seems to be at the beginning of (or immediately before) the marriage that the conflict between the man and the woman is greatest. The fisherman does not usually have many interests in common with his wife. Some men quickly come to regard their wives merely as providers of sexual and cooking services, in return for a weekly wage. With the passage of time, however, conflict tends to be reduced.

Among fishermen a rough agreement exists as to what is reasonable behaviour for a fisherman in his marriage. It is widely believed that during a turn-round time of three days between trips, a man should spend some time with his wife apart from eating and sleeping with her. On the other hand it is regarded as unusual for a fisherman to spend all three evenings with his wife. Men who only go out drinking when accompanied by their wives tend to regard themselves as unusually virtuous.

Strain is exerted on the marriage by the contrast between what happens when a fisherman has three days' turn-round time and when he has three weeks or more out of a ship. Wives say that a husband, who the last time home spent £40 in three days, now begs for money to buy cigarettes.

Fishing homes usually show evidence of recent decorating, painting, wallpapering—and wives usually report that this has been done by the man. Most fishermen find themselves doing such jobs, behaving indeed like the prototype 'companion' husband. But even though many fishermen at such times adopt more humble roles in the home, it seems to be during these periods that conflict really develops. We have already seen that when a fisherman comes home he disrupts the normal routine. At first this is welcome, he comes bearing gifts for the children. His coming is the main event by which the passage of time in the home is marked, he brings the family into focus.

The fisherman's marriage is shaped by his occupation. The very sequence of his presence and absence is determined by his trawler trips. But also his marriage comes to shape his attitude to work. The motives which sent a boy fishing in the first place are different from those which continue to make a man go fishing in later years. These motives are inevitably bound up with his marriage. After he has been ashore a while the fisherman feels that certain pressures are being exerted on him to go back. Money is shorter. 'Dole and rebate' usually is only roughly the same as the weekly 'wage' the wife receives when he is at sea, and the total sum declines progressively. The man inevitably finds himself differently regarded by his wife after a week or two from how she regarded him after a day or two.

As he goes back to sea again he cannot help feeling that these two things—the smaller amount of cash and his wife's different attitude—are suspiciously closely related. Does the wife only want him when he has money? When he is there more than a few days why does she grow weary of him? Why is he going to sea just to pay that ungrateful wife and her children? 'Legalized prostitution'. One sees the point and it explains why fishermen say so often and so savagely that women are just 'money-grabbing bitches' and less polite things. 'My wife is all "Gimme, Gimme",' one man commented.

The consequences of his marriage feed back into the structure of the industry a number of important implications. Though the fisherman may give more than just his basic wage to his wife, there still remains the belief that the basic wage is hers and the rest is his. This is why the fisherman says that his pay has never been put up for years. (The poundage payment between 1947 and 1960 has changed only from 11s. 6d. to 12s. 9d. per £100 of the catch's auction price.) If you point out that the basic rate has gone up a number of times the fisherman says that the basic goes to his wife.

Thus fishermen come to distrust increases in the basic, and might distrust even more a large negotiated increase in the basic rates to compensate a drop in the poundage. In this way attitudes to pay, which are shaped in the context of the family, carry over into the field of trade unionism and labour-management relations.

Relationships 2
Members of the Liverpool University Department of Social Science

Reprinted with permission from Liverpool University Department of Social Science: *The Dock Worker*, Liverpool, The University Press, 1954, pp. 48–50.

A traditional pattern of family life and of association between work and home developed in this area in the days of casual employment. The difficulty of obtaining a regular job made it impossible for the dock worker and his family to establish the mode of living based upon a regular system of working hours which is characteristic of modern industrial society. The dock worker was in and out of his house at all hours of the day, passing on information about what was happening on the docks and finding out for himself what was going on at home and amongst his neighbours. The routine followed by the dock worker's wife in her housework was directly affected by the hours her busband worked and by the kind of cargoes he handled. The children saw a lot of their father; and living near the docks they were familiar with the work he did and interested in the comings and goings of the different ships. The fluctuations in wages made a direct impact on household budgeting; the dock worker who was able to bring home to his wife a regular weekly wage was such an exceptional person that he acquired status in the community, both for himself and for his family. When dock workers went on strike, their whole families were affected, not only because of the financial hardship which followed, but also because the conduct of the father in relation to the strike affected the position of the family in the community. The family of the strike leader was given high status and his wife and children often assumed leadership roles in their own particular spheres. On the other hand, the family of the 'blackleg' who remained at work was subjected to abuse and ignominy and suffered as much as, if not more than, the man himself.

The close association between home and work which thus became characteristic of the dockside community has meant that the dock worker has developed a great interest in and high regard for family life. During the Manchester study, the investigators were impressed by the interest that dock workers showed in their families, for nearly all the men interviewed, both old and young, spoke freely and enthusiastically about their homes and children. Traditionally, the father is the unquestioned head of the household; and from what could be found out in Salford it seems that the older dock workers, at least, still occupy this position. Many of them have married children living with them, for it is as difficult for young couples to find new homes here as elsewhere, and all who live in the house have to conform to the standards set by the father, who is often referred to as 'the boss' by the other members of the family.

A patriarchal family structure is often associated with the tradition of son following father in the same occupation. The Port of Manchester is not yet old enough for more than three generations of the same family to be connected with it; even so, 75 per cent of the dock workers interviewed were sons of dock workers. About 10 per cent of the men interviewed had entered the docks when they married dock workers' daughters; some were themselves dock workers' sons but had been introduced into dock work by their fathers-in-law or brothers-in-law, rather than by their own fathers. This was most frequent where the husband had gone to live with his wife's family on marriage.

Relationships 3
N. Dennis

Reprinted with permission from *International Journal of Comparative Sociology*, Vol. II, 1962, pp. 86–8.

The need which can be satisfied *outside* the family with increasing difficulty only is the need to participate in a relationship where people are perceived and valued as whole persons.

In urban industrial society it is necessary to collaborate with one set of people in order to earn a living, with another to worship, with a third set to be educated, with a fourth for amusement, with a fifth in seeing to the affairs of the neighbourhood, and so on. Minute differentiation of function is the secret of productivity. But the one thing which this type of organization of roles cannot 'produce' are the values of what Toennies called 'mutual furtherance and affirmation'. In the elaboration of modern social institutions, marriage has become the only place in which the individual can demand and expect esteem and love. Adults have no one on whom they have a right to lean for this sort of support at all comparable to their right to lean on their spouse. The marriage relation, to a far greater extent than in systems where communal type solidarities exist between fellow-workmen, neighbours, and extended kin categories, is in a strategic position in this respect.

In contributing to one another love, dignity and emotional support in spite of failures in specific roles or particular tasks, the spouses are fundamentally alike. Yet this is a special case of cooperation where likeness of contribution nevertheless produces great interdependence. This is so for two reasons. Unlike, say, housework, where the task could be carried out by a single person, and more than one person does it for reasons of convenience, sociability essentially requires the interplay of feelings for its fruition. The man and woman give each other something they could not provide for themselves. Unlike, say, sexual intercourse, which is possible in casual liaisons, companionship needs time and conditions suited to the emergence of primary-type ties, and these conditions do not flourish outside the family. James Thurber's 'One is a Wanderer' well describes the futility in the big city of the search for companionship outside of the family setting. Not only is it practically difficult to find communal satisfactions in modern society. The norms do not allow men and women not married to one another to indulge in tender companionate relationships. Any friendship between males tends to be stigmatized by attributing to it a homosexual basis. These rules are functional. They prevent obligations arising in communal type relationships from contaminating complex and fractionalized utilitarian relationships in the economy and in society at large.

The changing grounds of recruitment to the role of spouse support this interpretation. Sentiments turn increasingly towards the notion of romantic love as not just preferable but as the inevitable and only valid basis for marriage. Values emphasize personal response to the exclusion of economic advancement or social standing. A second tendency has been the increased obscurity of standards of choice where these are not connected with the romantic motif. 'In all the conversation about courtship there appears to be a lack of any definite criteria for liking or disliking . . . expectations which are vague and diffuse are more easily met and adjustment between husband and wife . . . may therefore be less difficult than in cases where both partners know exactly what they want'.

The divorce figures themselves support this interpretation. Primary relations which are sought for themselves, as contrasted with those which emerge as the by-product of other cooperative activities, are difficult to sustain. The well documented and much discussed 'loss of functions' of the family has reduced the possible volume of by-product primary group satisfactions. It is not surprising therefore that the divorce figures should have reached their present level. When people marry under the influence of romantic love, as Bertrand Russell has said, 'each imagines the other to be possessed of more than mortal perfections and conceives that marriage is going to be one long dream of bliss. . . . In America, where the romantic view of marriage has been taken more seriously than anywhere else, and where law and custom alike are based on the dreams of spinsters, the result has been an extreme prevalence of divorce and an extreme rarity of happy marriages'. In so far as companionship, a close, durable, intimate, and unique relationship with one member of the opposite sex becomes the prime necessity in marriage, a failure in this respect becomes sufficient to lead to its abandonment. But it is significant that divorced people nevertheless remarry at about the rate at which bachelors and spinsters marry. They are discontented with a particular spouse. They cannot do without marriage if their primary social needs are to be met.

The spouse relationship, as has been indicated, is reorganized around this new balance of functions. Getting a living and making a comfortable and beautiful home are subordinated to companionship. Raising a family is also assessed within this context.

The Basis of Marriage
K. Little

Reprinted with permission from K. Little: 'The Strange Case of Romantic Love', *The Listener*, April 7, 1966.

I call romantic love 'strange' because in some societies a strong love attraction is socially viewed as a laughable and tragic abberation. Individual love relationships seem to occur everywhere; but a romantic complex is entirely absent from many societies, and our own Western civilization is almost unique in this respect. I mean by this the idea that falling in love is a highly desirable basis of courtship and marriage.

This special feature of our culture can be traced back to feudalism during the eleventh century. Among the ruling class at that time marriage was a mere commercial enterprise, an assignment forced upon the two interested parties by their overlords and guardians. It was destitute of love. Indeed, the wife of the knight or baron has been described as a serf and a chattel whom he kept in order by such corporal chastisement as circumstances might require.

With the ending of the struggle between Christendom and the pagan or infidel invaders, the castle became the centre of social intercourse. The knight who was now free to remain at home instituted a court. This gave women a chance to express feminine interests and graces.

This change of attitude, which lifted the woman of noble birth from conditions of savagery, was associated with the troubadours. They effected her rescue not by encouraging wives to love their husbands or husbands to cherish their wives but by propounding a code of gallantry. This required knights and squires as part of their chivalric duty, to gain the favour of a lady, and having won it to make it the lodestone of their lives. The relationship was supposed to be restrained on the physical side, rapturous, beautiful, and tender but entirely extra-marital. Marriage was regarded as the most formidable obstacle and dangerous enemy of love.

The medieval concept had drawn a line between the spiritual and the sexual aspects of love. The court society of the baroque and the rococo periods rewarded the gallant's deeds and duels with carnal favours. This integrated love and sex, though only outside marriage.

The idea that love and sex could be combined then filtered down from the castle to the city. It appealed to the rising merchant classes, but illicit relationships did not square with puritanism and thrift. Consequently, the verbiage of courtly love was now addressed not to the married woman but to the marriageable maiden. This meant that between engagement and marriage the man was expected to court the girl and display emotional fervour. Association with the opposite sex was not supposed to take place before the betrothal. Nevertheless, the aim at last was to integrate love and marriage. Young people were to make their own choice of partner on the basis of their feelings. Thus, for the first time, the spirituality of love and the marital sex relationship became the same. The conjugal union was to be sanctified by the former.

I have explained that romance first connoted love outside marriage. Marriage was arranged, hence it was assumed that only extra-maritally could people make true love choices. The significant change is that romance has come to be the predominant factor. The connubial state as well as courtship should be rapturous. At first romance was monopolized by aristocratic ladies and by conveying the idea that amorous dalliance was a mark of noble birth, gave to love-making a high social status. It encouraged courtship among the bourgeois family, placing its women members on a special pedestal. Their duty, by the middle of the nineteenth century, was to keep alive virtues and graces that the sterner sex had no chance of developing. The latter—the sons of manufacturers—had to be converted into gentlemen. So, protected from vice and from danger, protected even from serious work, the wife or daughter symbolized her menfolk's aspirations. She was their surrogate in the upper-class world of gentility.

How, then, did romance manage to survive the subsequent emancipation of women? George Bernard Shaw has given part of the answer. His plays show clearly how romance has adapted to feminine needs. Girls, he declares, are right to choose their own spouses; it enables them to deal with the opposite sex as equals. The ethic laid it down that love is profaned by marrying for money, but there is nothing wrong about marrying for love: on the contrary, it is everyone's simple duty. So popular proved this theme that with the development of mass media of communication it became the principal stock-in-trade of major industries. In other words, not only were the traditional barriers down, but the wheel had turned full circle. Who could question this when, as it appeared, thrones were abdicated and royal families did not deny commoners as suitors—all for the sake of romantic love?

I exaggerate, but only because some psychologists have dismissed this emotion as adolescent frenzy. Instead, perhaps romantic love is one of society's methods of rationalizing changes in the organization of marriage. Abstractions come easier in the context of a different culture and so, finally, an example from West Africa. Traditionally, among the people there the bride is chosen by the family, who expect her to produce children and help economically. There, unlike here, even in monogamy a man's closest relationship is not with his wife but with his kinsfolk.

Nowadays, however, educated young West Africans have discovered the alleged virtues of romantic love. They stress the idea of marriage being a true union of husband and wife as well as an economic partnership. Love will be the most important thing when they marry. These younger people have new opportunities in West Africa today. Particularly if educated, there are careers in which they can often rise quickly. But to advance individualistically may seriously offend respected older kinsfolk and relatives. Having partly paid for a man's education, they will expect a return and to share in his subsequent prosperity. It is difficult for him to refuse, because this wide family system has ingrained deep feelings of obligation. He has somehow to square personal interests—his ambition—with kinship sentiment.

Western marriage, therefore, may be an emotional solution. It emphasizes love for a single partner and so reduces the extent of moral obligation customarily felt. This is what I meant by romantic love having a rationalizing function. It helps in the dilemma described to ease an otherwise guilty conscience.

Broken Homes
R. Illsley and B. Thompson

Reprinted with permission from R. Illsley and B. Thompson: 'Women from Broken Homes', *Sociological Review*, March 1961, Keele, University College of North Staffordshire, pp. 27–8, 48–50, 51–2.

'Broken home' is only one of many terms used to describe abnormal family circumstances in which children are deprived of continuous care from two parents. The variety of terminology, 'abnormal upbringing', 'disturbed home', 'parental deprivation', 'deprived children', often reflects differences in definition and in underlying concept. In some studies illegitimate children are automatically included in the abnormal category, in others they are ignored. Sometimes the emphasis is on parental loss by death, separation or divorce, sometimes the term is widened to include marital disharmony, child neglect or extreme poverty. Distinctions are sometimes drawn between children whose homes were broken at different ages but more often than not the age at which the break occurred is not reported.

Equally important, however, is the omission to differentiate between homes broken in different ways (death of father or mother, divorce, desertion, illegitimate birth) and between different types of upbringing following the break. One might reasonably expect that a child whose father had died and who was brought up by a mother and grandparents would differ in some respects from a child whose mother deserted the family and who was subsequently reared in a number of temporary homes.

Little is known about the incidence and social distribution of broken homes in a general population. Most of our knowledge derives from the experience of pathological groups and their controls. Closely matched controls for a series of delinquent, promiscuous or psychotic individuals, are unlikely to be a true cross-section of the population. The position is well summarized by Wootton in a review of hypotheses and research into the connection between delinquency and broken homes: 'Attempts to assess the significance of their findings are thwarted, first by the absence of precise definition of what constitutes the "breaking" of a home, and, second, by lack of any information as to the frequency of the broken home amongst the population in general'. The material on this most popular hypotheses is, in fact, quite exceptionally difficult to sort out.

The term 'broken home' however is imprecise and any consideration of possible traumatic effects must take account of the different ways in which a home may be broken, the ages of the children and the great diversity of their subsequent upbringing. The commonest cause of a broken home, the father's death, has least repercussion on the unity of the family. Dispersal of the family is more frequent when the mother dies or leaves the home; much depends in these circumstances on the availability of older sisters and other kin, but in general the father finds it difficult to look after very young children who may therefore be brought up apart from the family. The young child, on the other hand, often finds a permanent and stable home for the rest of its childhood whereas the older children are faced with domestic responsibilities and recurring family crises as makeshift arrangements break down.

A distinction must also be drawn between social, economic and psychological effects. The father's death may cut the family's standard of living but need not drastically change its domestic habits, its cultural values or its relationship with neighbours, friends or kin; the mother may become preoccupied with outside work and domestic worries but this need not amount to maternal deprivation. On the other hand parental disharmony leading ultimately to separation could have a profound effect on the child's personality and its later social and sexual life.

Despite such diversity of experiences a few general conclusions may be drawn. Where the father dies but the home remains otherwise intact, the daughters, as adult women, differ little from other women reared in intact homes; such differences as do occur are not necessarily the result of paternal deprivation but might easily result from the slightly lower level of such families before and after the break. The father's death or absence might have greater repercussions on boys than on girls. This possibility warrants further study for more fathers than mothers die young and more boys than girls become delinquents; Andry suggests that young male delinquents are more likely to have a defective relationship with their father than their mother.

Judged by their educational and occupational experience, the social class of their husbands and their high rates of extra-marital conception, conditions of upbringing were least favourable for illegitimate children, those brought up in foster-homes and institutions and the children of separated and divorced parents—particularly where the final break was preceded by prolonged estrangement or periods of temporary separation. Unstable conditions, lack of continuous care and consequent insecurity were common factors in the lives of such children and it is difficult to disentangle such influences from the effect of parental deprivation per se. It seems significant in this respect, however, that children brought up by relatives and apart from both parents fared much better on all our criteria, being very little different from children brought up by their mother following the father's death. Nearly two-thirds of the children brought up by relatives were under five at the time of the break and most of them received continuous care from their relatives subsequent to the break. The circumstances leading to a broken home and the continuity and quality of care following the break seem, on this evidence, to be more important than parental loss itself.

Children from broken homes are demographically abnormal for they inevitably contain a higher than average proportion of youngest children and of those brought up as only children. An excess of youngest and only children in populations of delinquent or mentally ill individuals from broken homes does not necessarily mean that family break-up has a more disturbing effect on them than on children with different positions in the family. Indeed, if our findings are generally applicable it seems likely that youngest children may be comparatively fortunate in their conditions of upbringing after the break, for many are resettled in stable homes and receive continuous care from a parent or parent substitute for the rest of their childhood. Roughly a third of only children came from broken homes—twice as many as in other family sizes. A number of investigators have reported a high incidence of youngest or only children among delinquents and psychiatric patients and the indirect effect of family break-up and its aftermath may contribute towards this.

Early parental death is less common than a generation ago; divorce is much more common. Recent studies of young families show that more homes are now broken by separation or divorce than by death. Although, in our study, the children of separated and divorced parents appear to have fared worse than those whose parents died, a higher divorce rate does not necessarily mean more unhappy children. Many unsuccessful marriages which now end in divorce were preserved intact a generation ago and the children grew up in an unhappy rather than a broken home. In this study of adult women such cases are included in the category 'intact home' and their inclusion in that category may have dulled the contrast between broken and intact homes; in a contemporary study of young children they would be included among broken homes.

With our present limited understanding of family habits and their impact on child personality and behaviour the net effect of these changes is incalculable.

The changing composition of broken homes, the relative decrease of parental loss and the greater frequency of divorce, reinforces the need, revealed throughout this study, to treat the general concept of the broken home with extreme caution. Broken homes do not possess a monopoly of marital disharmony and childhood unhappiness—many children from intact homes suffer from family insecurity and emotional deprivation. Conversely many children from broken homes lead a happy normal life. This is particularly true in post-war Britain where social services and concern for child welfare have softened many of the harsher consequences of parental loss.

Widowhood
P. Marris

Reprinted with permission from P. Marris: *Widows and their Families*, London, Routledge & Kegan Paul, 1958, pp. 124–8.

At first the loss of her husband seems to spread a pervasive mood of frustration over all a widow's interests. For a while she may become indifferent even to the care of her children: her home, her future, her family—nothing matters any more. Bewildered by her loss, she can hardly at first believe it. She still hears his footsteps on the stairs, his voice calling, finds herself waiting for him at the door when the men come home from work, and as each habitual expectation is unfulfilled, she begins to realize the meaning of his death. Then she may cling all the more desperately to her memories, to his possessions, trying to deny that he is really gone, only to feel grief all the more poignantly when the power of illusion fails. Or she may try to escape from everything that reminds her of the past. But this seems a betrayal of the dead, and in its turn arouses all her latent anxieties about the sincerity of her love, the fear that she is in some way responsible for his death, even absurdly wished it. And she may defend herself against these self-accusations by an obsessive assertion of her grief. Thus bereavement seems to involve a conflict between the desire to acquire an indifference which the loss has no power to hurt, and to idealize the happiness of which it deprived her. But whether she tries to live in the past, or live as if it had never been, she cannot avoid grief, and she bitterly resents her fate. She looks for someone or something to accuse, and envies the good fortune of others.

It may take two years or more to become reconciled to bereavement, and the working out of grief seems to proceed uneasily, by contradictory impulses, isolating the grief-stricken in a struggle that they cannot share. Mourning itself seems to ease the conflict. The funeral, placing a memorial, wearing black, visiting the grave are tributes to the dead, and also continue a relationship with him that does not deny his death. As the mourner accepts her loss, as she gains assurance that she has established her loyalty beyond reproach, as her other interests revive, putting her loss in proportion, these conventional observances can be gradually discontinued. Mourning articulates grief, and gives it expression.

Grief, by its nature, seems to yield very reluctantly to consolation. The profound discouragement of bereavement tends for a while to devalue all relationships except that which has been lost, so that a widow, instead of turning to her children, her parents or her friends with all the more affection, becomes at times almost indifferent towards them. Moreover, there seems to be a need to mourn the dead, to show how much the loss has meant, and consolation must wait until this tribute has been paid. Hence it is difficult for friends or relatives to help a widow overcome her grief. Sympathy may only aggravate distress: exhortations to be practical and look to the future seem glib and insensitive, solicitousness seems officious —the comforters seem to fuss ineffectually outside a conflict that they cannot understand, when all she wants is to be left alone. They can best guide her recovery by encouraging her patiently to feel that she has mourned enough.

The apathy and withdrawal that follow bereavement tend

to isolate a widow from social life. Her indifference and depression make her poor company. When she meets old friends, she is painfully reminded of former meetings when her husband was beside her. She envies married couples their mutual companionship, and feels awkward going out with them by herself. And she seems to project her indifference and bitterness onto others, believing that she is unwanted or neglected. However sympathetic people may be, there is always something humiliating in misfortune, a sense of being pited or patronized. Hence the attraction of relationships where she does not feel inferior—with her children, companions at work, remarriage. Here she need not feel accepted only out of charity, but can give as much to the relationship as she takes from it.

But if relatives and friends cannot do much to ease the pain of grief, nor even at times to relieve a widow's loneliness, their practical help is invaluable. Minding the children and the sick, getting meals and shopping, advising, dealing with officials, helping out with a loan or a present of clothes, holiday expenses, a television set—family life in the East End of London provides a system of mutual services that spreads the burden on each household. It is useful at any time, and especially valuable to a widowed mother, who must be relieved of part of her household routine if she is to earn a livelihood for herself and her children. Not that the nature of these services changes so much in widowhood: she probably received the same kind of help, for the most part, when her husband was alive. But now she depends upon it more. Only in certain household jobs, and practical advice, does it seem that a brother, a cousin or a son may, in the most literal sense, sometimes take the dead man's place. If the nature of the help her relatives give her otherwise changes very little in widowhood, this is partly because at all times it provides insurance against just such hardship.

Her relationships with her husband's family are more radically affected. A man is more usually drawn into his wife's family than she into his. He visits his old home on his own, after work of an evening perhaps, or on Sunday morning with the children. When he dies, the common bond is broken. And where, before, there was rivalry between wife and mother-in-law, the conflict may break out in open recrimination, inflamed by the bitterness of grief. But even where there is no resentment, she tends to see less of her husband's family: there is no longer much obligation to overcome a mutually protective reserve that has always characterized the relationship. Only occasionally, having, perhaps, few close relatives of her own, or her husband's people living much nearer, may she be drawn to them by a mutual sympathy in their bereavement.

On the whole, therefore, widowhood tends to impoverish social life. A widow can take little pleasure in entertainment, feels awkward with her old friends, loses the only strong tie with her husband's family, and has moods in which her lonely struggle to master grief, her apathy and repudiation of consolation, isolate her even from her own family. These tendencies are reinforced because now she is poorer. She has less money to spend on entertainment, less for fares to visit her friends and relations, and less time, too, since she is more than ever dependent on her earnings. Poverty, besides, makes her sensitive, and she fears to be thought a tiresome poor relation, whose visits will be interpreted as a begging mission. Perhaps there is always a sense of failure in misfortune, however undeserved, and the more so when the misfortune involves poverty.

It would be wrong, therefore, to conclude that when her husband dies, his place must necessarily be taken, as if social relationships were organized like an army, closing its ranks about the fallen. Only in the day to day management of a household economy must a substitute be found, and his widow may prefer to provide this substitute by her own efforts. The love and companionship of a successful marriage are hard to replace at best, and grief, for the reasons I have tried to describe, makes it harder. Hence his widow seems rather to try to reconcile herself to the loss, to find consolation in the memory of her married life until the pain of bereavement sinks in time below the threshold of consciousness.

If this is true, then the adjustment to widowhood is not, most characteristically, to find in a second husband, parents, children, brothers or sisters someone to restore companionship and a secure livelihood, but rather to establish an independent status. But so long, at least, as women are paid less than men, it is likely to seem an inferior status. If a widow has children, her income will be less in proportion to her responsibilities even than a single woman, who besides will have had more opportunity to pursue a career. Thus a widow cannot maintain her standard of living after her husband dies merely by going out to work, because she cannot earn a man's wage.

Kinship 1
J. B. Loudon

Reprinted with permission from J. B. Loudon: 'Kinship and Crisis in South Wales', *British Journal of Sociology*, Vol. 12, No. 4, 1961, pp. 347–9.

It is on ceremonial occasions that people reveal the extent to which they are aware not only of the details of their own kin ties but of those of members of other 'families'. One of the chief difficulties facing newcomers is their lack of knowledge of the key kinship connections between their long-settled neighbours. This is not only or chiefly because they are liable in their ignorance to ally themselves irrevocably with the wrong people when they arrive, or with members of one or other faction in a long-standing local feud. The real point is that without some knowledge of kin ties they can take little part in local gossip.

Gossip is undoubtedly the most important channel for constant reaffirmation of shared values about behaviour. Those who cannot join in gossip about their neighbours, friends and relatives, especially gossip which requires that kind of intricate map-reading of kinship connections which comes as second nature to those with lifelong familiarity with the local genealogical landscape, soon find themselves excluded from conversations at local gatherings. Nuances of expression escape them when discussion turns on the relevance to the speaker's long held opinion of a particular family of the latest example of the behaviour of one of its members. Even where the individual under discussion is referred to by more than his Christian name, more often than not it is by one of half a dozen common Welsh surnames or by the name of a house or farm; and his behaviour may well be related to that of members of earlier generations of his family now all dead.

Conversely, the newcomer tends to be treated by his neighbours with that reserve which is appropriate towards people who have no easy way of expressing, in relation to particular individuals and instances familiar to their audience, their general ideas about what is right and wrong, still less of showing that they share the expectations of their neighbours regarding customary behaviour in specific contexts. It should not be thought that kinship as a means of evaluating behaviour and placing people is primarily employed by women. It is true that, in general, women appear to have a more detailed and systematic knowledge of kin ties than men do, in the Vale as elsewhere in Britain. Men's knowledge of genealogical connections, while usually pragmatic, is often no less extensive than that of women. People who live in small rural neighbourhoods in the Vale and who cannot be identified in terms of local kin ties are often regarded with latent suspicion by their neighbours.

The importance of this process is obviously dependent on the proportion of the inhabitants who have local kinship connections. In one typical village in the Vale there are 112 people living in 31 households. Only 5 households, comprising 21 individuals, lack kin ties with people living less than 10 miles away. A further 5 households, comprising 19 individuals, are linked through kinship with people living in neighbouring parishes. Each of the remaining 21 households, comprising 72 individuals, have kin ties with other households in the village as well as with other people living elsewhere in the Vale. It is sometimes said by informants that people who have moved into the Vale never 'belong' until at least one of their children has married a member of a local family. In general, informants have no clear definition of what they mean by a local family, though those who consider themselves to be members of one often differentiate between what they call 'real Vale people' and others in discussing marriage preferences. Such preferences, colloquially expressed in a variety of ways, oblique, derisive or simply practical, are often best identified by reference to the informant's evaluation of exceptions rather than in looking for statements of rules. A woman is said by her husband's kin and neighbours to be a successful farmer's wife in spite of the fact that she is not a farmer's daughter and was born and brought up in a town. A rich member of a long-established gentry family marries, as his second wife, a woman who was originally a servant in his household and his relatives say: 'But she's really a decent little woman and Freddy has never been looked after so well in his life', or the envious say, with a sigh, of a marriage between people much better off than themselves, 'Well, money marries money, doesn't it?'

Impressions gained from such items of gossip may be confirmed by survey material. The vast majority of farmers' wives are, in fact, the daughters of farmers. Most members of the upper class, however defined, marry members of the upper class. Affinal ties tend to reinforce business connections between entrepreneurs.

The evaluative function of kinship is of particular importance in any study of the ways in which members of a local community identify and deal with unusual behaviour. The social roles, including kinship roles, filled by an individual actor are related to the readiness with which his family, friends and neighbours regard certain kinds of behaviour on his part as unusual. Furthermore, the readiness with which some kinds of unusual behaviour are recognized as evidence of mental disorder, by doctors as well as others, is related to the perceived social status of the individual. In relatively small communities, especially among what have been described as the highly homogeneous sections of the local population, kin ties are often more important than factors such as occupation, education and economic resources in the perception of social status in certain contexts. Where an individual has no extensive local network of kin ties, evaluation of unusual behaviour is often in terms of general or 'national' norms of expectation regarding the performance, for example, of occupational or 'social class' roles. Unusual behaviour on the part of those with 'close-knit' networks is more likely to be assessed in terms of flexible local norms which are adaptable to particular circumstances.

Kinship 2
J. Hubert

Reprinted with permission from *International Journal of Comparative Sociology*, 1966, pp. 61, 63–5, 79–80.

This paper deals with a small sector of the results of research in progress among a set of middle-class families in London. The object of the study is to analyse the structure and estimate the magnitude and social significance of the kinship systems of British middle-class families.

It started with a pilot investigation of 30 families living on a private housing estate in North London, generally considered to be a 'good middle-class area', and having a high proportion of professional people living on it. Following the pilot survey, a random sample of 60 households was taken of the total population of electors' households on the estate (about 250 in all). This sample was heterogeneous in terms of marital status, family stage, age, religion and occupation, though the majority of individuals are married with children, Protestant, and the occupations of the heads of households fall within the broad band of 'middle-class' occupations. . . .

The majority of the individuals in the Highgate sample are not born Londoners. 22 out of 60 were born in London, the rest elsewhere. This is not surprising since one might expect a metropolitan population to be drawn from all over the country. But it contrasts with the origins of the working-class informants in Young and Willmott's survey of Bethnal Green, where 85% of men and 85% of women were born in London. Taking very crude geographical areas, a similar number of the Highgate individuals were born in the south (including the south-west) of England, and the north of England—11 in each: 6 were born in Scotland, 1 in Ireland, and none in either Wales or East Anglia. A surprising number, 9 out of 38 non-Londoners, were born abroad, but only in rare cases were they born of foreign parents—in most cases their parents were living abroad, which in itself has some kinship relevance.

Most of the Highgate informants are thus migrants to London, and come from a wide range of different areas. By definition, all 30 married couples now live in London, and over two-thirds of them also first met their spouses in London; of the 21 pairs who met there, in only 5 cases were both born there; only 2 couples first met in any other 'home town' of either of them, the rest elsewhere in the country or abroad. Thus there was in nearly every case some degree of mobility before marriage, on the part of both men and women. Spouses were not, on the whole, drawn from a home environment and very few met either directly or indirectly through kin.

The 2 couples who met in their home town first met as children, which may or may not be considered to be meeting through kin. Of the others, only four couples met through relatives of some kind. Eleven couples met through their training, or in connection with their work, the other 13 either socially or in some indeterminate way. The high proportion of couples who met through college and work is perhaps typical of a professional group of people.

The fact that most informants married spouses from different areas implies that either their parents moved from the place they were born, or that the informants themselves left home before marriage. In fact in most cases both men and women had been living away from home for some time before they were married. This is not unexpected in the case of the men, but is so with the high proportion of women. Exactly two thirds of the wives were living away from home before they married, all of them for over a year, and the majority of them for five or more years.

What emerges from this is that the informants, and in particular the women, are independent of their parents before they married, at least in terms of residence. This contrasts with the working-class situation usually described, in which a girl lives at home until she marries and possibly for some time after she marries, until the couple can afford a place of their own. This early independence of girls from their parents, and especially from their mothers, is significant because it affects the type of relationship they have with their mothers, and attitude towards them, in adult life. Certainly we have not found situations at all like those described by Young and Willmott in Bethnal Green, where married daughters depend on their mothers not only for day-to-day services in the house, but also for emotional support in their daily life. The fact that this does not commonly occur in Highgate does not mean that the young wives do not have strong affective ties with their mothers, but residential independence long before marriage, combined with professional training and general independence of outlook, must lead to at least a different sort of relationship between married daughters and their mothers; one expressed not in terms of daily contact and moral support, but in perhaps maturer ways, with dependence only in times of crisis, e.g. in confinements and illness, not in the daily running of their lives.

Independence from parents is not merely an accidental concomitant of professional life. In most cases there is explicit agreement that children should be independent of their parents. This is manifested in earlier life by the willingness to send children to boarding schools. This attitude is apparent, when their children marry, in the strong preference on both sides for the young couple to set up house on their own, and in order that this should be possible parents will provide money towards a house rather than let them have to move in with them.

This stress on independence is significant as one of the main factors in the formation and development of kin relationships and attitudes. It means that young people can choose to live where they like, or where their work takes them because the sort of relationship they grow up to have with their parents, and thus with their other kin, does not depend on frequent and intense contact of any kind. From childhood onwards there are different attitudes and expectations of parent-child behaviour; and different ways of expressing emotion.

This fact makes the assessment of relationships with kin somewhat more difficult. It means that frequency of contact cannot be taken in isolation as the criterion of a close relationship, and in fact it may sometimes be misleading as an indication of the strength of an affective tie between two kinsmen.

The relative freedom, in intellectual and emotional terms, of children from their parents, is important in various ways in their subsequent relationships with extra-familial kin in general. In one respect merely being residentially independent, especially in order to get professional training of some kind, enables persons to widen the scope of their contacts, and to meet people with whom they have things in common, e.g. similar training and intellectual disciplines. Young people will be freer to choose as friends people they like, and this may extend to members of the family as well. 'Community of interest' is often quoted as one of the most important things in the choice of friends from within the family. These people, by virtue of their background, education and occupation, have additional criteria to apply in their selection of kin. In fact one might have expected far fewer and less intense relationships with kin than is the case. What is surprising is not the paucity of kin relationships, but the number and richness of them considering the alternatives open to these individuals, and in many cases the lack of common interests between them.

To return to residential independence—it can be seen that it is not only our informants that have moved from their parental home or home area, but the majority of their kin have scattered too, in this and previous generations.

This does *not* mean that relationships are ineffective or necessarily distant between parents and children, or between other sorts of kin. The expected patterns of behaviour are based on strong affective ties which are not, however, expressed in frequent and intense interchange of contact and services or mutual dependence. Just because there is not frequent and intense contact does not mean that the affective tie does not exist. Nor that, in certain circumstances, kin are not called upon for assistance or advice. It is significant that certain services are given regardless of the geographical distance between kin. For example, one of the situations in which mothers are most frequently called in to help is at the birth of a baby. Nearly all the young wives had their mothers to stay in the house at least during one confinement, i.e. when she herself was in hospital. Many mothers travelled from great distances to do this, one or two even from abroad. Thus it can be seen that distance is no barrier to the sort of services these sort of people tend to need. Neither mothers nor daughters expect or want daily exchange of household services in normal circumstances, neither do they generally want constant contact with each other.

The type of relationship between parents and children obviously determines to a large extent the sort of relationships an individual will have with the rest of his or her kin. If a relationship with a parent is not manifested in constant interaction then two things result. Firstly, the ideology and attitudes with which a child is brought up will be of such a kind that he does not expect a close relationship with his extra-familial kin, and secondly, because of relatively infrequent contact with parents and siblings, genealogically more distant kin will enter into his life even less, and ties even with relatives who may be in constant contact with a parent may be dropped or maintained according to individual preferences. In this sense geographical distance may enable ties to be dropped without, generally, upsetting the relationships between other kin.

Considering a wide divergence of occupations and cultural interests and, in some cases, of class background, a great many ties are maintained with relatives. Generally, contact is not frequent, but this seems to bear little direct relation to geographical distance except insofar as the latter acts as an extreme limiting factor. Where people want to see their kin, wide distances are covered relatively often. Expectations of extra-familial kin behaviour do not usualy demand frequent contact, even when proximity allows it. With closer kin, specifically parents and siblings, there is more evidence to support the hypothesis (often held for all kin) that as much interaction will take place as possible at all times. Even for parents and siblings this is not entirely so, but here behaviour approximates more to this hypothesis, and this is so in spite of the ideology of independence with which children grow up, and the complex set of circumstances arising out of a wide range of occupations and cultural interests.

Ties with kin outside the family of origin are maintained on a more selective basis, and they are often manifested only in contact of an intermittent nature. Partly, this is because these ties are not often of a very strong kind—it is fair to say that to a great extent these people function independently of the majority of their kin. But it is also partly because more overt behaviour patterns of any more intense nature are not expected between members of these families.

Family and Society 1
S. Yudkin and A. Holme

Reprinted with permission from S. Yudkin and A. Holme: *Working Mothers and their Children*, London, Michael Joseph, 1963, pp. 156–63.

The social and educational background of the young mother often sets the pattern for the whole way in which she looks at married life, children and the question of going to work. The image of married life with children which a young woman brings to her family stems largely from this educational and social background. She may have absorbed the prevailing concept of the advertising media—of a mother with gaily coloured apron at a bright kitchen window with no care but to use the latest detergent or bake delicious cakes—or she may have the harsher reality of her own mother's drudgery in her mind when she determines that her life shall be different. She may have had opportunities for education which give her some inner resources to deal with the narrow if fully occupied life of the mother of young children: or she may have enjoyed a lively social life before her children were born, the reminder of which jars unpleasantly with the reality of napkins, feeds and dangerously agile toddlers. Her financial status may give her opportunities to choose temporary part-time work or not to work outside the home at all. Her husband may have strong views—socially determined for the most part—about women's place and whether a wife or mother should go to work at all.

These basic attitudes may come into conflict with or be reinforced by the new pressures that arise as a family arrives and grows up. The individual mother's decision to work outside her home and her feelings about doing so will be to some extent fashioned by these attitudes. Even in such an important matter as the arrangements a mother will make for the care of her children, her own background and the opinions of her own social group will give her views about children's independence and their needs which are reflected in the actual arrangements that are made. The attitudes held by one group often seem inappropriate or even ludicrous to another but they are so much part of an adult's personality as often to be accepted as axioms. It was significant that many of the husbands in Viola Klein's survey who disapproved of their wives working, or even of the idea of them working, simply stated that women's place was in the home, a cliché offered with no attempt at rationalization and clearly culled from a prevailing social climate.

The influences of the neighbourhood and its traditions can be equally strong. Families in Lancashire or the Potteries feel very differently from the families of miners in Wales about wives and mothers working. A mother in one part of the country may feel very guilty if she goes out to work: a mother in another area may feel equally guilty if she does not. Mothers may bring their own attitudes to a new neighbourhood and find more conflict. They may find arrangements, taken for granted at home, unsuitable or frowned upon in the new environment or, worse, they may adopt arrangements for the care of their children which may be positively dangerous where old relationships no longer exist. One thinks of many families coming to our big towns from their own homes abroad or in the countryside where the families were large and the communities friendly and close. The pressure of financial needs may make it very urgent for the mother to go out to work but there is no grannie, sister, aunt or close friend to look after the small children. Having taken so much for granted in her home community, a mother may well not realize how differently her children may fare under the new types of care that may be available. Sometimes the young children will be sent back to their original 'home' with the mother hardly realizing the effect this may have on her own relationship with her children.

In an area where there is an accepted tradition of mothers going out to work many of the problems may be lightened. There will, of course, be no feeling of guilt for the working mother. The school-children, and even those of nursery age, would find their own position to be the same as many of their fellows and would not be likely to feel that they were missing something. In areas like these there may be few neighbours staying at home who could care for the children; on the other hand an important feature of such a neighbourhood is that various arrangements for the care of the children are likely to be an accepted part of the social scene, whether in the form of day nurseries, after-school clubs, play centres or other facilities. It is such neighbourhoods, of course, that are most seriously affected by local or national economies in the provision of care. But even in an area where it is traditional for mothers to work outside the home, gradual and unheeded social and demographic changes may bring such fundamental changes in the structure of the community that traditional arrangements no longer apply. The change in the grandmother's own attitude to work outside the home is only one such example. The gradual disappearance of the unmarried aunt is another. A new light industry may itself change the whole basis of the social structure with its demands for women's work and movements of significant parts of the population may bring equally important if different problems.

Factors such as these cannot be ignored in discussion of the effects on children of mothers going out to work. In a sense they are primary and should be given priority in discussing the problems of any area, or perhaps even of any family.

Many mothers work part time and many others would like to. Those that do soon find that 'part time' rarely means hours that are conveniently suited to the hours that their children are at school. Part-time work may leave mothers with more time for household tasks and more time for relaxation with their families. These are most important considerations of which the mothers are deeply aware but it often still leaves problems of substitute care similar though less intense than those which face full-time workers. For mothers of young children especially, part-time workers are effectively excluded from using day nurseries.

It seems probable that most women find that the attraction of an outside job and the time and energy that they have available for it all increase as the children grow older and more independent. While these factors will obviously differ from family to family, the majority of women would probably like, if it were possible, to give a small amount of time to work outside their home whenever they first think it begins to be possible and then to increase the time they spend in this work step by step with the increasing maturity of the children. Unfortunately such desires rarely correspond with reality. Step by step increases in the amount of time given to a job are very rarely to be found except where a mother is prepared to take fairly unskilled jobs as the occasion arises and to move from job to job. Further, the financial pressures are often most acute when the children are small, the husband fairly young and a separate home not yet acquired. A family of three or four children on the other hand may effectively put off any possibility of outside work until the mother may find herself too old, even at forty, to be acceptable in many types of job.

Thus large numbers of women have to compromise between what they might like to do and what is either practicable or necessary, and the compromise is not always satisfactory. One of the most unfortunate features of this situation is that a number of adverse factors are often combined in individual families. For example, many of the mothers of very young children who are in full-time work are under strong financial pressure either because they have no husband living with them or because their husbands are invalids.

Where such pressures are great mothers may be forced to find some type of care for their children and this may be unsatisfactory or change frequently or both. Both Terence Moore in his study in London and Miller and Court in Newcastle noted how often a series of adverse factors combined to put enormous strain on the children of certain families. That special help is needed for such families goes without saying. In general, however, there is little doubt that for the majority of families the lack of varying opportunities to suit the changing needs of mothers as their children grow up is a major factor both in keeping many of them at home and in pushing many others into making relatively unsatisfactory arrangements for the care of their children.

Family and Society 2
M. Abrams

Reprinted with permission from M. Abrams: 'How and Why we Spend our Money', *Twentieth Century*, Autumn 1963, pp. 134–8.

The cycle of family life today runs, on average, as follows. At the age of twenty-two a spinster marries a bachelor of twenty-five. For the first eighteen months of her marriage the wife continues to go out to work. She then gives up her job because her first confinement is only two or three months off. Then, just before her twenty-fourth birthday she has her first child. Her second child is born three years later, and usually this will be her last child. For the next eight years her life is dominated by bringing up her two children. Then, when she is between thirty-five and forty years of age and the elder child is nearing school-leaving age, she will probably take a part-time job in a factory or a shop—partly for the sake of additional companionship, and partly so as to help her family, through her earnings, to enjoy a higher standard of living.

Soon after she can expect both her children to leave school, become economically independent, and even contribute something to the family income. For a few years the family is highly prosperous since it contains several earners and no dependants. This stage, however, is comparatively brief. By the time the housewife is in her late forties both children will have left home and got married. She and her husband are now on their own again; both of them probably have full-time jobs, and they remain reasonably prosperous while both are still in the prime of life. Then in their sixties both husband and wife retire from work, and their economic well-being is likely to suffer an appreciable setback as they adjust themselves to living on their pensions, their savings, and, in many cases, on these supplemented by National Assistance.

These, then, are for the average person the seven stages today in the typical life-cycle. For the women of this country the dimensions and definitions of these groups today can be set out, in broad terms, as in the table overleaf.

From stages 1 to 5 total income tends to increase, except for stage 3, and then falls off, with an abrupt drop from stage 6 to stage 7. In terms of income per head of the family, perhaps the biggest fall is from stage 2 to stage 3. These fluctuations

Stage in Life-cycle	Proportion of all women 1961 %	Economic Position	Prosperity Scale*
1. Young, single (aged 16 to 34)	11	Prosperous	4
2. Young married (aged under 35) with no children	4	Prosperous	4
3. Young married (aged under 35) with children	15	Tight	2
4. Middle married (aged 35 to 44)	16	Fairly prosperous	3
5. Older married (45 to to 64) with children at home	6	Very prosperous	5
6. Older married (45 to 64) with no children at home	20	Prosperous	4
7. Pensioners (65 and over)	18	Tight	1
8. Others	10	Varies	—
	100		

* This is very rough, with 5 representing the peak, and 1 the lowest point of prosperity.

in prosperity result from (a) the presence or absence of young children in the family; (b) the participation or non- participation of the housewife in paid employment outside the home.

At stage 2, roughly two-thirds of women are working, but at stage 3, the ratio is only one-fifth—and of these most are in part-time jobs; at stage 5, over half are at work again—and usually in full-time jobs.

These age differences in purchasing power lead to differences in consumption which are often very much greater than those generated by class differences. And, indeed, one of the new functions of consumption is to help to demonstrate to the consumer and to the outside world the age group to which the consumer belongs; this replaces to some extent the older function of consumption—to indicate the class identity of the consumer.

An increasing part of the rising standard of living takes the form of more leisure, and the use of this leisure comes to affect the sort of goods and services produced.

Since the early 1950s the number of hours worked each week by the average manual worker has shown only a slight reduction, but despite this the average person's quantity of leisure has increased. In part, this is because the length of holidays has increased; in part, because a larger proportion of the working population is now in white-collar jobs where the working week is usually little more than thirty-seven hours; and, more importantly, because for roughly half the occupied population the working week is now concentrated into five days and leaves two clear days at the weekend; there has emerged almost a separate weekend style of living when a clean break is made with earning a living.

For many consumers the additional leisure is taken up with fairly humdrum activities—if activities is the right word. Most of it goes on a few more hours of sleep, and a few more hours are spent on watching television. And for those with cars a few hours can be killed, when the weather is favourable, by driving to the coast and back.

There are signs, however, that these more or less passive forms of consuming additional leisure are being supplemented in three main directions. In recent years there has been a considerable growth in time spent on 'do-it-yourself' tasks round the home. For example, over the past twelve months nearly one-quarter of all men have spent some time in painting or decorating their homes. In part, this is an attempt by younger married men to save money, but more positively this leisure work is an expression of the ordinary person's greater concern to make his home the centre of his leisure interests.

A second expanding form of leisure consumption is in the field of cultural goods—books, music, art exhibitions, etc. Its growth so far has been modest and is likely to remain modest at least until a new generation has been trained as children in the skills of making music, making pictures and attempting imaginative and critical writing. Apparently growth in the demand for cultural goods is dependent not upon subsidies for the producers of these goods but upon more widely disseminated childhood experience in their production.

The third direction in which leisure consumption has lately shown some increase is into activities which provide consumers with opportunities for exercising individual (i.e. non-team) athletic skills—rock climbing, sailing, pot-holing, fishing, etc. The consumer here is apparently seeking to recover some of the autonomy he has given up in the consumption of non-leisure goods.

With the rise in material welfare and the relative expansion of the middle mass market, the average person finds that consumption is of considerable and growing importance as an area in which to have opinions, and as a body of raw material on which to build conversation and social relationships.

This growth is at the expense of work, sport and politics, which earlier fulfilled these functions.

The modern consumer apparently derives a good deal of satisfaction from talking about, rather than actually using or consuming, such commodities as motor cars, wines, holidays, hi-fi equipment, lawn mowers, etc. Various consequences follow from this. Commodities which do not provide opportunities for such talk are, other things being equal, likely to find themselves with stagnant markets. Secondly, this particular function of consumption works to favour the manufacturer with the ability to develop new goods. Thirdly, consumer leaders (e.g. the first families in the neighbourhood to install oil-fired central heating, the first teenagers to wear Italian shoes) acquire a new social prestige that enables them at least to equal, if not surpass, political leaders, sportsmen, etc., as figures of popular interest.

The growing importance of consumption as the raw material for conversation and social intercourse can hardly be exaggerated. There is, for example, the evidence of the use made by the middle class Sunday newspapers of their additional pages over the past five years. Much of their extra space has been given over to regular features concerned with consumption and with building the reputations of writers who are specialists in various areas of consumption. In the Britain of the 1960s the real deprivation of the relatively poor is not in any deficiency of calories and proteins, warmth and shelter, but in their insufficiency of money to buy the sort of consumer goods that are talked about and thus provide the basis of social relationships. Probably part of the loneliness of old people springs from the fact that they do not buy the sort of goods and services normally bought by the rest of society, and without these purchases they can no longer connect with younger age groups.

Consumption displaces birth, education and occupation as the basis of class differentiation.

In various recent surveys concerned with political attitudes people have been invited to indicate the social class they belonged to and then asked to justify their chosen identity. Invariably in all groups—white-collar workers and manual workers—large proportions have described themselves as middle class and then gone on to substantiate this claim by describing the sort of goods they consume and own. In a prosperous Britain people feel they are moving towards classlessness not because of any significant diminution in the unequal distribution of political and economic power and educational opportunity but because of the expansion in the proportion of households who buy cars, refrigerators, holidays, and frozen foods. It now goes without argument that 'what a man consumes, a man is'.

In many ways all the developments discussed here work together. Recent and present economic trends are producing consumption-minded citizens who see the spending of money as a social act which will enable them to enjoy a publicly recognized style of life and will enable them to enjoy in consumption some of the autonomy and sense of power that is not available to them in either work or politics.

The Home
W. V. Hole and J. J. Attenburrow

Reprinted with permission from W. V. Hole and J. J. Attenburrow: *Houses and People, A review of user studies at the Building Research Station*, London, Her Majesty's Stationery Office, 1966, pp. 57–60.

The standard of comfort which a family enjoys in their home obviously bears some relationship to the amount of money available for furnishings and equipment. It is therefore worth considering some of the recent changes in the pattern of consumer expenditure. The new affluence of the present day is now a household byword. A comparison of consumer expenditure in Britain in 1938 and 1959, with prices standardized, shows that there have been relatively small increases in expenditure on the 'essentials' of food, housing, fuel, light, power and clothing. The most spectacular increases are in spending abroad, travel (including the journey to work), communication services and entertainment. Increased spending on household goods is less marked, but is still substantial. The home therefore has claimed some of the extra money which is available, but even more is spent outside the home. This does not necessarily imply that the home is viewed as less important than entertainment and outside interests; there is probably more scope for spending outside and certainly more consumers than there are householders.

In the current (1964) pattern of expenditure by consumers, food represents 32 per cent of the total (food has taken around 30 per cent of expenditure for the whole of this century), housing 11 per cent, clothing 9 per cent, durable household goods 6 per cent, and transport, including running costs of vehicles, 11 per cent. Money spent on household goods, i.e. furniture, electrical appliances and so on, therefore represents a small but not negligible portion of the consumer's budget. Other items such as communication services or entertainment, for which the rate of increase is so striking, represent a much smaller part of the budget (0.5 per cent and 2 per cent respectively).

1. Ownership of household appliances—private households

	1948	1956	1961	1963
Electric Iron	86%	88%	90%	91%
Vacuum Cleaner	40%	51%	71%	72%
Washing machine	4%	19%	39%	45%
Refrigerator	4%	7%	20%	30%
Television set	—	40%	79%	82%
Food mixer	—	1%	3%	5%
Electric sewing machine	—	5%	13%	12%
Spin Dryer	—	—	5%	—
Electric floor polisher	—	—	—	2%

— no data

So far only the national picture has been considered. Much more can be learnt from family expenditure surveys which reveal how households at different income levels distribute their spending. The gross weekly income of families, included in a survey carried out in 1961, ranged from £4 to over £40 per week. There was a progressively smaller proportion of the weekly income devoted to three 'essential' groups of expenditure—food; housing; fuel, light and power—from the smallest to the largest income group. A trend which was equally distinct but in the opposite direction operated for clothing, transport and services (which included entertainment, holidays, education, hairdressing and medical attention). For these, expenditure was proportionately less in the lowest income groups and rose gradually towards the more affluent end of the scale. For 'household durables', however, the proportion of weekly income spent was around 7 per cent for all groups whose gross income was over £10 per week. In other words, if one accepts a crude distinction between 'essential' and 'luxury' expenditure, the households with income ranging from £10 to £24 per week have concentrated their 'luxury' spending on household durables and on this item have spent proportionately as much as do those whose income is £25 a week or more.

Unlike homes in the United States, comparatively few British homes contained major items of labour-saving equipment before the war. Estimates of the production of washing machines in 1938 for example represent about 5 per cent of present-day output. In this pre-war period 80 per cent of homes which were electrically wired had an electric iron and 27 per cent had a vacuum cleaner. But during the last fifteen years the rise in ownership of television, and of labour-saving appliances has been dramatic. Much has been written about the rate at which Britons are buying cars, but they are acquiring television and washing machines at an even greater rate. What is even more striking is that ownership of these appliances has filtered down the social scale. Families whose head is a skilled worker or is in a better paid clerical job are rising towards equality with the professional and middle classes in ownership of these goods. The order in which these possessions are acquired appears to be television, washing machine, vacuum cleaner, refrigerator.

More specialized studies of skilled workers in prosperous and expanding industries, such as the manufacture of motor cars, reveal even higher rates of ownership of these goods than are assigned to this group in Fig. 2. However, the impact of these appliances extends well beyond the new and prosperous housing estates. A recent study in Leeds of a slum area which is scheduled for demolition revealed that 74 per cent of the households had a television set, 41 per cent a vacuum cleaner, 38 per cent a washing machine and 11 per cent a spin dryer.

Very few of the houses had a means of heating water, fixed baths or inside W.C's, and in a number of cases the outside W.C. was shared between three and four families. The juxtaposition of obsolete housing with labour-saving appliances indicates the difficulty of achieving some simple measure of the general standard of comfort or living conditions of a family.

2. Social class and ownership of certain household appliances —private households

| | Business Professional & Middle Class | | Highly Skilled & Clerical | | Manual lower clerical & OAP | |
	1948	1961	1948	1961	1948	1961
Vacuum cleaner	83%	93%	61%	84%	26%	64%
Washing machine	9%	56%	5%	40%	2%	35%
Refrigerator	24%	49%	5%	32%	1%	12%
Television	—	82%	—	82%	—	76%

— no data

The evidence discussed so far shows that, as part of the rising standard of living, many families have been able to improve both the comfort and appearance of their homes by buying furniture and household appliances. This trend seems likely to continue and could conceivably reach saturation point; an even more radical change could occur if families decided to spend a higher proportion of their income on housing, i.e. to demand more space or a higher standard of design and amenity.

Further Reading: **Family**

† N. W. BELL AND E. F. VOGEL (EDS.): *A Modern Introduction to the Family*, New York, The Free Press, 1960.

* R. FLETCHER: *The Family and Marriage*, London, Penguin Books, 1962 (and 2nd Ed.).

* C. C. HARRIS: *The Family*, London, Allen and Unwin, 1969.

* M. LASSELL: *Wellington Road*, London, Routledge and Kegan Paul, 1962 (and Penguin Books, 1966).

A. MYRDAL AND V. KLEIN: *Women's Two Roles*, London, Routledge and Kegan Paul, 2nd Ed., 1968.

* J. AND E. NEWSON: *Patterns of Infant Care*, London, Penguin Books, 1965.

* P. TOWNSEND: *The Family Life of Old People*, London, Routledge and Kegan Paul, 1957 (and abridged, Penguin Books, 1963).

* C. TURNER: *Family and Kinship in Modern Britain*, London, Routledge and Kegan Paul, 1969.

* P. WILLMOTT AND M. YOUNG: *Family and Class in a London Suburb*, London, Routledge and Kegan Paul, 1960 (and Penguin Books).

* M. YOUNG AND P. WILLMOTT: *Family and Kinship in East London*, London, Routledge and Kegan Paul, 1957 (and Penguin Books).

* Available in paperback
† Reference

Chapter Two   Community

It is difficult to find an acceptable definition of the term community because it is used in so many different ways: for example, to describe an area on the one hand where all the inhabitants are able to have face-to-face contacts, or on the other hand an area the size of a large city. For some the boundaries of their area may reflect merely administrative convenience; for others they may represent strong feelings of common interest. Community tends to be a God word. In many circumstances, when it is mentioned, we are expected to abase ourselves before it rather than attempt to define it. It contains some or all of the following: a territorial area, a complex of institutions within an area, and a sense of 'belonging'.

The notion of territorial area is present in most definitions of community, though even here qualifications have to be made. The word has been used to describe groups of people, physicians, lawyers, and others, who are in the same kind of occupational or professional position. Locality is relevant in all the Readings which follow for one reason or another. Within the distinct area which it covers, the boundaries of which may be blurred for all kinds of reasons, the community contains certain types of institutions which lead to the development of distinctive sets of social relationships.

Communities vary a good deal in the ways in which they are independent of, or dependent upon, close ties with other communities. Isolation in Britain tends to exist only in remote rural areas, and the character of the fifth of the population living in rural areas is influenced by the increasing presence of former town dwellers who come to live in the country though often continuing to work in the towns. The sense of community, of belonging, is not confined to those living in close-knit villages: it has been documented in the studies of East London, by Young, Willmott and others. In his consideration of the characteristics of the city, Wirth emphasizes a set of social conditions, notably the size of the population, the density of settlement, and the heterogeneity of the inhabitants.

Certain factors help to determine the nature of the development of a community. They include: time and common residence, shared activities and the degree of involvement in them, the characteristics of members (especially where they come from), and the kinds of leadership which are present. Frankenberg provides a useful continuum of communities, from 'truly rural' to examples drawn from housing estates and central areas of cities. In some cases the feeling of community may be only a residue after the bonds which kept the community together begin to disintegrate.

A classification by Curle of villages in Devon into four types of social sub-system is discussed in Sprott's *Human Groups*. It provides a useful frame of reference, distinguishing as it does between two types which are 'closed' and two which are 'open'. Closed but integrated is the relatively static traditional type whereas closed but disintegrating represents its decay and loss of vitality (in part because of the age structure) in the interaction between the inhabitants. Open but not integrated reflects the 'atomized' pattern of new suburbs transported to a rural setting whereas open and integrated suggests open and flexible but equipped with common standards and a strong sense of community.

The first two Readings relate to the 'common bonds' which members of a community share. These are considered, in the first, in relation to five basic roles, of new householder, tenant, neighbour, parent, together with a residential community role, which assume different degrees of importance with the passage of time or because of the changed family circumstances of the inhabitants. Berinsfield, where the survey was conducted, is an untypical example of a new housing development in that most of the inhabitants previously lived together in a hutted group of buildings where levels of amenity were low. Their previous acquaintance made for certain differences, as did the scheme for rehousing whereby no pair of neighbours was housed together, but the bonds can be considered, with others, in relation to any neighbourhood.

Since 1919 a larger and larger proportion of the population have been housed in public housing on 'estates'. The Reading about Watling relates to one of the first of these developments raising questions about the community life which develops and the pressures which affect the forms it takes. In particular, brief reference here is made to the factors leading to differentiation, among them the growth of organizations and the economic standing of the families. One of the crucial points is the way in which the sense of community which originally arose from facing common problems dissipated itself when new and sectional loyalties began to develop.

Questions about the journey to work and the mobility of the population, and the effect of these on the level of commitment to any 'community', arise from the study since Watling and their life there 'belonged to only part of their day, and merely to a passing period of their lives'.

The theme of the next three Readings is of structure and change. In the first Glass and Westergaard consider redevelopment in Lansbury in London. This provides a view of a working-class population with strong links with their area who wished, despite some dissatisfactions, to be rehoused nearby. It presents evidence to suggest that even those who disliked their new environment, and the kind of high-density accommodation found there, were often able to come to terms with it and appreciate its advantages. Mobility within the urban setting, and in particular the different rates of turnover of the population in different kinds of areas, is one theme of the study of a redevelopment area in central Liverpool by Vereker and Mays. It is not fortuitous that areas of high mobility are reception areas for immigrants, and often have been traditionally so because of the combination of type of house and accommodation, level of amenities, and other factors. Rex and Moore's book on Sparkbrook is the best study of an 'immigrant' area.

The Reading from Illsley, Finlayson and Thompson, documents the movement of young adults into and out of Aberdeen. Its relevance to the community is in drawing attention to factors from outside, such as the demands of the occupational structure, which bring about movement and influence the commitment that is felt towards the place people live. Differences between the social groups emerge very clearly. Watson in Chapter V presents material about one social group from a different standpoint: the way of life of these 'spiralists' is geared to mobility.

The Reading from Stacey, about the small town of Banbury in Oxfordshire, documents the movement of immigrants into the town and how this arose from changes in the social and economic structure. In consequence of the growth of the town and the entry of new kinds of inhabitants a distinction arises between traditionalists and non-traditionalists, each with distinct systems of values and ways of life. This has implications not only for the organizations in the town but also for its social class and its political divisions.

Mobility, and the confrontation of 'old' and 'new', may lead to changes in the structure of power. Elias and Scotson, in the first Reading on the theme of leadership, discuss what they call the quality of 'sociological oldness' whereby working-class families living for a long time in the same area may exercise power by monopolizing key positions in local institutions rather than by the inheritance of property. This arises, the authors suggest, from the greater cohesion and solidarity, and the greater uniformity of norms of the group. The study was undertaken in a rural area of Leicestershire where the old-established 'villagers' came into conflict with the inhabitants of the new estate grafted on to the old village. This is shown to be the result of becoming interdependent as neighbours. Finally, the stereotyped image of the Estate in the minds of the villagers was reinforced by a minority of Estate youngsters whose behaviour was bad.

The tensions and conflicts which arise in the main from social class, leading in this case to the erection of a wall between old and new housing development (also owner-occupier and tenant respectively) is documented in a fascinating way in Collison's *The Cutteslowe Walls*. There is also material in it about the ways in which common residence and shared social class affiliations tend to go together.

Like the material on Banbury that on Glossop, by Birch, provides a historical perspective which helps to show how changes in the social structure have led to new sources of leadership. In the past high status, influence and political power went together in a clear hierarchical structure but now the leaders of industry, for instance, are not rooted in the community in the same way, nor do they play a prominent part in it. There is now no established elite. The opening of new avenues of social advancement by education have had disadvantages, it is suggested, for small towns like Glossop.

Miller, in the third Reading on leadership, provides a comparative focus on three cities, two in America and one, Bristol, in Britain, with regard to the influence of different groups on community decision-making. The differences are striking, notably the way in which the 'Key Influentials' in 'English City' come from a broad spectrum of community life. It is suggested tentatively that a different occupational prestige system and a different local political system explain the variations between 'Key Influentials' in the cities discussed.

The membership of Churches consist of distinct groups of people whose identification is often based not only on what they believe but also on their class position. Some, like the Church of England and the Roman Catholic Churches, cover a wide social spectrum, though by no means a microcosm of society as a whole, whilst others, such as sects, draw their members from an extremely narrow social range.

Sects are comparatively small groups of people aspiring to individual perfection. Wilson has distinguished different types of sects in terms of their relationship to the world and their social goals, some seeking to alter men, others to change the world, others to replace worldly values by higher personal values, and others to achieve their social goals by mystical means. In this Reading he raises questions about the existence of sects in rapidly changing and urbanized society, seeing their birth as an attempt to provide social integration in response to the rootlessness and diversity of values which prevail. The three sects discussed in his book, Christian Scientists, Elim Four Square Gospellers, and Pentecostalists, were, he points out, mainly an induced growth, owing their existence to a few leaders.

The final Reading from the Buchanan Report on *Traffic in Towns* raises some general questions about aspects of the urban environment. In particular the problems arising from the presence of cars in larger and larger numbers are discussed, since they are responsible for a great deal of

noise, as well as danger and anxiety generally. Consequences
for the planning of particular neighbourhoods and
for patterns of shopping and play are among the issues
which arise. Altogether the Reading emphasizes the
importance not only of looking at the situation as it is at
the present time but anticipating the changes which will
take place, and the problems they create from the point
of view of amenity and quality of life, in the future.

Common Bonds 1
R. N. Morris and J. Mogey

Reprinted with permission from R. N. Morris and J. Mogey: *The Sociology of Housing*, London, Routledge and Kegan Paul, 1965, pp. 44–53.

Informants perceived five common bonds which could be expressed in role terms. Firstly, all were new-house dwellers. The 'house-holder role' covers all references to problems of gardening, and the maintenance and furnishing of the new house. Secondly, all were tenants of the same local authority. The 'tenant role' covers activities in this role-set: notably the payment of rent and complaints about the house and amenities, in so far as these were actually voiced corporately through the tenants' association. Thirdly, everyone had to adjust to new neighbours, as no pair of old neighbours was rehoused together. 'Neighbour roles' include adjustments to the neighbours, and the establishment of norms of neighbourly behaviour.

Fourthly, nearly all informants had young children. 'Parental roles' comprised those needs which were related to the children's behaviour, or suggested provisions for their welfare. Finally, many families felt the need to join with other residents in organizing social activities and entertainments, or in providing other services designed to benefit all adults. 'Residential community roles' includes all references to the residential community as a whole. Most of these references were to the social centre, the need for more amenities, or to the provision of social events for the adults.

The common bonds of the householder role were mainly intangible. There was, firstly, widespread excitement and pride occasioned by living in a new house, after experience of a hut or of life with in-laws. This normally found expression through delight with the running hot water, the bathroom and the w.c. These correlated consistently and highly with house satisfaction. One respondent assured us that her ten-year-old son was so thrilled that he had insisted on taking a bath every day since they had moved into their new home. At the time of the interview, this remarkable performance had been maintained for three months. Similarly, many families took a new pride in themselves and their appearance.

The second common bond of the householder role concerned the process of adjustment to the new home—finding the appropriate furniture and cultivating the garden:

'This is the first place where we could take an interest in the garden and surroundings and home.'

For the first few months, this process was so universal that whenever a householder looked out of the window he could see others coping with the same problems. New furnishings and appliances were a constant source of interest:

'The usual way—you start off with a pushbike and finish up with a car.'
'Everyone's trying to be better, buying new furniture.'

The interest was not simply part of the competition for status which occurs in any relatively new group; it was also an attempt to establish new norms of equipment and behaviour which would be appropriate for their role as dwellers in a new house. Whenever a resident went out, or paused for breath in the garden, he could see neighbours engaged in the same activities, and glad to exchange a grumble or a tip.

The tenant role offered a second important potential link between families, for all came within the responsibility of the same local authority. This bond has usually been important in leading to the formation of a tenants' association to request and sometimes agitate for the rapid installation of important services; but in Berinsfield the situation was more complex. The history of the hutted camp had been marked by sporadic and sometimes open conflict with the R.D.C., and by intervals of sullen non-cooperation. In July 1958, only half the respondents believed that the council's allocation policy would be fair and open. In November 1958, about 70 per cent of the rehoused families thought that the council had been fair; but very few of the families still in huts retained this view.

In the first set of interviews, references to the tenant role were mostly concerned with the problem of finding the extra rent for the new house. For most families the increase was between 30s. and 40s. per week. Later, when most families had adjusted to the increase, this problem received references only from the most recent arrivals. There was little spontaneous suggestion of a cooperative campaign for lower rents, or of help for families who had difficulty in meeting the extra commitments. The rent issue was quickly overshadowed by references to the open front gardens; and to the desire for a tenants' association which would ensure a prompt response to tenants' complaints.

The 'open fronts' were the major point of conflict in November 1958 between the council and the rehoused families. The council's insistence on this feature of the plan meant that most families had no separate front gardens, and little defence against any children who chose to stare through their windows. This threat to privacy was reinforced by a fear that the standard of maintenance applied by the R.D.C. to the open fronts would fall below the tenants' aspirations. Our tape recordings of the tenants' association meetings for this period illustrate the importance of the open fronts controversy in the later months of 1958. The open fronts still gave rise to quite a few complaints in the following July:

'They should have put proper fences up in the beginning.'

'They should give us front gardens, more privacy.'

'They should do the front gardens; have a little wall in front, or railings.'

One family went further, and expressed the view that

'Half the rent you pay should be for privacy.'

The neighbour role was also crucial at first, and of diminishing importance subsequently. The 'respectables' voiced the fear that the new houses might be allotted to 'scruffy' families; and some wished that families had been grouped according to this standard:

'They tried hard to put people who were in bad conditions into a house. The only thing I think is wrong is to put all those rough people in. They should have been put all together —I don't think they will change.'

'If they wanted a model village, they got the wrong people— people who do not care how they live'.

Rehousing gave every family a new pair of next-door neighbours; most families had previously been acquainted only superficially with their new neighbours. As the neighbour role is usually of crucial significance on a new estate, it was to be expected in the first two sets of interviews that neighbour roles would be critical. Satisfaction with the neighbours consistently implied satisfaction with the residential community; while dissatisfaction with the neighbours almost always meant dissatisfaction with the residential community.

The importance of the neighbours was not, however, as striking on this analysis as had been expected. Since most families were previously acquainted, less status competition was necessary to crystallize the village's social structure. Prior acquaintance reduced the importance of nearness and unavoidable contact in determining relationships; from this point of view, Berinsfield was not a normal housing estate.

When families are tied to their homes, their range of acquaintances is very limited. They will tend to expect the immediate neighbours to fill the roles of both neighbour and friend. These two roles, however, may be interpreted in a variety of ways. If the families' expectations are compatible, they will generally play both roles towards each other, and the primary social relationships of phase one will then develop. These two roles are not completely compatible, however; if families' expectations are different, they will tend to play a narrow range of roles towards each other, and the secondary relationships of phase two will develop. When two families are already acquainted, the first exploratory phase may be unnecessary. This argument would account for the lack of evidence of obvious 'phase one' behaviour at Berinsfield, especially among the locals; for there was no indication that mutual help, borrowing and lending increased as families tried to adjust to their new environment.

The fourth common bond was the parental role. Unlike the first three, this tended to grow in importance with the passage of time. Respondents quickly noticed the lack of amenities for the children, and the need for cooperative action to discipline the more unruly ones. These were complementary, for it was hoped that good amenities would alleviate and in the long run remove the nuisance which the children represented to some residents. Many of the children from Field Farm had grown accustomed to roaming and playing wherever they chose; protests were largely futile:

'My children are getting out of hand since we moved up here: I want to get out.'

Many respondents hoped that this behaviour would not persist in the new village, for they regarded tidiness and the preservation of trees and grass as the most important means

of making Berinsfield beautiful. There were also requests for
a bus to take the younger children to their school, about two
miles from the village. This request was met, through the
efforts of the tenants' association, at the beginning of the
1959–60 school year; previously the children had had to walk
along a very muddy path, or along the edge of a fast and
dangerous main road.

The role of the children in determining the nature of the
contacts between neighbours was also important. Their
behaviour and needs may produce either cooperation or
conflict: much will depend on the adjustment which the
parents have already made to each other. The age of the
children is important in determining the radius of their
influence as a common bond. When they are young, it tends
to operate within the neighbourhood. As they grow older, it
tends to move to the residential community, and then farther
afield. Disciplinary action at the community level was accordingly sought in relation to the older children; while trouble
with the neighbours was the main threat represented by the
younger ones.

Residential community roles represented the fifth common
bond. References were mainly to social events for the adults
and to the need for amenities, and occasionally a parish council,
for the whole village. These references tended to become of
greater importance as families adapted themselves to their
new homes and neighbours. Social events were offered regularly by the social centre during the year of our survey; yet
in spite of the relative success of bingo and jumble sales, the
organizers felt that the centre attracted little sustained interest
and support. At the time of the move, they assured us that
attendance by the locals had become negligible; and very
few of the strangers ever attended. In this respect, too, the
phase hypothesis applied only weakly to Berinsfield.

Residential community roles had nevertheless become the
most important category by the end of the research, and
social events for the adults were one of the principal manifest
needs of the village. There was thus a contrast between the
expressed need for residential community roles and the
limited use made of the available opportunities. This may
reflect simply the absence of facilities to perform desired roles,
such as those of shopper, church member and drinker. In
part, it may be due to ignorance of the opportunities available.
It may also, however, be related to the community centre's

normal function of crystallizing differences within the residential community, which will alienate some groups and lead to a demand for activities which the centre cannot provide, or for existing activities in more congenial company. Finally, since the centre, like the general store, was still housed in a dilapidated hut, it may have lost status through its inability to acquire a new home.

Common Bonds 2
Ruth Durant

Reprinted with permission from Ruth Durant: *Watling, A Social Survey*, London, P. S. King & Son, 1939, pp. 42–9.

At the end of this early period, in the summer of 1931, the Estate had acquired much of the likeness of a town and had lost much of its earlier resemblance to an intimate community of people. The people themselves had become more like strangers to each other. In other words, a housing estate which is faced with its specific problems is more likely to develop social consciousness and keenness for local unity than a modern town pursuing its daily routine.

But it has to be remembered that a housing estate will never exactly resemble an ordinary town; a number of important differences remain which at least offer the possibility of its being favourably distinguished by the intensity of local social life. Indeed, so far as Watling is concerned, this seems to have been achieved. Its development was positive as compared, firstly, with the institutional bareness of Watling's early life, and secondly, as compared with the dreary social existence of suburbia. It was negative when its temper and tempo are set against Watling's early keenness on its own behalf. Whilst new instruments of corporate activity had been created, the old communal enthusiasm had markedly waned.

One set of causes had been primarily responsible for this result: forces inherent in the development of the Estate itself were destructive of community life. Growth of local organizations necessarily means decline of ambition to secure them. This is an obvious fact which needs no elaboration. Moreover, at first the desire to equip the Estate with amenities was common. There was no difficulty in getting various groups of people to agree on a plan of campaign. Later, it was more difficult for them to agree on the administration of existing amenities especially since new residents had arrived who had not shared the failures and successes of the early struggle. Moreover, there was no institution whose authority was recognized by all people and to which a final appeal could be addressed.

Economic and social differentiation was a further result of Watling's growth. In the early period the major difficulties were common to all people. For many, however, adjustment to their environment meant to become acutely aware of their individual worries. The financial burden of higher rent, more fares and instalment fees on furniture weighed heavily. The weariness of long train journeys made itself felt. Poverty loomed larger than loneliness. People were too worried to develop social interests, and often too tired to seek entertainment. Just when communal life was most in need of their support, when local societies were in their infancy, the economic crisis set in and endangered the existence of innumerable households. For at least one-quarter of all families the margin of comfort was extremely small. That means that illness or unemployment, or the loss of a wage-earner, completely upsets their carefully balanced budgets. Hence the crisis not only enhanced the difficulties of needy families but it also pushed more households into that category.

Simultaneously, it sharpened the cleavage between poor and well-to-do people on the Estate. There were amongst the small families of the Civil Servants, transport workers and other people in secure positions, a considerable number who were not immediately affected by external influences, such as the crisis. In fact, they profited from the fall in prices and felt richer, whilst the others became poorer. Thus complaints about snobbishness and also apathy were repeatedly heard during the same period. None of these tendencies was very beneficial to social development.

A further factor created and accentuated differentiation. From 1928 immigration to the Estate slowed down; it became subject to vacancies only. Although large in total, immigration henceforth became an individual event, problems of adjustment to the Estate an individual experience for each particular family, and their solutions became extremely individualistic too. People either completely shut themselves up in their homes or they went to one of the existing local societies which competed for their favour. Each of these, whether it provided politics, garden seeds or nursing services, was now a closed unit. Hence, by joining, the newly acquired member was not hindered from himself becoming self-contained.

Moreover, it became increasingly difficult for the residents to identify this place with their existence. They realized that, sooner rather than later, they would have to leave it again: the individual family was so mobile. During the ten years which have passed since the first houses were occupied the total number of families who have lived on the Estate is nearly twice its maximum capacity. One out of every two families which have ever come to the Estate moved elsewhere before the end of ten years. Almost half of all families stayed there less than five years. Watling belonged to only one part of their day, and merely to a passing period of their lives.

Structure and Change 1
Ruth Glass and J. Westergaard

Reprinted with permission from Centre for Urban Studies *London, Aspects of Change*, London, MacGibbon & Kee, pp. 164–73.

Local Roots

The visual benefits of high density development are apparent; its social benefits are even more marked. The experience of Lansbury shows that an alternative policy of low density reconstruction and consequent large-scale dispersal would come into conflict with the strong local attachment of the population.

Physical continuity has been matched by social continuity. Indeed, the population of the East End has a social continuity of its own. Local roots and local loyalty are strong. And like other East Enders, most of the people in Lansbury are tied to the area by tradition, by choice and by the necessity to be near the industries on which they depend. Their birthplaces and workplaces, their family and social associations are in and around Poplar. They 'belong' to Poplar: they have the same social status and folkways as their neighbours in Lansbury and nearby.

Like their neighbours in the old area around Lansbury, and like the population of the East End in general, most families in Lansbury belonged to the working class: about 90 per cent of the chief wage earners interviewed in the survey were manual workers—dockers and stevedores, lorry drivers, skilled and semi-skilled factory operatives, building workers and general labourers.

The majority of earners—chief wage earners and subsidiary earners alike, worked nearby. In 1951, 40 per cent of all male earners (those who were then employed and had a fixed place of work) had less than a mile's journey to work; another 23 percent had a journey from one to two miles. The female earners, too, generally worked in the proximity; and the same was true of the earners—young and old, men and women —in the old area around Lansbury. Moreover, in that respect conditions were the same in the borough as a whole. In 1951, almost two-thirds of the occupied population of Poplar worked either within the borough or in adjacent areas— Stepney, Bethnal Green, Shoreditch and West Ham.

The view that Lansbury offered a satisfactory environment was shared by most of the people within and around the new neighbourhood. And there was no reason to suppose that their opinions were irrational. They were not uncritical, and they gave valid reasons for their criticisms.

Most housewives in the flats were, for example, full of praise for the communal laundry provided in each block, though they talked of some technical deficiencies, such as shortage of drying facilities. Opinions about the new market, on the other hand, were less unanimous: it was criticized by many people, both in Lansbury and in the surrounding area. It was said to be too congested—'you can't take a pram round'. While the stalls of the old Chrisp Street Market were strung out in two single rows on either side of the street, the stalls of the new market were—and still are—arranged in four double rows with rather narrow gangways between; and many people complained that this had reduced their chances of 'having a look round': they have to wend their way through the crowded gangways. 'You have to decide where and what to buy before you go in.' The stallholders, too, disliked this arrangement: they believed that it reduced the number of potential customers passing any particular stall. To begin with, there were also some complaints by shopkeepers and stall-holders that 'casual traders' were kept out by the relatively high licence fees in the new market; they feared that this would reduce the attraction of the market for the public. In retrospect, it seems that such misgivings were exaggerated. Ten years after its opening, despite its shortcomings, the market is still as lively as ever; and, on a Saturday morning, especially, as busy, crowded and gay as it used to be. Undoubtedly, the translation of the East End tradition of street trading into a new setting has been successful.

However, in the early days of Lansbury, the provision of communal facilities, in general, was incomplete. There was a shortage of public open space: most children played in the streets, and not only those from the flats, but also the children who lived in houses, since their small gardens—and private gardens generally, irrespective of size—are hardly suitable for group games. Eventually there will be some improvement in this respect: in the plan a large area, immediately north of the site first developed, has been designated as an open space. (By the end of 1962, this area had been cleared and laid out with grass; but even then it was still unfinished and closed off with wire fencing.) The plan makes scarce provision, moreover, for all the varied needs of mothers and children, especially of children under five; it is based on yesterday's definition of a rather autonomous family life, and on the picture of the housewife who is irrevocably tied to her home, day in and day out. For all sorts of reasons most young mothers in Lansbury did not share this view. Above all, they wanted to go out to work to contribute to the rent of their new homes and to keep pace with the rising cost of living. But they often could not do so, because Lansbury had no day nurseries and originally only comparatively few nursery school places.

The Lansbury tenants also recognized deficiencies in the interior design of their dwellings. Indeed, it was clear once again that more consumer research among rehoused families would be eminently worth while. It might prevent the kind of mistakes which, in retrospect, are often difficult to understand: a shoddiness of thought in design, and of detail and finish, particularly in several of the blocks of flats; the provision in some terrace houses of a 'dining' recess in the living-room, which is so located and also so small that it can serve no useful purpose and often has to be curtained off to keep out draughts; or the frequent provision of small, unheatable 'working' kitchens, although many households prefer, and find it more convenient, to have their meals in the kitchen rather than in the living room. Some of the tenants also complained that they had not been shown how to use backboilers and immersion heaters economically.

However, to the tenants many of these shortcomings were of minor significance when set against the improvements they found at Lansbury. Praise was heard more often than criticism. And it is perhaps surprising, as well as gratifying, to find that the people in and around Lansbury, though set in their ways, were by no means as conservative as they were supposed to be. They liked novel features in the design of houses and community buildings just because these were 'new'.

Moreover, few Lansbury tenants would have agreed with the visitors who criticized the new neighbourhood for its comparatively high density. The majority were delighted with Lansbury's layout; they often said it is so 'open'; they liked it because 'you've got everything nice and handy'. They appreciated the fact that this new spaciousness in their surroundings had been achieved within easy access of workplaces, shops and entertainment, without loss of the advantages of metropolitan life.

Of course, there were some who had been conditioned to dislike high density in as much as they 'never did like buildings'. But these people, too, were prepared to change their minds. A few had done so already when they had found that the new flats, though frequently inferior in appearance and convenience to the new houses and maisonettes, were quite different from the tenements which they had known before. Even so, criticisms, especially of the six-storey blocks, were heard. These flats are not sufficiently satisfactory to resolve the dilemma of which many Lansbury families were acutely aware: 'We'd like to move down the line to get a garden for the children's sake', said a young woman who was living in a fourth-floor flat with her husband and two small children. 'But my husband's work is here, and we'd both feel lost out of Poplar.'

Most Lansbury tenants, especially the East Enders, were attached to their new homes and wanted to stay. 'I wouldn't leave Poplar if they paid me for it. I only wish there'd been a Lansbury when I was a kid.' 'I'm an East End woman and I feel at home.' While such remarks were typical, a minority—

about one in five of the tenants interviewed in the main survey—expressed some desire, though often vague and qualified, to leave the East End. But three out of four of these had special difficulties: they were some of the families with young children in flats, or they were strangers to the East End. The latter, though no less delighted with their new homes than their 'native' neighbours, had some difficulties in settling down, often far from their workplaces and previous contacts. By March 1953, one in seven of the tenants who had been interviewed during the winter of 1951 had applied for a transfer or already left Lansbury; but more than one in two of these had asked for, or gone to, another place within Poplar itself. Moreover, it seemed that the intended or actual departures from Lansbury were usually dictated by necessity: people were forced to leave for two, often related, reasons— changes in family size or financial difficulties.

Structure and Change 2
R. Illsley, A. Finlayson and B. Thompson

Reprinted with permission from 'The Motivation and Characteristics of Internal Migrants', *Millbank Memorial Fund Quarterly*, Vol. XLI, No. 3, July 1963.

This paper documents the movement of young adults into and out of the city of Aberdeen in the post-war years. Fifty-nine husbands had come to Aberdeen before marriage. Of these, ten came with their parental families as dependent adolescents. As with the premarital migration of women two distinct reasons are discernible: (1) the father's promotion, change of job or retirement; (2) the family migration consequent on parental death or marital breakdown.

Most of the others came to Aberdeen independently as adolescents or young adults.

The composition of this group of young job-migrants clearly reflects the relation between migration and the structure of professional and managerial careers. For example, 32 per cent of this group of pre-marital immigrants had Class I or II occupations (i.e. professional or managerial), compared with 13 per cent in the whole sample. Two promotion mechanisms are apparent, each involving migration and each of roughly equal importance. On the one hand are those who move within the same organization: bankers, insurance officials, industrial managers, salaried employees of large-scale organizations with many branches, for whom promotion means a larger branch, often in another town; unwillingness to move in these circumstances is often tantamount to withdrawal from the promotion race. For the other group, promotion is obtained by a move from one organization to another, each move representing a step up the professional ladder. In our sample this group included university lecturers, teachers, local government officials, newspaper reporters, lawyers and some industrial and commercial managers. It might be said that since migration for these men generally involves formal application for a job, it has more of the character of a voluntary act than it has for those who move within an organization; nevertheless, disinclination to move often means losing opportunities of promotion and, consequently, migration has become a generally accepted part of the way of life for many in these professions.

The impulse towards migration is regulated by two factors, the pulling power of the new place of residence and the strength of ties with the old. In this type of survey and analysis the positive element is easy to detect; men say 'I came here because I was transferred by my office', 'because I was appointed as a lecturer', or 'because there were plenty of jobs in my line in Aberdeen'.

With out-migration, as with in-migration, the motives are complex and we are aware that a broad sociological analysis gives only part of the picture. The factors, however, which emerge as important at this level of analysis are: the social and industrial geography of the area; the places of origin of husband and wife; and the husband's occupation. This last factor is discussed more fully below.

The data on out-migration in this study refer to the 5-year period following the birth of the first child. At this stage most wives are not employed outside the home and the wife's job or career has little bearing on family decisions. The husband's occupation automatically assumes greater importance in that he is the sole wage-earner and the family's standard of living is directly dependent upon him. Many young middle-class men are still at the beginning of a career which may entail further geographical and hierarchical moves;

most manual workers, on the other hand, have reached the peak of earnings in their occupation and further advance may be obtained only by change of occupation or by moving to an area with higher wages. The occupational basis of migration was still very evident in our population at this stage. The highest rate of out-migration occurred in Social Class I—63 per cent within the 5 years; the rate fell sharply with decreasing status—to 33 per cent in Class II, 19 per cent in Class III and 10 per cent in Classes IV and V. Broad class differences, however, conceal some of the most interesting industrial and occupational differences.

Two of the highest rates occurred in 'occupational' groups which are intrinsically mobile—university students and members of the armed forces; they assume prominence in this study only because Aberdeen is a university city and because military conscription was in force at the time. The high rate among university-trained or professionally-qualified workers, however, has a more general relevance, for it indicates a way of life and a career structure current in a large and increasing section of society. It is in sharp distinction to the rate among men in managerial occupations, the group most similar in income and responsibilities; within this latter group the migration rate is high only among the employees of large-scale national organizations; it is lowest in the peculiarly local industries such as fishing, fish handling and granite working which require skills unprized in other centres, or in small business (catering, retail distribution) in which success depends on a stable clientele or a local reputation. Somewhat similar considerations apply to clerical workers whose rate of out-migration is identical, for here, too, it is the employees of large organizations (banks, insurance companies) who are most likely to move.

Among manual workers in our population the most mobile were skilled mechanics, fitters and electricians, their rate of out-migration in fact exceeding that of the remaining non-manual workers. This is probably in part a local phenomenon stemming from the relatively limited outlets for their skill compared with the opportunities available to them in larger industrial centres in England and abroad. Educationally, socially, and physically, however, these engineers are the aristocrats of local manual work and they may be particularly susceptible to the attractions of a higher standard of living elsewhere when they find their occupational pathway blocked locally. They are very largely Aberdonian in origin, not earlier in-migrants from the countryside. They differ sharply in their rate of out-migration from other skilled engineers in the city, many of whom are employed in shipbuilding, in industry which is stationary or declining throughout the country and which is not conspicuously more prosperous in other areas than in Aberdeen. The engineering industry thus provides an excellent example of the impact of both local and national conditions on rates of migration, of the push-pull forces which have received so much attention in migration research.

The other manual-worker industry experiencing relatively high rates of migration in Aberdeen is transport, particularly railway transport. Here again, the national character of the industry is important, for transference within the organization is possible and may be the quickest method of obtaining promotion; the habit of long-distance travel, cheaper and easier communications and familiarity with other centres may possibly help to break down resistance to geographical movement.

The lowest rate of out-migration occurs in the fishing industry, which is largely manned by local workers. Employment in the same industry or occupation is available at only a few British ports, so that the incentive to move is low. It is probably relevant that this industry has had a low status locally and has not been attractive to workers with high social and economic aspirations. In terms of education, housing, and various aspects of reproductive behaviour and health, the members of this industry tend to rank lower than Social Class V and it seems likely that limited cultural outlook and aspirations heavily influence the low rate of migration.

The out-migration material confirms the earlier analysis based on in-migration statistics in showing that mobility is part of the way of life of young professional people. Mobility is less common in the lower white-collar occupations where skills are less specialized and where local candidates are more readily available. At lower occupational levels, the position is more complex and the volume and character of occupational migration is relatively more affected, not only by personal and family factors, but also by the relationship between opportunities at the local and national level. Knowledge of the local context is consequently crucial to an understanding of the occupational drives towards migration; analysis on a national or even regional may, scale by an averaging process, conceal motivation.

Structure and Change 3
M. Stacey

Reprinted with permission from M. Stacey: *Tradition and Change, A Study of Banbury*, Oxford University Press, 1960, pp. 12–20.

According to the findings of the schedule inquiry, immigrants now make up about half the adult population of the town, as Table 1 shows. True immigrants, those who were at least seven years old when they came to Banbury, outnumber born Banburians by nearly 4 per cent. But when these are reinforced by those born in the district and by those who came in early childhood, the local people outnumber the immigrants in the ratio 11:9.

Table 1

Proportion of Banburians and Immigrants

	%
1. Born Banburians	41·4
2. Secondary Banburians	3·5
3. District born	10·0
4. True immigrants	45·1

Many of the immigrants coming from great industrial cities, and particularly those who came from the north, found it difficult to adapt themselves to Banbury. Some found it unsociable. One Lancashire woman described how, in her first months in the town, she used to sit down and cry: 'I thought I'd never get to know anyone; they're so much more friendly at home.' Others found it self-centred and self-important: 'If they get a shower of rain in Banbury they think it's raining all over the world.' Many remarked on the slow tempo of life: 'I even found I was walking faster than anyone else.'

Banburians consider the industrial immigrants 'foreign' because they came with values and customs greatly different from those of the town. Many of the men were used to working in large-scale industry for absentee owners; they had been brought up to take it for granted that a worker belonged to a trade union. One said that the Banbury workers were 'like sheep'; another, anxious to build his union, that they were 'pigs to organize'.

Professional people of a kind new to Banbury came too, men who were graduates in metallurgy or engineering. Banbury could not place them: many of them were not 'Oxford or Cambridge', but came from provincial universities. They did not hold time-honoured positions as the priest and the doctor did.

As the town grew, and later the war came and the welfare state was further developed, new government offices were opened and old ones enlarged and rehoused, bringing with them more executive and clerical civil servants. The schools were extended and there were more posts for qualified teachers.

So today, in Banbury and district there are traditionalists: those who are part of the traditional social structure and who live by the traditional values and customs of old Banbury. There are others, the non-traditionalists, who do not belong to the traditional social structure and do not accept its values and customs; they do not share any common social system or system of values and customs for they are composed of many different, and sometimes opposed, groups; they include those who have come in with quite other systems of values and customs and those who are developing new ways to meet the changed circumstances of their life and work.

The traditionalists still judge people by 'who they are', by reference to their social status, their family and social background as well as their occupations. They are actively aware of fine status divisions. They accept their position and behave with the manners appropriate to it.

They all, for example, look up to Sir William, who comes of an old local family and who has lived in the same village, just outside Banbury, for the past thirty years. They acknowledge his public service and his work for charity. Sir William accepts his status. He is an active County councillor because he regards 'public service as a duty which a man in (his) position owes'. He feels, too, that he should 'set an example' and is, therefore, punctilious in his dress and manners. He is a member of the Church Council in the village and reads the lessons at Matins.

In the town itself, Mr. Shaw, a prosperous tradesman who owns a business, which has been in the family for three generations and in which his son also works, is an acknowledged leader. He, too, knows where he stands in the old-town society and accepts his position. Like Sir William, he considers that 'service to the community' is a duty. He has been Mayor of the town and gives freely to local charity. Mr. Grey, another of the leading trades-people, is very like him in his social position and in many of his attitudes. But Grey is a 'pillar of the Methodist Church' and a Liberal in politics, while Shaw is a sidesman at the parish church and a member of the Conservative Association.

George is an example of a traditional worker in Banbury. He has been employed at one of the old family businesses for twenty-five years. He accepts the leadership of Sir William and of the Shaws and the Greys in the town. For he feels that 'the ordinary working man hasn't got the education' and that 'it's better to leave things like that to people who know about them'. So he does not belong to a trade union and avoids political discussions. He votes Conservative and is 'Church', but his neighbour, a native like himself with a similar job, is a staunch Baptist and a Liberal.

Accepting time-honoured status divisions, traditionalists like these find associations in the town and district which cater for their 'own sort'. They join according to their interests, but it is by the social side of an association's activities that they judge it. They would feel uncomfortable in one which catered for a different 'class' from their own; the sociability of the association would suffer, the relations would be too formal.

Thus, Sir William rides with the hunt. Shaw and Grey play bowls with the Chestnuts, while George and his neighbour belong to the Borough Bowls. Shaw drinks at the 'White Lion' in the town centre, but George goes to the pub at the end of his street. Grey, like George's neighbour, does not drink. George is a member of the British Legion (Sir William is its President).

These traditionalists, too, are all closely associated with the town and district. Men of the upper class, like Sir William, divide their associations between those which are local and those of their class which are national. Many of the traditionalists are natives as are the men in the examples. But by no means all of them are. Some are people who have come into the town from similar social backgrounds to follow traditional occupations, or who have accepted enough of Banbury's traditions to fit into it and to make their life in the locality with Banbury as their principal frame of reference. They, as much as the Banbury-born traditionalists, rely on the local papers as essential sources of information about the fortunes and misfortunes of local people and families and of the clubs and societies.

In all these respects, the life, the values, and attitudes of the traditionalists are similar to what was described for the town before 1930 by informants like X. But, in those days traditionalists like these probably made up the greater part of the town. This they no longer do. Although they do not all know each other, it is possible to think of traditionalists as belonging to one social system. For traditional society is made up of a network of face-to-face groups, based on family, neighbours, occupations, associations, and status.

This is not true of the non-traditionalists who now make up a considerable and increasing part of the town. Non-traditionalists, as the name implies, have for the most part only negative characteristics in common: in one way or another they do not follow the traditional pattern of life. They are composed of two broad groups: those for whom the traditional structure has no place and those who reject that structure.

Many non-traditionalists do not apply 'Who is he?' as a test of a man's social acceptability. Their test is rather 'What does he do?', judging him on his merits as an individual both at work and at home, rather than on his family connexions and original social background. And on this basis they wish to be judged. Occupation is, therefore, more important for them than it is for the traditionalist. Furthermore, they do not belong to, or they do not accept, the status structure of Banbury. This is not to say that they do not recognize status. They do, and, in one way or another, are deeply concerned with it.

Sir William is matched, for example, by Lord A. who is chairman of a group of engineering companies. Lord A. owns a Hall in the district, but he is not often there because his work takes him to various parts of the country, to London, and to the United States. He has no roots in the locality and belongs rather to an international society, for he has face-to-face relations with people in and from all parts of the world. He does not belong to the traditional status system, for he derives his status, not from his family as Sir William does, but from his position in industry. He 'made his own way in the world' and, although he sent his son to a major public school, he expects him to make his own way too. His son had a post in Lord A.'s company, but he subsequently left.

Similarly, in the middle class, in the town itself, there are many who do not have a place in its traditional status system for there is no answer to the question 'Who is he?' in the way that Banbury understands it. Mr. Brown, for example, is a technologist on the staff of the aluminium factory. He is a graduate from a provincial university. Like Lord A. he did not inherit his position but has earned it on merit. He came to Banbury to work and, if he does not get promotion in the factory, he will apply for a better post elsewhere: his social aspirations are more closely linked to his job than to the status 'sets' of Banbury.

The second broad group are those who not only do 'not fit in' to Banbury society, but who actively reject its traditional standards. They follow a system of values and customs of an altogether different sort—in another place they might be traditionalists. George is matched today by people like Ted, who was brought up in an industrial city. He, like his father, has been a 'union man' ever since he started work. He is a Labour councillor. The class system for him is a matter of worker or not worker ('the boss class'). He accepts his status as a worker and is proud of it, but, unlike George, he will not receive patronage from his 'betters'. 'The workers look after their own,' he says. He does not accept that he has 'betters' and rejects the leadership of people like Sir William, Shaw, and Grey. He supports the Labour Party. He wants to improve the lot and the chances of the workers as a class.

Many non-traditionalists had difficulty in finding associations to suit them in the town and district and have created or tried to create new ones. Some middle-class non-traditionalists have interests which are more intellectual than those of old Banbury. Brown, for example, is an active member of the Banbury players, a new organization which is supported by immigrant non-traditionalists and which has also considerable support from the old-town society. But his friends who are interested in music and painting find it difficult to get people together for them.

The trade unionists found that there was no union in the aluminium factory and that, when they tried to form one, they had to meet in secret for fear of victimization. Indeed, they were not successful until the war and Ernest Bevin came and 'changed all that'. Now the factory has nearly 100 per cent membership and relations with the management are said to be good. They found, too, that the Labour Party was weak. But their activities there were sufficiently successful for the Conservative majority to be reduced to less than 2,000 votes at the 1945 election.

Furthermore, non-traditionalists found that the associations which catered for their interests had values they did not appreciate. Many non-traditionalists are, for example, less interested in the social side of a sports club than in the standard of play. In one tennis club there was serious friction as a result of this between non-traditionalists who wanted the social atmosphere preserved. As a result, Brown, who was at one time a member, and others resigned.

Most non-traditionalists claim membership of one of the Christian denominations, but, in general, they are less active in the life of church or chapel than the traditionalists. Religious differences are not an important basis of grouping among them.

While many of the non-traditionalists are immigrants, by no means all of them are, any more than all traditionalists were born in the town. There are Banbury-born workers, for example, who have joined a trade union and vote for the Labour Party. Other Banburians have accepted the merit basis of judging people (perhaps because they do not wish to be tied to the position of their family). Others, again, are less concerned with church and chapel than they used to be. All these have, to a greater or lesser extent, joined the ranks non-traditionalists. But perhaps the majority of non-traditionalists are immigrants, as emigrants from Banbury might also be found to be if enough of them could be traced.

The traditionalists themselves, although in many ways they still live by the customs and values of the period before 1930, have not been unchanged by the activities of the non-traditionalists and by the social and economic changes that have been going on around them. In the middle class, for example, people like Shaw and Grey, the tradesmen, are closer together than they used to be. They agree that 'private enterprise' means a business owned by an individual or a family. This agreement seems more important now that they are faced with international companies which run factories in their own town and with a growing number of 'company shops'; faced also with a large and active trade-union movement, a Labour Party branch, and the Co-operative Society. They are united in their anti-socialism, which now seems more important than their disagreements about conservatism and liberalism. Indeed, Grey, although he is a Liberal, has appeared at recent general elections on the platform of the Conservative candidate. In their opposition to the Labour Party they are joined by the middle-class non-traditionalists (like Brown) who dislike socialism as much as they do. Furthermore, traditionalists belong to some of the newer organizations, like the Rotary Club, where they meet non-traditionalists.

In short, Banbury today is a mixture of old and new and all its inhabitants are influenced by the old and the new. Its established practices and customs, its institutions and the values associated with them are being modified by men who practise new techniques and new forms of organization. This division between old and new is not one between Banburian and immigrant so much as between traditionalist and non-traditionalist. The former cling, so far as they can, to the old values based on personal face-to-face relationships, preferring the small organization to the large. For the latter the old ways are irrelevant. Non-traditionalists judge people as individuals, are not afraid of large-scale organization and abstract ideas, and belong to groups (industrial hierarchies and nation-wide trade unions, for example) which extend beyond Banbury.

But a deeper division than this, for traditionalist and non-traditionalist alike, is the division into social classes. It is a division looked upon and operated differently by the two groups but which affects each as profoundly. A traditional worker like George accepts a total status system. He accords leadership to the gentry and to the business men on all counts, social, economic, political, and religious. Non-traditional 'trade-union-minded' workers like Ted concede the economic power of owners and managers, 'the boss class', but do not concede them a 'divine right' of social or political leadership. The middle-class non-traditionalist has a status in relation to his occupation of which Banbury is not the arbiter, for his status follows from the hierarchy of industry (be it aluminium processing or government department). He has also a status which he has made for himself in Banbury among the neighbours and friends. But it is not a total status position as it is for the traditional middle class. For them many factors count towards one final social-status position: occupation, income, manner of life, reputation, and by no means least, family background, in the sense not only of the start their family gave them, but of lineage. Nevertheless, in terms of how and where they live and in their assumptions about the 'right' way to behave in everyday living, George, the traditional worker, and Ted, the non-traditional worker, have a great deal more in common than they have with middle-class traditionalists like Shaw and Grey or middle-class non-traditionalists like Brown.

Furthermore, social status, looked at broadly in terms of major social-class divisions, is allied to political divisions and cuts across the frontier between traditional and non-traditional. The alignment of Conservative and Liberal against Labour draws most of the non-traditional middle class together with traditionalists of all classes in opposition to the non-traditional (for Banbury) Labour working class. The widest gap, therefore, lies between the traditional middle class and the non-traditional working class.

Leadership 1
N. Elias and J. L. Scotson

Reprinted with permission from N. Elias and J. L. Scotson: *The Established and the Outsiders*, London, Frank Cass & Co., 1965, pp. 130–2, 152–3, 155–9.

For a very long time groups of families could only acquire the sociological quality of 'oldness' if they rose above the lower orders who had no or little property to transmit. The 'village' of Winston Parva seems to indicate that property is no longer as essential a condition of sociological 'oldness' as it used to be. Old peasant families based on the inheritance of land have of course been known in the past; so have old craftsmen families whose 'oldness' was based on the monopolized transmission of special skills. 'Old' working-class families appear to be characteristic of our own age. Whether they are a freak or an omen remains to be seen. Because sociological oldness in their case is not noticeably connected with inheritance of property certain other conditions of power which are normally to be found in other cases too, but which in other cases are less conspicuous, stand out more clearly in their case, particularly the power derived from the monopolization of key positions in local institutions, from greater cohesion and solidarity, from greater uniformity and elaboration of norms and beliefs and from the greater discipline, external and internal, which went with them. Greater cohesion, solidarity, uniformity of norms and self-discipline helped to maintain monopolization, and this in turn helped to reinforce these group characteristics. Thus the continued chance of 'old groups' to stand out; their successful claim to a higher social status than that of other interdependent social formations and the satisfactions derived from them, go hand in hand with specific differences in the personality structure which play their part, positive or negative as the case may be, in the perpetuation of an old families' network.

That 'old families' are known to each other and have strong ties with each other, however, does not mean that they necessarily like each other. It is only in relation to outsiders that they tend to stand together. Among themselves they may, and almost invariably do, compete, mildly or wildly according to circumstances, and may, often by tradition, heartily dislike or even hate one another. Whichever it is, they exclude outsiders. A good deal of common family lore is floating in the air of every circle of 'old families' enriched by each generation as it comes and goes. Like other aspects of the common tradition it creates an intimacy—even between people who dislike each other—which newcomers cannot share.

'Oldness' in a sociological sense thus refers to social relationships with properties of their own. They give a peculiar flavour to enmities and to friendships. They tend to produce a marked exclusivity of sentiment, if not of attitude, a preference for people with the same sensibilities as oneself, strengthening the common front against outsiders. Although individual members may turn away and may even turn against the group, the intimate familiarity of several generations gives to such 'old' groups for a while a degree of cohesion which other less 'old' groups lack. Born from a common history that is remembered it forms another strong element in the configuration of chances they have to assert and to maintain for a while their superior power and status in relation to other groups. Without their power the claim to a higher status and a specific charisma would soon decay and sound hollow whatever the distinctiveness of their behaviour. Rejecting gossip, freezing-out techniques, 'prejudice' and 'discrimination' would soon lose their edge; and so would any other of the manifold weapons used to protect their superior status and their distinction.

Thus, concentrated in the form of a model, the configuration found at Winston Parva in miniature shows more clearly its implications for a wider field. The task is not to praise and to blame; it is rather to help towards a better understanding and a better explanation of the interdependencies which trapped two groups of people in Winston Parva in a configuration not of their own making and which produced specific tensions and conflicts between them. The tensions did not arise because one side was wicked or overbearing and the other was not. They were inherent in the pattern which they formed with each other. If one had asked the 'villagers' they would probably have said they did not want an Estate at their doorstep, and if one had asked the Estate people they would probably have said they would rather not settle near an older neighbourhood such as the 'village'. Once they were thrown together they were trapped in a conflict situation which none of them could control and which one has to understand as such if one wants to do better in other similar cases. The 'villagers' naturally behaved to the newcomers as they were used to behave to deviants in their own neighbourhood. The immigrants on their part quite innocently behaved in their new place of residence in the manner which appeared natural to them. They were not aware of the existence of an established order with its power differentials and an entrenched position of the core group of leading families in the older part. Most of them did not understand at all why the older residents treated them with contempt and kept them at a distance. But the role of a lower status group in which they were placed and the indiscriminate discrimination against all people who settled on the Estate must have early discouraged any attempt to establish closer contacts with the older groups. Both sides acted in that situation without much reflection in a manner which one might have foreseen. Simply by becoming interdependent as neighbours they were thrust into an antagonistic position without quite understanding what was happening to them and most certainly without any fault of their own.

This, as has already been said, was a small-scale conflict not untypical of processes of industrialization. If one looks at the world at large one cannot fail to notice many configurations of a similar kind though they are often classified under different headings. Broad trends in the development of contemporary societies appear to lead to situations such as this with increasing frequency. Differences between sociologically 'old' and 'new' groups can be found today in many parts of the world. They are, if one may use this word, normal differences in an age in which people can travel with their belongings from one place to another more cheaply under more comfortable conditions at greater speed over wider distances than ever before, and can earn a living in many places apart from that where they have been born. One can discover variants of the same basic configuration, encounters between groups of newcomers, immigrants, foreigners and groups of old residents all over the world. The social problems created by these migratory aspects of social mobility, though varying in details, have a certain family similarity. Sometimes they are simply conceived as geographical aspects. All that happens it seems is that people move physically from one place to another. In reality, they always move from one social group to another. They always have to establish new relationships with already existing groups. They have to get used to the role of newcomers who seek entry into, or are forced into interdependence with, groups with already established traditions of their own and have to cope with the specific problems of their new role. Often enough they are cast in the role of outsiders in relation to the established and more powerful groups whose standards, beliefs, sensibilities and manners are different from theirs.

If the migrants have different skin colour and other hereditary physical characteristics different from those of the older residents, the problems created by their own neighbourhood formations and by their relations with the inhabitants of older neighbourhoods are usually discussed under the heading 'racial problems'. If the newcomers are of the same 'race' but have different language and different national traditions, the problems with which they and the older residents are confronted are classified as problems of 'ethnic minorities'. If social newcomers are neither of a different 'race', or of a different 'ethnic group', but merely of a different 'social class', the problems of social mobility are discussed as 'class problems', and, often enough, as problems of 'social mobility' in a narrower sense of the word. There is no ready-made label which one can attach to the problems that arose in the microcosm of Winston Parva because there the new-comers and the old residents, at least in the 'village', were neither of a different 'race', nor, with one or two exceptions, of different 'ethnic descent' or of a different 'social class'. But some of the basic problems arising from the encounter of established and outsider groups in Winston Parva were not very different from those which one can observe in similar encounters elsewhere, though they are often studied and conceptualized under different headings.

In all these cases the newcomers are bent on improving their position and the established groups are bent on main-taining theirs. The newcomers resent, and often try to rise from, the inferior status attributed to them and the established try to preserve their superior status which the newcomers appear to threaten. The newcomers cast in the role of out-siders are perceived by the established as people 'who do not know their place'; they offend the sensibilities of the established by behaving in a manner which bears in their eyes clearly the stigma of social inferiority, and yet, in many cases, newcomer groups quite innocently are apt to behave, at least for a time, as if they were the equals of their new neighbours. The latter show the flag; they fight for their superiority, their status and power, their standards and beliefs, and they use in that situation almost everywhere the same weapons, among them humiliating gossip, stigmatizing beliefs about the whole group modelled on observations of its worst section, degrading code words and, as far as possible, exclusion from all chances of power—in short, the features which one usually abstracts from the configura-tion in which they occur under headings such as 'prejudice' and 'discrimination'. As the established are usually more highly integrated and, in general, more powerful, they are able to mutual induction and ostracism of doubters to give a very strong backing to their beliefs. They can often enough induce even the outsiders to accept an image of themselves which is modelled on a 'minority of the worst' and an image of the established which is modelled on a 'minority of the best', which is an emotional generalization from the few to the whole. They can often impose on newcomers the belief that they are not only inferior in power but inferior by 'nature' to the established group. And this internalization by the socially inferior group of the disparaging belief of the superior group as part of their own conscience and self-image powerfully reinforces the superiority and the rule of the established group.

The 'bad behaviour' of a minority of Estate youngsters which reinforced again and again the 'villagers' stereotyped image of the Estate was not confined to branches of sex morality. One of the standard complaints of the 'village' people was that about the bad behaviour of the 'swarms of children' from the Estate. Tales were constantly repeated about the 'masses' of children who grew up to be delinquents and criminals and who destroyed the 'old peace' of the 'village'.

Complaints about the 'swarms of children' who disturbed the peace of the 'village' were not entirely unjustified, but it was not so much the actual number of children on the Estate which mattered as the conditions under which they lived. The children which roamed the streets and disturbed the peace of the 'villagers' came from the minority of 'notorious' families which has already been mentioned. Living as they did in relatively small houses, children from these large families had nowhere else to go but the streets after school or work. Those who tried to join the older youth clubs were soon shown that they were not welcome. They had learned a certain reserve on the Estate and applied it, as it seemed, quite easily to their relations with 'village' youngsters. But a minority of youngsters from the Estate, mostly children of the problem families, reacted differently. They enjoyed embarrassing the people who rejected them. The vicious circle, the see-saw process, in which the old and new neighbourhoods, the established and the outsiders, were involved ever since they had become interdependent, showed its full force in the relations between their young people. The children and adolescents of the despised Estate minority were shunned, rejected and 'frozen out' by their 'respectable' contemporaries from the 'village' even more firmly and cruelly than were their parents because the 'bad example' they set threatened their own defences against the unruly urges within; and because the wilder minority of younger people felt rejected, they tried to get their own back by behaving badly with greater deliberation. The knowledge that by being noisy, destructive and offensive they could annoy those by whom they were rejected and treated as outcasts, acted as an added incentive, and perhaps, as the major incentive, for 'bad behaviour'. They enjoyed doing the very things for which they were blamed as an act of revenge against those who blamed them.

Some groups of this type, mainly composed of boys aged between 14 and 18, 'got a kick out of' trying to enter one of the church or chapel clubs. They would enter the club noisily, shouting, singing and laughing. When a club official approached them one of them would ask to join the club while the others stood around grinning. The boys knew beforehand that they would be asked to agree to attend church services regularly. When this provision was put to them they would begin to groan and to shout in protest. Then they were usually asked to leave, though in some instances they were allowed to stay for one evening in order to see what advantages club life had to offer them. The request that they should leave was the anticipated climax of the performance for the group. They expected to be asked to conform to the established standards of behaviour as laid down by the churches; they expected to be rejected or to be accepted only on terms of their complete acceptance of 'village' standards. When this stage was reached the group would leave noisily, shouting abuse, slamming doors and then gathering in the street to shout and to sing for a while. Sometimes a group might agree to stay for the evening and would then 'make a nuisance' of themselves by knocking over chairs, by 'being rough with the girls', or by making loud obscene comments about club activities.

Leadership 2
A. H. Birch

Reprinted with permission from A. H. Birch: *Small-Town Politics*, London, Oxford University Press, 1959, pp. 34–5 and 37–40.

Looking back, it seems as if the social structure of the town fifty years ago was fairly clear-cut. At the very peak of the social hierarchy, in a category by themselves, were the members of the Howard family, the only people in the town who would be ranked as aristocratic in the wider society of the county or the nation. Beneath the Howards were the industrialists who comprised the town's upper class. They were wealthy men, some of them wealthier than the Howards and some even millionaires, who had either grown up in Glossop or moved into it at an early age, and who owed both their fortunes and their social status to their success in developing the town's industries. At the bottom of the hierarchy were the great mass of factory hands and their dependents who comprised the working class. In an intermediate position were a relatively small number of shopkeepers, professional people, and office workers. The only clear way to rise in the social scale was to make money in business. Given the right qualities, however, this was not particularly difficult, and if success was achieved there were no cultural barriers to social acceptance. Some of the millowners had themselves come from humble origins, and in Glossop nobody thought any the worse of them for that.

The structure of influence and political power in the town corresponded almost exactly with this social structure. The Howards had great potential influence but by the last years of the nineteenth century they had become rather aloof from local affairs. The real rulers of the town were the industrialists, who dominated its political and social organizations. They led the political parties, controlled the Borough Council, took turns to be mayor, and competed with each other to represent the constituency in Parliament. They also played a major part in the life of the churches, the sports clubs, and the charitable organizations. Their common leadership in business, social, and political affairs served to unify the community.

Today the social system is a good deal more complicated. The departure of nearly all the leading industrialists has left a gap which nobody has filled in the same way, and the present leaders of industry play a much less active part in social and political affairs. To explain this we must mention two aspects of the social revolution that England has experienced in the first half of the twentieth century.

The first of these is the development of new avenues of social mobility. Fifty years ago the standard way to get on in the world was to leave school at fourteen, go into industry or commerce, and rise to fortune by a combination of hard work, bright ideas, and good luck. People who succeeded in this way generally made their careers in the towns in which they were brought up, and they were normally keen to raise their status in the community by participating fully in its civic life.

In recent years this avenue of advancement has been largely replaced by the examination system. The way to grammar school and university is now open to all children who can pass the required examinations, and the importance of this is not lessened by the fact that the proportion of middle-class children who pass is higher than the proportion of working-class children who do so. At the same time, formal education has become a requisite for economic advancement in more and more fields. To an increasing extent, it is the educational system itself which now selects the people who will fill positions of responsibility in industry and commerce, and the main stepping-stones to a successful career are the selection for grammar school at the age of eleven, the selection for technical college or university at the age of eighteen, and the academic and professional qualifications that are subsequently acquired.

From the national point of view, this development has been almost wholly advantageous: it has opened a new avenue of social advancement for the children of poorer families and it has widened the field of recruitment to managerial and professional occupations. However, from the point of view of small- and medium-sized towns, it has been a mixed blessing. For although intelligent young people in such places have greater opportunities than ever before, most of those who benefit move to other parts of the country and thereby deprive their home towns of their services. People who get ahead in this way tend to become geographically as well as socially mobile, and to join the increasingly large class of professional and managerial workers who do not have strong roots in any local community.

The sample survey we conducted indicates that something like 60 per cent of the professional and managerial workers are immigrants to the town, compared with only 35 per cent of the adult population as a whole. If only the persons in the most influential positions are included—the chief industrialists, the senior public officials, the clergymen, the headmasters—the proportion is higher still. Our estimate, based not on the sample survey but on our discussions with local people, is that about four-fifths of these people are immigrants.

In the industrial field, the wealthy millowners of the past have been replaced by men of two types. In the first place, there are the owners of the seven or eight small firms that have moved into the town in the past twenty-five years, several of them central Europeans who came to England during the age of Hitler. Secondly, there are a larger number of salaried managers of the factories that are owned by combines, some of whom may move on to other branches in the future. When posts fall vacant in these firms, they are advertised over a wide area and the local man does not have any appreciable advantage over the outsider.

One of the results of this situation is that the present leaders of industry are not rooted in the community in the way that their predecessors were, and they do not play a prominent part in its social and political life. The consequence is, however, that the influence of the leaders of industry is largely confined to their own firms and they play very little part in the public life of the community as a whole.

The people of managerial and professional rank, although accorded superior status by the rest of the townsfolk, do not constitute an established elite as did the industrialists of a generation ago. Since most of them are immigrants and they do not play a prominent role in civic affairs, this is not surprising, but two other elements in the situation need to be noted. One is that these people are not so wealthy as their predecessors and do not spend money so conspicuously, either for their own or for the public benefit. The other is that although the economic gap between them and the industrial workers of the town is much smaller than it was, the cultural gap is somewhat greater. Most people in the managerial and professional groups have enjoyed a higher education, and in consequence have developed interests which are not generally shared by people who left school at the age of fourteen. One result of this is that there is much less contact between people of different economic groups in their sparetime activities than used to be the case.

Leadership 3
D. C. Miller

Reprinted with permission from 'Industry and Community Power Structure—A Comparative Study of an English and American City', *American Sociological Review*, Vol. XXIII, 1958, pp. 9–15.

The role of business leaders within a local community poses some challenging questions about the on-going processes of community decision making. Why do business leaders take an active interest in community affairs? What is the extent of their influence in the community? How do they exercise this influence?

The purpose of this paper is to describe and analyze the characteristics of decision makers in an American and an English city. It has been repeatedly asserted that business men (manufacturers, bankers, merchants, investment brokers, and large real estate holders) exert predominant influence in community decision making. This is the central hypothesis under test.

Research Design

Two cities with similar economic, demographic, and educational characteristics were selected. "Pacific City" is located in the Pacific Northwest, U.S.A., "English City" in South-western England. Both are comparable in many features with Hunter's Southern City. The following summary shows the close similarity of the three cities.

Southern Regional City in 1950 had a population of 331,000. It serves as the commercial, financial, and distributive center for the Southeastern section of the United States. It manufactures aircraft, textiles, and cotton waste products; is a transportation center of rail, air, bus, and truck lines; and is a center of education possessing a large university and many small colleges.

Pacific City had a population of 468,000 in 1950. It is the commercial, financial, and distribution center for the Pacific Northwest. Major transportation lines are centered in the city and it has a fine port. The city is the largest educational center of the region with a state university and many small colleges.

English City, also a regional city, serves as the commercial, financial, and distributive center of the West of England. Its population in 1950 was 444,000. The major manufactures are airplanes, ships, beer, cigarettes, chocolate, machinery, and paper. It possesses an ocean port. The city houses a provincial (state) university and many private grammar schools.

The Community Power Structure is composed of key influentials, top influentials, the community power complex, and those parts of the institutionalized power structure of the community that have come into play when activated by a community issue. When not active, the community power structure remains in a latent state. In this paper attention is centered upon the role of the top influentials and the key influentials as representative of a significant part of the community power structure.

The Top Influentials (T.I.) are persons from whom particular members are drawn into various systems of power relations according to the issue at stake.

The Key Influentials (K.I.) are the socio-metric leaders among the top influentials.

Table 1. Key Influentials as Selected by Top Influentials and Ranked by Status as Influential Policy Makers

Pacific City	English City	Southern City
1. Manufacturing executive	1. Labor party leader	1. Utilities executive
2. Wholesale owner and investor	2. University president	2. Transport executive
3. Mercantile executive	3. Manufacturing executive	3. Lawyer
4. Real estate owner—executive	4. Bishop, Church of England	4. Mayor
5. Business executive (woman)	5. Manufacturing executive	5. Manufacturing executive
6. College president	6. Citizen party leader	6. Utilities executive
7. Investment executive	7. University official	7. Manufacturer owner
8. Investment executive	8. Manufacturer owner	8. Mercantile executive
9. Bank executive —investor	9. Labor leader	9. Investment executive
10. Episcopalian bishop	10. Civil leader (woman)	10. Lawyer
11. Mayor (lawyer)	11. Lawyer	11. Mercantile executive
12. Lawyer	12. Society leader	12. Mercantile owner
Business representation: 67 per cent	Business representation: 25 per cent	Business representation: 75 per cent

This marked difference between the American cities and English City raises questions about community organization. Why should two labor leaders be among the outstanding leaders in English City while not one labor leader appears among the key influentials of the two American cities?

Evidence for the influence of the K.I. was sought by establishing measures of actual behavior for all the T.I. These measures included the activity of T.I. in committee work as reported in the newspapers over a two year period, and by their own statements of committee participation. Likewise, we sought evidence of their activity as spokesmen in community life as reported by the newspapers.

K.I. are very active in community affairs. However, this activity may not be reflected in newspaper accounts. There is no significant correlation in Pacific City between committee choice status and newspaper mentions of community activities; in English City there is a low negative correlation indicating that K.I. have received less newspaper publicity than T.I. This lack of publicity is in keeping with two features of civic activity as engaged in by K.I.: (1) much of their activity is policy making and is carried on quietly, and (2) there is a social convention that 'key' leaders do not seek publicity. In England, a deliberate effort is made by some K.I. to keep their names from the newspaper as a role requirement of their social class. The similarities exhibited by K.I. in the two cities suggest that there are many common role patterns. The influentials participate widely in social, civic, and professional organizations.

Business men appear to exert a predominant influence in community decision making in Pacific City and Southern City. However, in English City the hypothesis is rejected. The K.I. come from a broad representation of the institutional sectors of community life. Why should this difference exist between the two American cities and the English City? Two major factors seem to explain much of this difference. The first is the difference in occupational prestige values between the United States and England. In contrast to the United States 'the social status of industry in England, and so of its captains is low by comparison with the law, medicine, and the universities'. Top business managers are recruited from the universities (and upper-class families) where the tradition of a liberal education predominates, and this kind of education emphasizes humanistic values and minimizes the business orientation that characterizes the social climate of the typical American university campus. Many top business leaders, educated at Oxford and Cambridge, reported during interviews that they regarded business life as a very useful activity but did not view it as occupying the whole man. They expressed a respect for scholarly pursuits. Indeed, specialized courses in business administration in the University are very few, and the tradition continues that business management is learned by experience within the firm. This value system plays a role in the selection of community leaders in English City just as the larger emphasis and prestige of business leadership influences the selection of community leaders in the two American cities.

A second major factor is the structure of city government. In Pacific City the city council is composed of nine members elected at large on a non-partisan ballot.

A background of small business predominates. None of the council members was chosen as a top influential by our panel raters or by top influentials. There is every indication that the top community leaders do not regard the council as a strong center of community power. The council tends to make decisions on community issues after a relatively long period of debate and after power mobilization has taken place in the community. During this period such groups as the Chamber of Commerce, the Labor Council, Municipal League, Parent-Teachers Association, and Council of Churches take stands. Council members may be approached and appeals made to them. Newspaper editors write articles. K.I. may make open declarations for or against the current issues and use their influence with the 'right persons or groups'. The mayor as administrative head and an elective official is both relatively powerful as patronage dispenser, and, at the same time, exposed to pressure from citizens to whom he may be indebted for his position either in the past or in the future. In contrast to this pattern, English City has a city council composed of 112 members. When the council is organized, members are appointed to committees that meet once or twice a week. Issues that arise in any part of the community are quickly brought to the Council's attention. The city clerk is the administrative head of the city government. He is a civil servant appointed by the council on the basis of his administrative ability and serves under a requirement of impartiality as elections come and poliical parties change in power. The members of the Council are released by their employers from work at the time of meetings. They are paid a stipend by the local government for time lost from work and

Table 2. Occupational Composition of English City Council in 1955

32 Per Cent Trade Union Members N = 37	30 Per Cent Business Group Members N = 33	37 Per Cent Other Community Sectors N = 40
2 Foremen	4 Manufacturers	2 Solicitors
16 Skilled workers	7 Wholesale and retail owners	1 Doctor
5 Semi-skilled workers	1 Cinema owner	1 Dentist
8 Clerical workers	4 Contractors	1 Engineer
4 Trade union officials	8 Company directors and secretaries	1 Accountant
2 Unskilled workers	1 Bank official	1 Auctioneer
	8 Insurance officials	1 Teacher
		2 Ministers
		3 Political party organizing secretaries
		3 National government officials
		12 Housewives
Note: two vacant seats		12 Retired workers

for any personal expenses incurred in attending meetings within or outside the city. Table 2 shows the occupational composition of 110 members (2 vacant seats) of English City Council in 1955.

The Council is composed of three major groups, trade union members (32 per cent), business members (30 per cent), and other community members (37 per cent). Five of the twelve K.I. of the community are members and play major roles in their respective parties. The council is the major arena of community decision. Issues reach it directly, are investigated by Council committees, and are decided upon by a vote taken in the full council. Community organizations play important roles in debating the issues, but these are definitely secondary or supplementary activities. The community value system condemns any pressure tactics on the Council as 'bad taste'. However, in the council a caucus of elected party leaders is held before any important vote and a position is taken by the leaders for the party. The 'whip' is applied and members are expected to vote as instructed. Such action is rationalized as necessary for responsible party government.

Two factors, a different occupational prestige system and a different council-community power complex, seem to explain the variation in the composition of key influentials who come to power in Pacific City and English City.

Religion in the City
B. R. Wilson

Reprinted with permission from B. R. Wilson: *Sects and Society*, London, Heinemann, 1961, pp. 8–11.

The sect life of the modern British city appears to be thoroughly institutionalized. The sects treated in this study are all established religious bodies, and all relied on direction, inspiration or doctrine from elsewhere. It is possible that conditions really conducive to spontaneous sectarian expression prevail only in the rapidly changing, untraditionalized society, with mass immigration, clash of cultures, racial and national antagonisms, and rapid impersonal urban growth. There the spontaneous emotional sect arises as a first and necessarily naive attempt to provide a new social integration in a circumstance of social and cultural chaos, as a response to conditions of acute social anomie. Immigration into the British city of today tends to be individual, without the association of national, racial and ideological antagonisms; the pattern of life into which the individual moves is little differentiated from that which he has left, except perhaps in migration from country to city, and even here the cultural distance, in an age of mass-media and standardization, tends increasingly to diminish. The means of minimal accommodation are institutionally provided; the forms of entertainment (and it is the leisure time of the individual in which his anomic circumstance will be most acutely felt—and this, of course, much more so in an age of full employment) are familiarly impersonal. No specific adaptation is required—in social life there is no obvious department in which the immigrant is markedly underprivileged. The new resident is undifferentiated from the old in every observable dimension; the old residents themselves are not integrated into a community, they have no cultural pattern into which a stranger cannot fit, since the old residents are strangers one to another, and are unaware which stranger is new and which is old. The immigrant into present-day large cities will tend to drift into existing institutions in the spiritual as well as in the recreational sphere: his situation is too atomized and impersonal to allow a radical accommodation to occur. Such an accommodation would be the spontaneous expression in religious terms of the needs of the displaced and migratory. The stranger in the modern city need not be markedly more rootless than the residents; their mild and general anomie is itself a vaccine against his contraction of a more acute infection. There is, too, a wide provision of secular institutions in which, in an impersonal way, the individual can immediately find a place, so obviating the need for distinctive religious organizations. There is no economic or social inferiority, and no cultural dissonance and impoverishment on a wide scale, for which groups might need to compensate themselves by sanctifying their norms with the irrefragable transcendental sanctions of religious group-expression. Such personal maladjustment as arises today in this changed circumstance cannot automatically find fellow-feeling; it must seek accommodation and compensation in the established order where the impersonal state or commercial undertaking offers a minimal amenity, but in doing so perhaps saps the spontaneous initiative of the maladjusted and neurotic who might, otherwise, seek to make their own provision.

The sects which exist in Britain today are not very often the spontaneous creations of the people involved in them. The last crop of sects to emerge and gain wide adherence were the Pentecostal groups in the period immediately before and after the First World War, and even these were largely the creation of revivalists; they were mainly an induced growth. Their early success indicated the need felt by many for a radical emotional reorganization of their lives. But the solution was not spontaneously found, it depended upon the pump-priming activity of the revivalist to generate a distinctive form of religious expression. The sects of today are established sects, and those who belong to them have, in the vast majority of cases, and certainly in almost all cases in the three sects treated here, come to a sect which was already an established institution. It is already an established pattern of theory and practice when they enter it; they are not themselves creating a new way of life, and providing for themselves patterns appropriate to their needs, but they are rather fitting and moulding themselves to a given way of life, the terms of which are already laid down. This type of sect offers a different sort of accommodation from that of the spontaneous, emotional and unstructured group. The established sect provides an objective social environment for the individual, and imposes constraints upon him, for ultimately the moral codes of the group are identified with the behests of God, acknowledged as external, transcendent and impersonal in their authority. The spontaneous sect, which, of course, if it persists, generates the established sect, may ease psychological tensions by encouraging individuals uninhibitedly to express their feelings; but the established sect finds need, even when using devices of this type, to discipline in some measure the spontaneous expressions of its members, and to pattern enthusiasm into institutionally approved channels. The individual is unaware of the process whereby the initial psychological appeal of the movement's teachings induces him to accept a whole range of new motivations which condition his behaviour.

The sects of this study have all been called into being by one, or, at most, a very few leaders: in all three there has been a strong charismatic element, and this would appear to be a very common feature among the sects which have emerged within the last century. Not only is it evident in the groups arising autonomously, but it is also apparent in the schisms which occur in these groups. The charismatic leader conditions, if he does not determine, the development of the attitudes and Weltanschauung of the sect, as well as of its doctrines and organization: the leader's personality may, indeed, as in Christian Science, be built into the movement. I have attempted to pay particular attention to the role of the leader in the three movements here reviewed. Sectarians often display a high regard for the charismatic authority whether this be offered as the incarnation of God in man, as the special anointing by God of a prophet, or merely as a marked natural ability, special wisdom, knowledge, lucidity or unction. The leader is responsible, at least initially and in part, for the precepts and example which his votaries accept, and for the primary articulation of values to which they subscribe: his self-interpretation conditions their behaviour and beliefs.

The three movements have been considered both as collectivities and as institutions, in terms of structure and function, and of sect dynamics. Although the three movements are dubbed 'established sects', the tendency of sects to compromise with the world, over time, has been freely termed 'denominational tendencies'. The breakdown of sect values which a changing clientele may demand is met by the sect's mechanisms of conservation, and these three sects have all experienced, in varying measure resisted, pressures for change. The process itself fosters dissentions, and is the occasion for schism, whatever the rationalization of such divisions may be. Schisms produce independent groups, but do not at once generate essentially new sects; they signalize disintegration of original orientation towards the world, and the increasingly diverse needs of members; or they are the creation of would-be charismatic leaders, asserting a conscious or unconscious will to power.

Urban Environment
Buchanan Report

Reprinted with permission from *Traffic in Towns*, London, Her Majesty's Stationery Office, 1963, pp. 19–22.

Whilst delays in traffic jams, and difficulties of parking have already caught public attention, and whilst road accidents have become the subject of a steadily mounting campaign to try to catch public attention, the deterioration of our urban surroundings under the growing weight of traffic has passed almost unnoticed. Part of the explanation is doubtless the fact that we have all grown up with the motor vehicle, and it has grown up with us, so we tend to take it and its less desirable effects very much for granted.

Of all the influences which the motor vehicle has on the environment the question of safety should be put foremost. It is not really possible to separate this from the matter of accidents, which has already been discussed. To be safe, to feel safe at all times, to have no serious anxiety that husbands, wives or children will be involved in a traffic accident, are surely pre-requisites for civilized life. Against this standard, subjective though it may be, the conditions in our towns resulting from the use of motor vehicles obviously leave a great deal to be desired. There are now virtually no urban streets that are completely safe. Even ten years ago there were residential streets where few people owned cars, and where the only traffic was the occasional coal lorry or furniture van, but now most domestic deliveries are made by motor vehicles, and many of the residents have cars. These changes have resulted in continuous movement of vehicles up and down the street; and where, as is so often the case, there are no private garages, the cars stand in the street and create additional hazards for children. Moreover, as main roads have become congested with traffic, drivers have sought alternative routes, only too often using streets unsuitable for the purpose, or invading areas which by any standard should have a measure of peace and quiet about them. Some of this infiltration has taken place by drivers on their own initiative, in other cases it is the result of official policies for expediting the movement of traffic.

In addition to danger and anxiety, the motor vehicle is responsible for a great deal of noise. This is a matter which has recently been under consideration, along with other aspects of noise, by an official committee set up under the Minister for Science. In their Report, the Committee concluded that 'in London (and no doubt this applies to other large towns as well) road traffic is, at the present time, the predominant source of annoyance, and no other single noise is of comparable importance'. They discerned three possible lines of attack on the nuisance of traffic noise:

(i) *Reducing the noise emitted by vehicles*
The Committee concluded that, while there was clear evidence that amongst certain classes of vehicle the noise levels were higher than they need be having regard to the knowledge available to manufacturers, there were nevertheless considerable difficulties in reducing the noise levels from the most frequent offenders—namely diesel-engined buses and heavy commercial vehicles.

(ii) *Smoothing the traffic flow*
Vehicles produce their maximum noise when accelerating in low gear. Therefore anything that can be done to keep traffic moving smoothly will tend to reduce noise.

(iii) Reducing traffic flows past any given spot
This would be done by diversionary roads and other measures
of a town planning nature.

The Committee considered that the better sound insulation
of buildings against external noise could be achieved only
at the expense of modern methods of building, such as light
cladding and they concluded therefore that it would be unwise
to look to better insulation for any great contribution towards
the mitigation of the problem of external noise.

We accept the Committee's general conclusion that traffic
noise is now the predominant noise nuisance in towns. The
Committee found little evidence to show that noise causes
direct physical ill-effects on people, or mental or nervous
illness, but they concluded that one of the commonest and
most undesirable effects is the interference with communication based on sound (e.g. conversation, teaching). Our own
conclusion, based on observation and many discussions, is
that traffic noise is steadily developing into a major nuisance,
seriously prejudicial to the general enjoyment of towns,
destructive of the amenities of dwellings on a wide scale,
and interfering in no small degree with efficiency in offices and
other business premises. But again, this is something which
people have mostly grown up with and so tend to take very
much for granted.

The conclusions of the Committee that not a great deal
can be expected towards the abatement of traffic noise either
from the improved design of heavy vehicles, or from the
better insulation of buildings, are extremely important.
They suggest that the long term remedy must lie with town
planning, encompassing at one extreme the diversion of
heavy traffic flows from areas where people live, to the detailed
layout of buildings and building groups at the other. At
every turn in our consideration of traffic problems, we have
been impressed by the need for vehicle users to be aware of
their responsibilities to the rest of the community.

Fumes and smell constitute a further unpleasant by-product
of the motor vehicle. Fumes are emitted mainly from engine
exhausts, but also from ventilation holes in carburettors and
tanks, and from 'breathers' in crankcases. They contain,
amongst other substances, carbon monoxide (especially from
petrol as opposed to diesel fuel), unburnt elements of fuel,
and carbon dust. Carbon monoxide is toxic, and carbon dust

can act as a carrier for carcinogenic (cancer producing) compounds. In conditions of sunlight, fumes can develop as eye and throat irritants.

In Britain, engine fumes do not yet rank as a major cause of atmospheric pollution, though they are certainly already contributive to smog. But it is scarcely open to question that fumes are now rendering urban streets extremely unpleasant, though once again, since it is a situation that most of us have grown up with, it needs a conscious effort to comprehend what has happened. This nuisance is now all-pervasive through towns, no street that carries traffic is free from it. It seems to be a widely held view that fumes gather only in canyon-like streets, but a walk across any of London's river bridges demonstrates the fallacy of this. Nor is there any freedom from fumes even for drivers and passengers inside vehicles, for they breathe air sucked in at 'fume level'. This is in contrast to noise, for it is a characteristic of most modern forms of transport that the passengers are largely unaware of the noise their conveyance is making, even though the din to outsiders may be unbearable.

The motor vehicle has been responsible for much else that affects our physical surroundings. There is its direct competition for space with environmental requirements, at its greatest in city centres where space is limited and traffic at its most dense. In very few towns is the record other than one of steady encroachment by the motor vehicle, often in small instalments, but cumulative in effect. There are the visual consequences of this intrusion of motor vehicles, the crowding out of every available square yard of space with vehicles, either moving or stationary, so that buildings seem to rise from a plinth of cars; the destruction of architectural and historical scenes; the intrusion into parks and squares; the garaging, servicing and maintenance of cars in residential streets which creates hazards for children, trapping the garbage and the litter and greatly hindering snow clearance; and the in-direct effect of oilstains which render dark black the only suitable colour for surfaces, and which quickly foul all the odd corners and minor spaces round new buildings as motor-cycles and scooters take possession. There is the other kind of visual effect resulting from the equipment and works associated with the use of motor vehicles: the clutter of signs, signals, bollards, railings, and the rest of the para-phernalia which are deemed necessary to help traffic flow;

the dreary, formless car parks, often absorbing large areas of towns, whose construction has involved the sacrifice of the closely-knit development which has contributed so much to the character of the inner areas of our towns; the severing effects of heavy traffic flows; and the modern highway works whose great widths are violently out of scale with the more modest dimensions of the towns through which they pass.

Further Reading: Community

* R. FRANKENBERG: *Communities in Britain*, London, Penguin Books, 1966.

*† R. WARREN (ED.): *Perspectives on the American Community*, New York, Rand McNally, 1966.

P. COLLISON: *The Cutteslowe Walls*, London, Faber & Faber, 1963.

* H.M.S.O.: *The Needs of New Communities*, 1967.

B. JACKSON: *Working Class Community*, London, Routledge and Kegan Paul, 1968.

* JANE JACOBS: *The Death and Life of Great American Cities*, London, Penguin Books, 1964.

H. JENNINGS: *Societies in the Making*, London, Routledge and Kegan Paul, 1962.

G. D. MITCHELL AND OTHERS: *Neighbourhood and Community*, Liverpool, Liverpool University Press, 1954.

J. M. MOGEY: *Family and Neighbourhood*, Oxford, Oxford University Press, 1956.

* J. REX AND R. MOORE: *Race, Community and Conflict*, Oxford, Oxford University Press, 1966.

C. VEREKER AND J. B. MAYS: *Urban Redevelopment and Social Change*, Liverpool, Liverpool University Press, 1961.

P. WILLMOTT: *The Evolution of a Community*, London, Routledge and Kegan Paul, 1963.

* Available in paperback
† Reference

Chapter Three   **Socialization**

In general the term Socialization is used to describe the
ways in which the individual learns the values, beliefs, and
roles which underwrite the social system in which he
participates. For the child living in Britain learns to be
not only a performer of roles which are applicable to his
age and sex but also to his position in the society to which
he belongs. Crucial to socialization is the idea of culture
which may be defined as learned behaviour which is socially
transmitted. The idea of culture involves 'a complete design
for living'. From certain points of view culture may be
seen as a set of rules.

Since socialization is concerned with preparation for
roles in society it begins in the relationships which develop
between those with whom the child is in a position of
subordination, principally the parents, and those with whom
he is in a position of equality, principally in the early
stages brothers and sisters. By degrees the child takes over
standards from the parents and others with whom he is
in contact. There are many differences according to social
class background in the way in which this develops. These
have been illustrated graphically in the comparison between
a group of children living in slums and children going on to
public schools in B. M. Spinley's *The Deprived and the
Privileged*. The differences in early experience, she suggests,
'seem to be numerous, important and fundamental'.
Little overlapping was found in this study between the
groups in terms of their experiences. Two of the most
significant differences arose in the ways in which children
were brought up. In the case of the slum children there was
said to be no interference with the physiological satisfactions
of feeding or excretion in the first year but the period of

indulgence in this respect ceased at the birth of the next child in the family. In the case of the children of higher social status there was a consistent attempt to improve performance in all respects, and this was also true in the second significant area of difference, that of attitudes towards the future. The high status child is taught to think consistently in terms of deferring immediate gratifications whereas the slum child has no consistent set of values presented to him.

The middle-class model of socialization involves a great concern by parents for the performance of their children and training geared ideally to 'independence of action and a show of initiative'. Competitive behaviour is rewarded and success is acclaimed. For parents in many social groups the child is typically the hope of the future and in particular where parents have not themselves gone as far as they had hoped.

Some of these issues arise in the Readings concerned with relationships between parents and children to be found in Chapter I. Later other processes of socialization become important. For a considerable period of time before maturity the individual is socialized by the formal processes of the educational system. Contacts with the peer groups to which the individual belongs are also of considerable importance particularly during the time when the 'youth culture' begins to become more influential as the influence of the parents and the school wanes. All three of the sources of socialization are considered in the Readings which follow.

In the first Reading Bernstein considers the relationship between socio-cultural factors and educational performance. In particular he looks at the position of children from extreme social groups who are exposed to separate and distinct patterns of learning even before their formal education begins. He relates the kind of language the child uses to his eventual level of performance. Again differences between working- and middle-class children emerge not only in their upbringing at home but also within the context of the school. In the whole extract the crucial importance of the early stages of education is stressed. However, Professor Bernstein wishes to point out that the extract from his article was published originally in 1958. Since that time the theory, basic concepts and their elaboration have been revised.[1]

In the second Reading Little and Westergaard present information about changes in social inequalities as far as these relate to access to selective secondary education over the past two generations. It appears that marked social inequalities persist in educational opportunity and this is linked with other evidence about the constancy of class divisions within society.

Both the third and fourth Readings in the section on social class influences are by American authors. In that by Elder the consequences for the life opportunity and personality of secondary school children is considered. The main point which emerges is that those who develop low opinions of themselves as students tend to perform in accordance with their self-assessment. Streaming and the irrelevance of much of the subject matter in modern schools is also considered an element in producing the negative self-image of the products of that educational background. The importance of commercialized youth culture as having an influence on decisions to leave school early is also apparent. The question of youth culture is also raised in the article by Worsley in Chapter VII. Gerstl and Perrucci look at the mobility of the elite within a particular occupation and compare the situation in the United States and Britain. Trends in the recruitment to one occupation, that of engineering at a qualified level, are considered and the conclusion for both Britain and the United States is advanced that engineering is the best example of a career open to talent whatever the social background of its recruits.

The problems of children brought up in a situation where two cultures are present, one in the home and the other in the school and often the neighbourhood, are posed in the Reading by Butterworth. Little systematic work has been done on the kinds of adaptation necessary for newcomers

[1] B. Bernstein, 'Social Class, Language and Socialization', in N. Minnis (ed.), *Language at Large* (Gollancz, 1970); B. Bernstein,' Education Cannot Compensate for Society', *New Society*, 26 February 1970; B. Bernstein and D. Henderson, 'Social Class Differences in the Relevance of Language to Socialization', *Sociology*, Vol. 3, No. 1, Jan. 1969.

to British society, in particular those like the migrants from Asia who have to contend not only with problems of language but also of different cultural and religious traditions. These problems of socialization continue to arise for adults and it would be true to say that all members of a society continue to be socialized in response to new organizational arrangements and new values which arise with social change.

The segregation of roles between men and women in Muslim society, which is also true of Sikhs and Hindus to a slightly different extent, is a consequence of a particular social structure. Added to conflicts between generations which are a commonplace of life in a modern society are others which follow from these cultural differences. Attitudes towards people in authority, whether parents or teachers or others, may be modified in consequence of life in Britain, with long-term effects on the self-image and the capacity to identify with a particular group of the individual concerned.

The kind of education which is provided for particular groups within the population reflect in part the historical development of the system and the needs of society as these are perceived by the policy-makers. Glass, in the Reading on 'Education and Social Change', looks at the different levels of provision and the assumptions which underlay them. In place of the view of a relatively static tradition he presents one which has experienced a considerable number of changes in consequence of new priorities being established but which remains in general strongly elitist in the distinctions made between middle classes and the rest in terms not only of potential but of educational opportunities.

The Readings on 'Institutions and Teachers' concentrate on three main themes. The first examines the changes in commitment to the school of boys entering a particular grammar school in a northern area over a period of time. Two examples are given by Lacey of boys whose careers, for reasons within the class situation, did not conform to the established relationship between social class and academic achievement.

The Newsom Report was concerned with those attending secondary modern schools. It makes the connection between the kinds of schools attended and educational

success. One important influence, which the Reading is
selected to illustrate, is in the differential 'holding power'
of schools in terms of the length of stay of their staffs in
different kinds of neighbourhoods. The consequences,
especially where this influence is one of a number of others
including the mobility of the student population, the age of
the school, its equipment and level of amenity, the attitudes
of staff, and relations between home and school, are far-
reaching.

The role of the teacher is obviously a crucial one,
particularly when the school is not only an agency of social
promotion but one of the few remaining agencies of social
demotion. How he performs will reflect not only his
training but his social attitudes and expectations. Floud
considers the crisis in the teacher's role and in particular
the bases of the moral authority of the teacher. Their
traditional authority tends to be undermined by certain
social pressures and it is also suggested that they are
generally ill-equipped by their social and educational
history to cope with the tasks confronting them.

Social relationships within the group form an increasingly
important element in the process of socialization. Downes
looks at the delinquent gang and how factors such as
teenage culture and re-housing have undermined the
traditional gang framework. He distinguishes clearly
between adolescent peer groups, where young people can
experience for the first time relationships embodying
equality and democracy, and the gang, which tends to be
hierarchical and tightly knit. This has consequences for the
treatment of the seriously disturbed delinquent, and also
how we view the types of adolescent protest. Spencer, in
Stress and Release in an Urban Estate, about an area in
Bristol, provides a contrasting view of the adolescent gang
which sees it much more in terms of similar kinds of
behaviour—in general outline though not in specific
content—to that of young people in other countries from
similar social backgrounds.

Social Class Influences 1
B. Bernstein

Reprinted with permission from 'Some Sociological Determinants of Perception', *British Journal of Sociology*, Vol. IX, June 1958, pp. 161–6.

The child in the middle-class and associative levels is socialized within a formally articulated structure. Present decisions affecting the growing child are governed by their efficacy in attaining distant ends, affectually and cognitively regarded. Behaviour is modified by and oriented to an explicit set of goals and values which create a more stable system of rewards and punishments, although the psychological implications of this may vary from one family to another. The future is conceived of in direct relation to the educational and emotional life of the child. Consequently, the child grows up in an ordered rational structure in which his total experience is organized from an early age. Within middle-class and associative levels direct expressions of feeling, in particular feelings of hostility, are discouraged. The word mediates between the expression of feeling and its approved social recognition, that is, a value is placed upon the verbalization of feeling. This is so in all societies but the important determining factor here is the nature of the words and the type of language-use, not necessarily the size of vocabulary, but the degree to which the social emphasis on an aspect of the language structure mediates the relation between thought and feeling. Language exists in relation to a desire to express and communicate; consequently, the mode of a language structure —the way in which words and sentences are related—reflects a particular form of the structuring of feeling and so the very means of interaction and response to the environment.

When a middle-class mother says to her child, 'I'd rather you made less noise, darling', the child will tend to obey because previous disobedience after this point has led to expression of disapproval or perhaps other punitive measures. The operative words in this sentence which the middle-class child responds to are 'rather' and 'less'. The child has learnt to become sensitive to this form of sentence and the many possible sentences in this universe of discourse. The words 'rather' and 'less' are understood, when used in this situation, as directly translatable cues for immediate response on the part of the middle-class child. However, if the same statement were made to a child from the family of an unskilled worker it would not be understood as containing the same imperative cues for response. 'Shut up!' may contain a more appropriate set of cues. Of course, the last statement is meaningful to a middle-class child, but what it is important to stress is the fact that the middle-class child has learned to be able to respond to both statements, and both are differentially discriminated within a finely articulated world of meaning. We are discussing two modes of language and the working-class child has only learned to respond to one, and so although he may understand both, he will not differentiate effectually between the two. Further, if the first statement is made by a middle-class person to a working-class child, the child will translate it into 'Shut up' and will relate the difference between the statements to the different social levels. What he will not have, and what he cannot respond to directly, is the different language structure of the first sentence. The working-class child has to translate and thus mediate middle-class language structure through the logically simpler language structure of his own class to make it personally meaningful. Where he cannot make this translation he fails to understand and is left puzzled.

One of the aims of the middle-class family is to produce a child oriented to certain values but individually differentiated within them. The child is born into an environment where he is seen and responded to as an individual with his own rights, that is, he has a specific social status. This early process of individuation is accomplished by two important factors: the scrupulous observation of the child by the parents so that the very fine stages of development and the emergence of new patterns of behaviour are the object of attention and comment; together with recognition and communication in a language structure where personal qualifications are significantly used and which the child learns to use in response. The child's relation to the environment is such that his range and expression of discriminating verbal responses is fostered by the social structure from the beginning. A vicious circle is set up which is continually reinforced, for the mother will elaborate and expand the embryo personal qualificatory statements that the child makes. It would follow that the greater the differentiation of the child's experience the greater his ability to differentiate and elaborate objects in his environment.

The next fact to consider is the way in which the order of communication, the mode of expression of language, modifies perception. It is necessary to make a distinction between non-verbal expressions of meaning and verbal expressions of meaning in any communication. The role of gesture, facial expression, bodily movement, in particular volume and tone of the speaking voice, will be termed 'immediate' or direct expression, whilst the words used will be termed 'mediate' or indirect expression. What is important is the emphasis placed upon one or the other and the nature of the form of the verbal communication. Now if the words used are part of a language which contains a high proportion of short commands, simple statements and questions where the symbolism is descriptive, tangible, concrete, visual and of a low order of generality, where the emphasis is on the emotive rather than the logical implications, it will be called a public language. Feelings which find expression in this language will themselves be affected by the form of the expressions used. Feelings communicated will be diffuse and crudely differentiated when a public language is being used, for if a personal qualification is to be given to this language, it can only be done by non-verbal means, primarily by changes in volume and tone accompanied by gesture, bodily movement, facial expression, physical set. Thus if the language between mother and child is a public one, as it is in the working-classes, then the child will tend to become sensitive to the quality and strength of feeling through non-verbal means of expression, for the personal qualification will be made through these means. And this has many implications for the structuring of experience and relationships with objects.

The language-use of the middle-class is rich in personal, individual qualifications, and its form implies sets of advanced logical operations; volume and tone and other non-verbal means of expression although important take second place. It is important to realize that initially in the middle-class child's life it is not the number of words or the range of vocabulary which is decisive but the fact that he or she becomes sensitive to a particular form of indirect or mediate expression where the subtle arrangement of words and connections between sentences convey the feeling. It is the latter which the child originally strives to obtain in order to experience a full relationship with the mother and in so doing learns to respond to a particular form of language cues. Because of the importance of this type of mediate relation between mother and child a tension is created between the child and his environment such that there is a need to verbalize his relations in a personal, individual way. Thus the child at an early age becomes sensitive to a form of language-use which is relatively complex and which in turn acts as a dynamic framework upon his or her perception of objects. This mode of language-use will be termed formal. It was stated earlier that the pressure within a middle-class social structure to intensify and verbalize an awareness of separateness and difference increases the significance of objects in the environment. Receptivity to a particular form of language structure determines the way relationships to objects are made and an orientation to a particular manipulation of words.

The child in the middle-classes and associative levels grows up in an environment which is finely and extensively controlled; the space, time, and social relationships are explicitly regulated within and outside the family group. The more purposeful and explicit the organization of the environment with reference to a distant future, that is the greater the rationality of the connections and inter-relations between means and distant ends, the greater the significance of objects in the present. Objects in the present are not taken as given, but become centres for inquiry and starting points for relationships. The effect of this on the experience of the child is to make him more generally and specifically aware of a wide range of objects at any one time which will intensify his curiosity and reward his explorations. Here the critical factor is the mode of the relationship and this is a function of his sensitivity to structure. A dynamic interaction is set up: the pressure to verbalize feelings in a personally qualified way, the implications of the language learnt, combine to decide the nature of the cues to which he responds—structural cues. An orientation towards structure allows many interpretations or meanings to be given to any one object, which increases the area and intensity of the child's curiosity and receptiveness. This leads to an awareness of the formal ordering of his environment, notions of its extensions in time and space and so is the beginning of the formation of primitive interpretative concepts. This, of course, is part of the socializing process of any child but it is the mode of established relationships which is of decisive importance because the mode determines the levels of conceptualization possible. Different children will be able to benefit more from this environment as a result of other factors, e.g. specifically psychological factors, but the means of utilizing and exploiting formal educational facilities are provided.

The school is an institution where every item in the present is finely linked to a distant future, consequently there is no serious clash of expectations between the school and the middle-class child. The child's developed time-span of anticipation allows the present activity to be related to a future and this is meaningful. There is little conflict of values between the teacher and child and more importantly the child is pre-disposed to accept and respond to the language structure of communication. The school aims at assisting the development of consciousness of self, cognitive and emotional differentiation or discrimination, and develops and encourages mediate relationships. There is, in the child, a desire to use and manipulate words in a personal qualifying or modifying way and, in particular, a developing sense of tense (time) which together combine to reduce the problem of the teaching of English: reading, spelling, writing. The middle-class child is predisposed towards the ordering of symbolic relationships and more importantly, imposing order and seeing new relationships. His level of curiosity is high. There is a conformity to authority and an acceptance of the role of the teacher, irrespective of psychological relationships to his personality. This is not to say that at times feelings of rebellion will not appear. The middle-class child is capable of manipulating the two languages—the language between social equals (peer groups) which approximates to a public language and a formal language which permits sensitivity to role and status. This leads to appropriateness of behaviour in a wide range of social circumstances. Finally, the school is an important and socially approved means whereby the developing child can enhance his self-respect. Thus the social structure of the school, the means and ends of education, create a framework which the middle-class child is able to accept, respond to and exploit.

Social Class Influences 2
A. Little and J. Westergaard

Reprinted with permission from 'The Trend of Class Differentials in England and Wales', *British Journal of Sociology*, Vol. 15, No. 3, 1964, pp. 311–14.

The analysis gives as accurate a comparison of pre-war and post-war educational opportunities as it seems possible to present from available data. The results are easily summarized. Social inequalities in access to selective secondary education have been somewhat reduced over the past 50–60 years. But the reduction has, in the first place, been small—so small as to disappear should one choose to look at the differentials in failure to obtain a grammar school type education, rather than at the differentials in successful admission to such an education. In the second place, the reduction of social inequalities is not a new, post-1944 phenomenon, but the continuation of a long-term, gradual trend. And in the third place, it has been confined to entry into selective secondary education, while access to the universities has remained more or less unaffected. The general increase of grammar school places has benefited children of all social classes, but working class children proportionately rather more than others. The general increase of university places has perhaps, if anything, benefited children of the upper and middle strata more than those from the lower stratum. Certainly, the overall expansion of educational facilities has been of greater significance than any redistribution of opportunities.

The persistence of marked social inequalities in educational opportunity is in line with a good deal of other evidence on the relative constancy of class divisions in our society. While average levels of living have increased in absolute terms, and crude economic insecurity has been reduced, relative differences between the strata remain sharp—in the distribution of wealth and welfare, in the incidence of infant mortality, in patterns of fertility, for example. Some of these or other social differentials may perhaps be in process of modification. Boundary lines between the strata are inevitably imprecise; and there is considerable movement of individuals across them—though probably no more now than fifty years ago. Nevertheless, the social classes constitute genuine groupings, 'quasi-communities' distinct from each other in their typical life chances and styles of living.

To recognize this, however, is not to assume that particular patterns of inequality are fixed, or embedded in so tightly interlocking a complex of economic and cultural factors as to defeat attempts either to identify particular causes or to pursue particular policies designed to reduce such inequalities. Differentials in educational opportunity coincide with many other social differentials: their causes need still to be separately traced. A good deal of recent work has pointed to the important—and almost certainly increasing—role of cultural, rather than crude material, factors in perpetuating educational inequalities: class differences in educational aspirations, occupational orientations, language, intellectual climate, and so on. Fruitful or promising as much of this work has been, it should not blind one to the continuing influence also of other factors, less subtle in their operation—and more immediately amenable to change through deliberate policy. Among this latter group of factors are the gross economic facts of educational provision—the continued existence of a private school system, closed to most of the population; the persistence of wide differences in educational provision between different areas; and the low level of total educational provision in a society which—like most European countries—reserves formal schooling beyond a fairly rudimentary stage for a small minority of its young people. The effect which this latter feature, in particular, may have on the social distribution of such educational facilities as exist has still to be explored in precise terms. But almost certainly it helps to give the patterns of educational inequality the character of a self-perpetuating cycle. The education of the great majority of children finishes at 15 or shortly after. As a result the working class child who strives or is encouraged to stay on at school is deviating from the pattern of early entry into the labour market which is the typical experience of his age-mates of the same social background. Because successful completion of a full grammar school course is thus at present inevitably exceptional, it is not surprising to find hints in the evidence available that fairly often the working class child who manages it comes from a family which, by virtue of origins, style of life or aspirations, is somewhat detached from the general working class environment.

The adoption of an educational policy and philosophy,

through which early school leaving became the exception rather than the rule, would change this situation. But it could not be expected to eliminate the social inequalities in educational opportunity. Such inequalities would more likely be shifted to those later stages of education where selection would then operate—and where at present in Britain, as we have suggested, competitive social pressures are not so strongly felt. A comparison with the United States, where the typical age of leaving school is much later than in Europe, is illuminating. An estimate for the early 1950s indicated that the chances of graduating from a university or college varied from over 40 per cent for children from professional and semi-professional homes to some 6 or 8 per cent for children from manual workers' and farm families. There is a strong general similarity between these differentials and those found in England and Wales, at about the same date, in the proportions staying on at school till 17 or more—with the big difference, of course, that the American figures relate to college graduation.

Consideration of the trends in educational opportunity in Britain may help to throw light on the wider question of trends, past and future, in social mobility generally. It may also help to explain the contradiction between the empirical finding of constancy in social mobility rates over time in this country and others, and the expectations that mobility rates would have changed over time. Class differentials in educational opportunity have been diminishing somewhat throughout this century. The fact that social mobility rates have remained roughly stable during the same period therefore suggests that mobility through channels other than the educational system—in particular, career mobility through promotion and demotion—has been correspondingly reduced. This is precisely what might be expected. But if this is so, and if the opportunities for career mobility continue to become gradually more restricted as the result of continued professionalization, bureaucratization and automation of work—then it would seem unlikely that the rather modest further narrowing of class inequalities in educational opportunity which has followed the 1944 Act will be sufficient to bring about any significant net increase in total social mobility. For the probable continuing restriction of career mobility to be more than just about counter-balanced by widening of the educational channel of mobility, a far more radical attack on the causes of educational—and related general—inequalities would be necessary than appears to be envisaged as a matter of current policies.

Social Class Influences 3
G. H. Elder, Jr.

Reprinted with permission from 'Life Opportunity and Personality: Some Consequences of Stratified Secondary Education in Great Britain', *Sociology of Education*, Spring 1965, Vol. 38, No. 3, pp. 184–99.

Presumably assignment to a low-status school or to a low academic stream within a school affects a British youth's public esteem which, in turn, affects his private self-esteem. Typically, youth who have a low opinion of themselves as students perform in accordance with their self-assessment. Since low self-esteem is associated with anxiety, defensiveness, low achievement, and low future aspirations, the consequences of eleven-plus failure and of allocation to streams within the grammar and modern school are likely to be substantial. The enduring consequences of being typed as a failure during childhood are revealed in the experience of the head of one comprehensive school in Western England: 'After extensive enquiries, I have not found any pupil who failed the eleven-plus who has overcome his sense of inferiority at this failure, irrespective of his performance even at university level.' In addition to the psychological harm produced by the eleven-plus, this selection procedure contributes little towards developing every youth's ability to the fullest capacity.

The restriction of a youth's opportunities, coupled with the punishment associated with failing, tends to engender a negative self-image which, in turn, is apt to be associated with an under-utilization of mental abilities. Instead of coping with and exploring scholastic tasks, the student with a negative self-image is apt to avoid such demands.

The effects of streaming within primary schools on academic achievement are comparable to the consequences of being assigned to selective and non-selective secondary schools. Among students of equal measured ability in primary school, Douglas found that those of middle-class status were more likely than working-class students to be assigned to upper streams. Academic deterioration was characteristic of students in lower streams, especially those of working-class status. Relatively low-ability students seemed to benefit most academically between ages 8 and 11 if placed in upper streams, while brighter students suffered most in the lower streams. (From a probabilistic standpoint it should be noted that large gains are more possible for low-ability youth as are large losses for bright youth.) Jackson and Marsden, in a study of the educational careers of 88 working-class children in Marburton, observed that few of the working-class children in grammar school who were placed in ability groups below A lasted for the sixth form. 'Once declared "C" children, did they not begin to learn, play, act, think, and feel as "C" children? Precisely that.' The mobility aspirations of youth in different streams conforms in ordinal progression to their respective status levels in the school; 'A' stream youth are more upwardly mobile in their aspirations than 'B,' 'C,' or 'D' children. Persistence in Secondary School—variations in scholastic achievement by social class and secondary school—are paralleled by differences in student persistence in grammar and modern school.

The lack of meaningful courses for modern school youth who desire to remain beyond the age of 15 is an important condition producing this response on the part of able students in modern schools. Children of high ability in modern schools are commonly aware of the difficulty in obtaining adequate preparation for the G.C.E. In one or two years of extended courses, modern students are frequently faced with accomplishing what grammar school youth achieve over four or five years of schooling. In the words of one modern school student: 'It takes a long time at my school to get enough G.C.E. subjects; you would need about twenty years before you got enough.' Boredom, and complaints about lethargic teachers were common themes among 200 students from five modern schools in Sheffield. 'Many boys and girls seemed to have spent a lot of their time at school in a state of boredom and learning little. Occasionally they "had fun"—notably when they managed "to get a teacher off the subject". To achieve this was one of the satisfying accomplishments.' Some of the more ambitious boys were highly resentful of the slow pace; 'We didn't do enough work there,' said one boy, 'It was terrible. Most of the teachers just said do something without explaining it, and when you had finished it, instead of going on to teach something more advanced, they just told you to get out a book and read.' Many of them felt that 'they had reached a dead end at school. They preferred to get out into the world and devote their energies to something new, rather than vegetate at schools or struggle against the odds to get on terms with grammar school children. It was better, too, not to take an examination at all than to take one and fail.' Although there are substantial variations among modern schools, students from these schools are generally less positive toward school and are aware of the low status of the school in the community. Findings from the Gallup survey are similar.

The seeming irrelevance of modern school for the life situations of many enrolled youth has left a void in their lives which has been filled in large measure by commercialized youth culture. This culture and the seeming irrelevance of school are major pressures encouraging modern school youth to leave school as soon as possible. As a result, teachers in some modern schools are faced with the frustrating task of teaching youth who could not care less about their course work.

Social Class Influences 4
J. Gerstl and R. Perrucci

Reprinted with permission from 'Educational Channels and Elite Mobility', *Sociology of Education*, 1965, Vol. 38, No. 2, pp. 226–32.

As a contribution to the accumulation of case studies in comparative mobility, we are concerned with changes over time in the recruitment into one elite occupation in Great Britain and the United States. The specific occupation for which we have comparable information is that of the engineer —an elite by dint of professional standing, with similar prestige in the two countries.

The general framework for this comparison is necessarily the total mobility pattern for the two countries involved. Three separate indices of upward mobility in Britain and the U.S. from Miller's analysis are shown in Table 1. The rates of intergenerational movement from manual to nonmanual categories are very similar for the two countries. However, consideration of movement into elite occupations from either the manual or middle-class level shows the two to have dissimilar patterns. Britain has much less mobility into elite occupations than does the United States.

Part of this difference is due to the relative size of the elite category and is thus not only a reflection of the amount of individual movement or pure mobility. In America, with larger elite strata, there is a structural push toward a higher rate of mobility into the elite. In addition, the mechanisms for gaining access to elite occupations are very different in the two societies. The contrast is that of contest and sponsored mobility, seen most dramatically in the proportions gaining access to higher education.

Table 1. Upward Mobility Rates for Great Britain and the United States

	Manual into Nonmanual	Middle Classes into Elite I and II	Manual into Elite I and II
Great Britain	24·8	8·6	2·2
United States	28·8	19·8	7·8

The more recent U.S. engineers are increasingly the sons of professionals (21 per cent to 30 per cent). Younger British engineering graduates, on the other hand, are less likely to be the sons of professionals than are their older colleagues (52 per cent to 28 per cent). The increasing proportion of high status sons moving into engineering in the U.S. seems to have paralleled the upgrading of engineering as a profession. The increasing emphasis upon mathematics and the physical sciences as necessary for engineering has also enhanced its respectability. In addition, these prerequisites for engineering as a career are more likely to be a part of the high school curriculum of the high status son than of the low status son. A similar pattern of upgrading the engineering profession does not seem to have occurred in Great Britain, despite the continued concern regarding recruitment into the profession. This may account for the lack of attraction which engineering in Britain has for sons of professionals. The contrasting status of engineers in the two countries is indicated by the one-way flow of the 'brain drain', England constantly losing personnel to the U.S.

While there has been little change in recruitment patterns for American engineers in the two most recent time periods, the amount of upward mobility for the British has been steadily increasing. Interestingly, for the most recent engineers, the proportion coming from professional backgrounds is similar for the two countries. The total pattern that emerges with respect to changes over time is one of declining mobility in American recruitment as contrasted with increasing mobility in Britain.

It is, of course, possible that the relatively small shifts in recruitment that have occurred in the U.S. sample (as compared to the British sample) may be due to changes in the proportion of the labour force in various occupational categories. Thus, the increasing proportion of engineers coming from professional origins would be due simply to an increasing proportion of the labour force who are professionals. An examination of the occupational structure over the last half-century in the U.S. does not indicate that our changing patterns of recruitment are only reflections of the changing composition of the labour force. Between 1910 and 1960 there has been a steady increase in the proportion of the labour force in professional occupations and in clerical and sales occupations. Our recruitment data show similar increases in the proportion of engineers having fathers of professional and clerical and sales occupations. However, census data also indicate that there has been a sizeable increase in the proportion of the labour force in skilled and semi-skilled occupations. Our recruitment data, on the other hand, indicate that the largest recruitment decline has occurred among sons of skilled and semi-skilled fathers. An additional consideration is that for this same time period of 1910–60 the number of engineering graduates coming out of the universities has gone from approximately 1,000 to 36,000. Thus, the marked growth in engineering enrolments has not come from any increased recruitment of manual working-class sons to this occupation.

We may hazard a few guesses as to the continuation of these recruitment trends for the two countries in question. The increasing proportion of recruitment from manual strata in Britain is likely to continue. The changes in British education beginning with the 1944 Education Act concerning secondary education, are only now affecting higher education as indicated in the Robbins report. On the other hand, the trend of increasing recruitment from high status origins in the U.S. will probably continue considering the apparent flow of high calibre students into engineering and science. It would appear that even the increased manpower needs for engineers, as suggested by several personnel projections, will not necessarily increase the recruitment of lower class youth, since the increased needs will occur in management and basic research functions, while traditional engineering functions will remain stable. In this connection, we would suggest that it is the traditional engineering image that would most likely attract the mobile lower-class youth, while the basic research and managerial functions would require academic knowledge and social skills that are differentially distributed in the class structure. Thus, the lower-class youth in the U.S. is disadvantaged both by the lack of social supports and inducements to undertake science oriented curricula, and by the absence of such programs in the schools he is most likely to attend.

A refinement in the analysis of the degree of mobility attained may be introduced by considering the degree of success achieved in professional engineering careers. Clearly, not all engineers are of equal status. If success is independent of social origins, this would be an additional indicator of the openness of the social structure.

As access to the means for mobility (i.e. engineering training) becomes wider, differential rewards are more likely to be related to social origins. For access to training operates as a screening mechanism which, if highly rigorous, is more likely to result in equal treatment once the initial hurdle is passed. Since university entrance is much more selective in Britain than in the U.S., we would expect that this is the stage at which the crucial sorting out process takes place. Just as almost all British entrants to university survive through their final year while Americans do not, so the success of British graduates in the same field should be more independent of their social origins than it is in the U.S.

All British engineering graduates are seen to have good chances of success, whatever their origins. Although those of manual origins do somewhat less well, there is no difference between sons of professionals and those from middle-class backgrounds.

Our most general finding emerging from the comparison of one elite level occupation in two countries, both in terms of changing patterns of recruitment over time and in the relation of social origins to degree of success, suggests the degree of fluidity in Britain to be greater than in the U.S. This does not by itself refute the conclusion of the broad similarity of trends in industrialized countries. It may well be, for example, that the pattern for other occupations is very different and may off-set trends that apply in the case of engineers. However, the importance of engineering as indicative of patterns for elite occupations must not be underestimated. For, engineering is the single largest professional category in an industrial society (excluding teaching, of course, which is primarily female). Furthermore, it is likely that engineering is the one profession most open to entry, engineers tending to have lower status origins than members of other professions. In addition, once entry to the engineering profession is realized, success should be more susceptible to intrinsic career criteria than in other professions. For example, in medicine and law, family influence, as manifest in contacts and financial aid in starting a practice, is much more relevant than it is in the organizational world of the engineer. It is in this respect that engineering is most exemplary of 'careers open to talent'. These considerations apply equally to engineers in Britain and in the U.S.

Two Cultures
E. D. Butterworth

Reprinted with permission from D. Martin (Editor): *A Sociological Yearbook of Religion in Britain* 2, London, SCM Press, 1969, pp. 151–4.

There is much stronger emphasis within the Muslim family on the authority of its senior members and in particular of the father. In a society without social security and welfare the obligations of children to support parents are stressed. In the presence of parents the child must be docile and quiet, and a degree of formality develops in the relationships between fathers and sons as the sons get older. One aspect of this is the way in which fathers lay down what their children should do. In more permissive situations there is a conflict between what children from this background see as being the practice of their schoolfellows and what their parents expect of them at home. In addition there are great distinctions between the roles of men and women. Generalization is difficult because so much depends upon the personal circumstances of the individual, and women of a higher social group, especially if living in cities, may have more freedom than their rural counterparts. In Pakistan there is a discrepancy between the rights which women are accorded by the teachings of religion and their actual situation. Under Muslim law women have rights, for example, to inheritance and divorce, but there is a great discrepancy between what their situation is according to law and what it is in practice if they live in remote rural areas.

The activity of women is mainly confined to the domestic sphere. Men spend their leisure time with companions of their own sex and marriage is an alliance of families. Girls are protected, after puberty, from contact with men who are not related. When a girl marries she is expected to have had no contact with young men at all. One informant said, in contrasting British and Muslim practice:

It is really unfortunate that even some teachers approach Muslim parents to allow their daughters to adopt the English way of life, such as having boy friends, which is totally unacceptable to our culture.

The kind of problems which arise in practice in the school situation include girls sitting next to boys and talking to them. In a Muslim society they cease to mix at an early age. Girls adopt traditional female dress which covers the legs and they remain in a secluded world. Any hint of irregular behaviour on the part of the girl, such as conversing with boys, may affect not only her marriage prospects but also those of her relatives.

The difficulties of preserving this degree of separation, and the institution of 'purdah', by which women are protected from contact with males outside their family circle, are obvious in Britain. At first some women were taken to clinics by their husbands but conflicts arise between the need for husbands to be at work and to protect their wives. Modifications of practice are inevitable in many cases and have taken place. Often women look upon the visit to the clinic or shops as an excursion. If possible they go with another woman, who is usually related.

Preserving dietary practices may also be difficult. Quite large numbers of Muslim men appear to drink alcohol, and it is not always possible to check where the foodstuffs come from and in particular whether meat is being killed in the approved way. Children who stay for school meals may be particularly liable to eat food which is not prepared according to precept.

In the sphere of education the demands of parents, or the conflicts between the values of the family and the values of the school, cause tensions for the child. One practical issue is that the desire to teach the child about Muslim culture and religion may mean that children, often quite young, spend long hours at the weekend or after school or both, learning about their traditions. Though not all children attend the classes which are provided there are increasing contraints to do so. However, if parents become aware of the strains which this is imposing they may well question the importance of traditional studies of their religion and culture as compared with the subjects taught in the school situation. Those with a strong motivation for their children to do well and adapt themselves and obtain better jobs may be more resistant to this development.

The methods employed by the teachers at the schools set up by the communities or groups are far more formal and authoritarian than those in an English school. The reverence for learning which is inculcated stresses forms of rote learning and knowledge of 'facts' rather than power of analysis. Thus even for the child in a good school environment problems of adaptation frequently arise and the teaching models reveal considerable differences between the situation in which he learns about his background and that in which he learns to adapt himself to English society. There is also the problem of the 'helpful' parent, teaching in a way alien to the tradition in this country. Parents adopting an inflexible, authoritarian attitude may well dominate their children and, for example, keep them within the confines of the home quite effectively, but in a number of cases there may well be open discontent and the possibility of family breakdown. To specify the kinds of breakdown which could arise, and put a relative value on them, would be difficult at this stage of the settlements, but undoubtedly delinquency is one possible area of deviation. Others include relationships with people of the same age group of the opposite sex. The fears in this respect are almost always expressed on behalf of the girls rather than the boys.

The changes going on in patterns of life and consequent effects on religious beliefs and cultural practices seem to be anticipated hardly at all by the Muslim community in Britain. On the whole the attitude of the religious leadership is to ignore the kinds of consequences that are likely to arise from life in a more affluent, sophisticated and urban environment. Some informants suggested that parents were aware of some of the considerable problems but hoped that they would not arise in an acute form in their own lifetime. Those in a position to make a choice and who move to the edges of the areas may well accommodate themselves to some aspects of life in Britain and obtain far more benefits both for themselves and for their children. On the other hand these are people in the front line of integration, as it were, and the response to them will depend on the general character of race relations in the country. Accommodation that does take place will reflect the growing similarity of interests, at least in certain respects, between migrants and native-born.

With increasing affluence and the extent to which the society remains, or becomes, more 'open' in terms of opportunities linked to ability, changes are more likely to take place. One of the more significant developments in recent years has been the emergence of a definite class structure which, professional people apart, is not entirely based on the working class. There are two main groups of the upwardly mobile. One is of those professional people in medicine or law who provide services both for the minority group and for the host community. The other, a much larger section, is of people who have begun as workers but, by dint of saving, have acquired business and commercial interests. The form this takes is either through the ownership of property or the ownership of shops or businesses. Styles of life in some cases may begin to approximate more closely to those of the equivalent groups in the host community. Many similarities exist between those who have emerged from the working class and those who have stayed in it, but it is conceivable that, for some, class and social group interests may come to outweigh the ethnic loyalties which previously have prevailed.

Not all will be influenced, especially in a situation where there is a high density of settlement. It is possible that the greater the concentration in the ghetto situation the more the need for a siege mentality will develop. At the same time great changes are likely to come about in traditional structures of authority. How far the Muslim religion can retain its hold in a completely different situation and in a modern society which has few similarities with those in which the majority of Muslims live is an open question.

Education and Social Change
D. V. Glass

Reprinted with permission from M. Ginsberg (Editor): *Law and Opinion in the Twentieth Century*, London, Stevens & Sons, 1959, pp. 322–7.

In the late nineteenth century England was still educationally a very under-developed society. It would, of course, be both incorrect and unjust to minimize the part which religious and philanthropic bodies had already played in establishing schools. The incidence of illiteracy could not have been as high as it is in some underdeveloped countries today. Even so, a third of the men marrying in 1840 in England and Wales, and half of the women, signed the registers by a mark; the proportions in 1870 were still 20 per cent and 27 per cent. The rate of change in the provision of education since 1870 has been so rapid that it must be taken into account when considering present-day educational deficiencies.

It must be equally clear that the phrase 'the English tradition of education' not infrequently used in arguing against further rapid change in the character of secondary education, has a very limited validity. It can scarcely apply to the public system which, even during its brief history, has greatly altered in respect of objectives, structure and methods of selection. Nor, in the sense of a centuries-old persistence of character, is the term really applicable to the private sectors, whether secondary or university. It is true that, as an institution, the grammar school 'has a thousand years of history behind it'. But the present character of grammar schools derives from action taken during the nineteenth and twentieth centuries, action originally taken because, however deeply rooted the grammar school idea may have been, the schools themselves had ceased to be effective as educational institutions. In any case, most grammar schools today are not private. They are maintained by the local education authorities; they are thus part of the public system; and they have been exposed to powerful pressures for change in the curriculum, in the universe from which pupils are drawn, and in the qualifications of teachers. The public schools, too—the schools belonging to the Headmasters' Conference and the most firmly imbedded and 'traditionalist' part of the private system—bear little resemblance to their original form. They were, on the contrary, the first schools to be reconstructed in the nineteenth century. Indeed, it was the reforms introduced by Arnold and others which, as G. M. Young has said, 'reconciled the serious classes to the public school', and which encouraged the establishment of additional schools; fifty-one out of the present one hundred and sixteen independent public boarding schools were founded in the nineteenth century. The curriculum has also changed, though more slowly, and half the present public schools specialize in science and mathematics. The process of change has applied equally to the universities. The history of university reform is too well known to need documenting here. But it is evident that Trevelyan's description of Oxford and Cambridge in the days of decay as 'little more than comfortable monastic establishments for clerical sinecurists with a tinge of letters' would scarcely apply now. Moreover, the larger part of the university complex is itself the creation of the nineteenth century, and almost two-thirds of today's university students are studying in institutions established since the 1830s.

Much of the present educational system is thus not traditional. Moreover, many of its characteristics are not particularly English. Even during the first half of the nineteenth century, once the memory of the French Revolution had become a little clouded, educational reformers in England drew markedly upon the experiments which were being conducted on the Continent. And this was just as well, for the new influences helped to replace the more specifically British contributions of Lancaster's mutual system and Bell's 'Madras' system, which appeared to require a school to be a combination of factory and of Bentham's Panopticon. Later in the century Matthew Arnold imported from France the term 'secondary education' and with it the objective of a reorganized and comprehensive system. Technical education, too, especially in its shifting emphasis from craftsmanship to general principles and their application, was influenced both by foreign competition and by foreign models. All this has clearly been to the good. But along with these innovations there has been one underlying continuity—the influence of the class structure on the images of education and its function. It is this continuity and its consequences which I should now like to discuss.

During the nineteenth century, educational developments reflected two fairly distinct sets of considerations, one relating to the mass of the population and the other to the middle classes. Public concern with elementary education was in large measure concern to meet certain minimum requirements in a changing society—the need to ensure discipline, and to obtain respect for private property and the social order, as well as to provide that kind of instruction which was indispensable in an expanding industrial and commercial nation. Though many individuals and groups showed a far broader vision, these minimal considerations are evident in the very limited objectives of the system which grew up at that time. In the earliest period, the Bible and the catechism were sufficient, Hannah More thought; she would 'allow no writing for the poor.' Later, the sights were set a little higher. Speaking of the working-class child, James Fraser, subsequently Bishop of Manchester, told the 1858 Newcastle Commission that: 'we must make up our minds to see the last of him, as far as the day school is concerned, at ten or eleven . . . and I venture to maintain that it is quite possible to teach a child soundly and thoroughly, in a way that he shall not forget it, all that is necessary for him to possess in the shape of intellectual attainment, by the time that he is ten years old.' The Commission accepted the fact that most children would go to work at the age of ten or eleven. A similar assumption underlies the 1870 Act. It is not surprising that H. G. Wells referred to it as 'an Act to educate the lower classes for employment on lower-class lines, and with specially trained, inferior teachers.'

To gentle the masses was another explicit purpose. 'A set of good schools civilizes a whole neighbourhood,' said the Newcastle Commission; and Forster, when he introduced his 1870 bill in Parliament, spoke of 'removing that ignorance which we are all aware is pregnant with crime and misery, with misfortune to individuals and danger to the community.

And he continued, 'I am one of those who would not wait until the people were educated before I would trust them with political power. If we had thus waited we might have waited long for education; but now that we have given them political power, we must not wait any longer to give them education.' Some of these notions were changed when the 1902 Act provided a framework for both elementary and secondary education. But the civilization motive had a longer currency, and even in 1929 Sir Cyril Norwood argued that it was largely elementary education which had prevented 'Bolshevism, Communism, and theories of revolt and destruction from obtaining any real hold upon the people of this country.' 'I hope,' he added, 'that those who attribute the scarcity of domestic servants to the unreasonable institution of elementary education, by which they are made to pay for the teaching of other people's children, will lay in the other scale this other service, which has made of Bolshevism only a bogy which sits by their pillows and frightens them in the night.'

Concern with secondary education sprang from different motives. The effectiveness of the public schools and the endowed grammar schools as educational institutions for those groups who could afford to make use of them was the main issue. In the early part of the century an attempt had been made to compel the public schools to give the local poor the rights to entry provided by the founders' statutes. But the attempt failed, and the place of the public schools in the national system of secondary education was not again discussed by a Government committee until 1942. Instead, in 1861 a Royal Commission was appointed to study the quality of the education in what have ever since been known as the 'Clarendon schools'—nine schools with 2,815 pupils. And the Clarendon Commission was immediately followed by the Taunton Commission, which inquired into the education given in the endowed grammar schools. Though expressing some disquiet at existing class distinction in education, the Taunton Commission in the main accepted the situation as they found it, and their recommendations were drawn up for the benefit of the middle classes by whom the schools were being used. What is particularly interesting is the emergence at this stage of a fresh criterion of the effectiveness of secondary education, the criterion of providing an avenue to the universities; and there were unfavourable references to the fact that 550 grammar schools sent no boys to universities, in sharp contrast to the large numbers now going from the nine Clarendon schools and from some of the recently founded proprietary schools.

For university education, like secondary education, was coming to have a new meaning. The changing society needed individuals of greater educational maturity and tested qualifications. The old and the new middle classes needed avenues of employment which would provide both prestige and relatively high income for their sons. Considerations of both scientific and social status were causing the existing professions to raise their standards of entry, and additional professions, including the higher civil service, were beginning to develop, also demanding considerable educational attainments.

Institutions and Teachers 1
C. Lacey

Reprinted with permission from 'Schools and Academic Streaming', *British Journal of Sociology*, September 1966, Vol. XVII, No. 3, pp. 245–62.

The Local Education Authority of Hightown sends about 15 per cent of its 11-year-olds to grammar schools each year. This clearly does not imply that 15 per cent of the pupils in *any* junior school in the town will find themselves in the same grammar school. There are six grammar schools in Hightown and these are specialized in a number of ways; there are two Roman Catholic grammar schools (one for boys and one for girls) which serve the separate R.C. education system in Hightown and the surrounding area; and four L.E.A. grammar schools (two for girls and two for boys) which draw their pupils almost exclusively from Hightown. For non-Catholic, 11-year-old boys in Hightown there are then three possible grammar school avenues; entry to a direct grant school outside the town, Hightown Grammar School and Hightown Technical Grammar School. (A very small fraction attend public schools.)

The boys entering Hightown Grammar are selected from a large number of junior schools, and the selection test tends to scoop a few pupils from each school. Over half the boys come from schools that send six or less pupils. Evidence from a variety of sources (junior school reports, autobiographies and the statements of junior school teachers etc.) clearly shows that these contingents include the vast majority of top scholars, team leaders, school monitors, head boys and teachers' favourites. In short they are the 'best pupils'.

When the boys arrive at Hightown Grammar they are divided at random into four classes. The classes are also House Groups. The pupils in them remain together for prayers, school meals and registration as well as lessons.

A more comprehensive picture of the degree of isolation of the first-year boy, on his arrival at Hightown, must therefore take into account the effect of the school organization: 58 boys out of 118 questioned had no friend from the same junior school in their class. Thus almost half of the first-year intake spend the great majority of their time at school in a class in which they are isolated from their previous friends.

It can be seen from the foregoing analysis that any batch of new boys assembling at Hightown Grammar School are likely to make up a highly selected and homogeneous group. The annual intake being about 120, they represent under 4 per cent of their age group in the community and all are boys who have ostensibly been selected on the basis of their sex, religion and academic achievement.

The homogeneity of the intake and the relative isolation of individual new boys from their junior school friends are both important factors affecting patterns of behaviour in the first-year classes. The first-year pupils show a high degree of commitment to the school. School uniform is rigidly adhered to; caps and blazers are proudly displayed, school functions and clubs are attended disproportionately by first-year boys. Their behaviour in the classroom is characterized by eagerness, cooperation with the teacher and a high degree of competition among themselves. 'Please sir, Willy Brown is copying my sums' is a remark that could only come from a first-year boy. I once tried to measure the response rate to a narrative and question-and-answer lesson given by a History teacher. So many responded to each question that I could not record them. As the tension mounted boys who did not know the answers looked around apprehensively at those who did. These were in a high state of excitement and they smiled triumphantly at those who did not know the answers; they stretched their arms and bodies to the utmost as they eagerly called, 'Sir', 'Sir', 'Sir', every time the master glanced in their direction. When the master said 'All right Green, you tell us,' there were quiet sighs and groans as those who had not been called upon subsided into their seats. The whole performance was repeated as soon as the next question was asked.

During such spells the desire to participate was so great that some boys would put up their hands and strain for notice, even though they had no idea of the answer. And, if asked to give the answer, they would either make a gesture suggesting that they had suddenly forgotten, or else subside with an embarrassed and confused look, to the jeers and groans of the rest of the class who would then redouble their efforts to attract attention.

The type of enthusiasm characteristic of a first-year class was occassionally found in second- or third-year forms but there were a number of observable differences. The second and third forms were more likely to 'play dead' and to allow five or six people to 'do all the work'; and, even if the master succeeded in getting a larger proportion to participate, there was always a residue of boys who hardly participated or who only did so by giving obviously wrong or funny answers. Finally there was the possibility that the form would use any excitement of this kind to sabotage the lesson or to play the fool. For example, a boy will stretch so hard that he falls out of his desk, another will accidentally punch the boy in front as he puts up his hand and the form's 'funny man' will display his wit in response to an ambiguous question—sometimes isolating the teacher from the class by referring to a private class joke.

On one occasion, for example, a master asked three boys to stay behind after the lesson to help him with a task calling for a sense of responsibility and cooperation, the master called 'Williams, Maun and Sherring.' The class burst into spontaneous laughter, and there were unbelieving cries of 'What, Sherring?' The master corrected himself. 'No, not Sherring, Shadwell.' From the context of the incident, it was clear that Sherring's reputation was already inconsistent with the qualities expected of a monitor. On another occasion, Priestley was asked to read and the whole class groaned and laughed. Priestley, a fat boy, had been kept down from the previous year because of ill health (catarrh and asthma) and poor work. He grinned apprehensively, wiped his face with a huge white handkerchief and started to read very nervously. For a few moments the class was absolutely quiet, then one boy tittered, Priestley made a silly mistake, partly because he was looking up to smile at the boy who was giggling, and the whole class burst into laughter. Priestley blew his nose loudly and smiled nervously at the class. The teacher quietened the class and Priestley continued to read. Three lines later a marked mispronunciation started the whole class laughing again. This performance continued with Priestley getting more and more nervous, mopping his brow and blowing his nose. Finally, the master with obvious annoyance snapped, 'All right, Priestley, that's enough!'

This short incident, one of several during the day, served to remind Priestley of his structural position within the class and to confirm the opinions and expectations of the class and the teacher towards him. Priestley's behaviour was consistent with his performance in the examinations at the end of the Autumn Term when he was ranked twenty-ninth out of thirty-three.

During this period of observation I also noticed the significance of the behaviour of another boy, Cready. Cready first attracted my attention because, although his form position was similar to Priestley's (twenty-sixth) he habitually associated with a strikingly different group. He behaved very differently in class, and had a markedly different reputation.

A sociogram for the class showed an apparent inconsistency. In class Priestley was frequently in the middle of a group of mischievous boys. If there was trouble Priestley was in it. I expected him to be fairly popular with some of the boys who led him into trouble, but none of them picked him as a friend. He chose five boys as his friends but the only boy to reciprocate was the other Jewish boy in the class.

The other boys used Priestley to create diversions and pass messages, and because he was so isolated he was only too pleased to oblige. He could never resist the temptation to act as if he was 'one of the boys'. However, when he was caught out they deserted him and laughed at him rather than with him. He was truly the butt of the class.

These incidents, seen in the context of the structure of the class, show how Priestley had fallen foul of the system. He was not in control of his own situation, and anything he tried to do to improve his position only made it worse. His attempts to answer questions provoked laughter and ridicule from his class-mates. His attempt to minimize the distress this caused, a nervous smile round the class, a shrug of the shoulders; pretending either that he had caused the disturbance on purpose or that he did not care, served to worsen his position with the teacher.

He compensated for his failure in class and lack of academic success by learning the stocks and shares table of the *Financial Times* every week. This enabled him to develop a reputation in a field outside the sphere in which the school was competent to judge. He would emphasize the *real* importance of this in his future career and thus minimize the effect of his scholastic failure. Even this did not improve his standing in the school, especially with the staff. It served only to explain his laziness, his bad behaviour and lack of concern with school work.

It is interesting to note the family background of these two boys. Priestley is Jewish, second in a family of three and lives in an area of expensive detached houses. His father is a clearance stock buyer. Cready on the other hand lives on a council estate, is fourth out of six in the family and his father is a quality inspector in an abrasives factory.

Cready and Priestley do not, therefore, conform with the established correlation between academic achievement and social class. Cready, a working-class boy from a large family on a council estate, is making good, while Priestley, an upper-middle class boy from a smaller family, is failing academically. However, this negative case highlights the point I want to make; there was a measure of autonomy in the system of social relations of the class room. The positions of Cready and Priestley are only explicable in the light of an analysis of the system of social relations *inside* the classroom. This system is open to manipulation by those who are sensitive to its details. Hence Cready, who had all the major external factors stacked against him, was able to use the system of social relations to sustain and buoy himself up, while Priestley, despite all the advantages that he brought to the situation, had fallen foul of the system and was not only failing but also speedily losing any motivation to succeed in the sphere in which the school was competent to judge him.

I reiterate that this is not an attempt to disprove the general established trend but to highlight the fact that there are detailed social mechanisms and processes responsible for bringing it about, which are not completely determined by external factors. By studying these mechanisms it will be possible to add a dimension to our understanding of the general processes of education in our schools.

Institutions and Teachers 2
Newsom Report

Reprinted with permission from *Half Our Future*, A report of the Central Advisory Council for Education (England), London, Her Majesty's Stationery Office, 1963, pp. 245–9.

'Are you going to stay with us, Sir?' was the question which greeted the hero of a recent novel about a modern school as he got to know the boys in his form. They had had a long experience of transient teachers and had not enjoyed it. Were they particularly unfortunate, or is this what must be expected? The Schools in our sample were asked to report their staff changes since September, 1958, so that we might know how many comings and goings of teachers the Browns, Jones and Robinsons of our report had known in their secondary modern schools.

There must, of course, always be changes in school staffs. Experienced teachers reach retiring age, promising men and women get promotion and young men and women are appointed to fill their places. This is a natural and a healthy process. In addition the years covered by our enquiry have been years of increasing numbers of pupils in secondary schools and extra teachers have been appointed to meet the bulge. There were 14 per cent more men and 11 per cent more women teachers in the schools in our sample in 1961 than in 1958.

There is no precise way of deciding from the information in our possession what a normal and healthy turnover would be, but it is necessary to have some kind of yardstick by which to judge the present position. Probably few heads of schools would wish to appoint a man or woman to the staff who would not stay at least three years with them. Heads of training colleges and university departments of education would probably advise their students to stay three years in their first post. Allowance must be made for young teachers who run into difficulties in their first school and are well advised to move to another school where they can avoid the mistakes they have made. Older men and women may find promotion unexpectedly come their way within three years of joining a school staff. It seems reasonable to suppose that somewhere between 10 per cent and 15 per cent of new appointments may rightly move on within three years for one or other of these reasons. The period under review in our survey was one of three years. We know for each school how many men and women were appointed to the staff after September, 1958, up to and including September, 1961. If the argument of this paragraph is sound, we should hope that the schools would still have on their staffs somewhere between 85 and 90 per cent of those appointed during this period. A school with a holding power of this order is in a healthy condition.

An index of 'holding power' was calculated for all schools. Holding power was defined as the proportion of teachers appointed to the staff after September, 1958, who were still in post in September, 1961. On this basis the overall holding power of schools where men teachers are concerned was 65 per cent and for women teachers 58 per cent. Even if our estimate of a healthy situation in the last paragraph proves somewhat too exacting, the contrast between it and these figures indicates an unhealthy state of affairs in modern schools generally.

To some extent this is clearly a national problem—one consequence of the general shortage and wastage of teachers and the greater opportunity of promotion to graded posts since 1956. The difference between the holding power index for men and women teachers is no doubt associated with the early wastage of married women teachers. In the conditions which prevailed in the 1930s both generally and among teachers, the holding power of the schools was almost certainly greater.

But excessive turnover is not only a national problem. The differences in holding power between schools are more than can be explained by sampling fluctuations. Some variation is in any event to be expected just as it is when twenty coins are each tossed ten times. But undue variation—and what is undue in this context can be evaluated mathematically—would be evidence of something odd in the coins themselves. So here the variation is more than would arise accidentally, and is evidence of real differences in holding power not only between categories of schools but between schools in the same category.

The distinction between various kinds of neighbourhood has often been useful in interpreting the data from our survey. The school staffing situation is no exception. Thus, while the average holding power index for men in modern schools is 65 per cent, in socially mixed neighbourhoods it is 70 per cent and in rural schools 76 per cent. In the special group of slum schools it is only 34 per cent. The full picture by neighbourhoods is given in Table 1.

Table 1. Index of Staff Holding Power by Neighbourhoods

	Rural	Mixed	Council	Mining	Problem Areas
Men	76%	70%	67%	58%	55%
Women	69%	57%	58%	60%	56%

These differences are not unexpected and they are certainly important, but perhaps even more important is the fact that these groups are far from homogeneous. The differences between schools in the same type of neighbourhood are often greater than can be explained by chance in the sense in which we have used it. It is reasonable from our data to infer that the quality of the school as a community can on occasion increase or lower its holding power, proving stronger than the effects of the neighbourhood in which its work is done. Some schools at least can help themselves.

Institutions and Teachers 3
J. Floud

Reprinted with permission from 'Teaching in the Affluent Society', *British Journal of Sociology*, September 1962, pp. 301–6, 307–8.

The prestige of the teacher's office and the social and intellectual characteristics of the profession are closely bound up each with the other and with the opportunities for teachers to develop the personal influence over their pupils implied in the notion of 'leadership', which depend on the state of the relations in the wider society between the generations and between family and school. The point about the affluent society is that by its influence in all these interrelated matters it presents formidable obstacles to the successful exercise of institutionalized leadership in teaching; indeed, it precipitates a crisis in the teacher's role which is a familiar feature of the American scene and in this country incipient and potentially severest in the secondary schools. I want briefly to review the familiar social factors at work before turning to the teachers— incumbents of a social role which they are both predisposed and taught to conceive in traditional missionary terms, but which must be performed in the affluent society under conditions which all but transform it.

'The Affluent Society' is a fancy name for an advanced industrial society in which pre-Keynesian economics of scarcity are giving way to post-Keynesian economics of plenty as the results of the twentieth-century technological revolution are assimilated and its dynamic imposes itself, bringing about an unprecedented rate of all-embracing social change. The revolutionary consequences of these developments for education are being explored by economists and sociologists. I do not want to dwell on them here, but merely to recall that they involve, firstly, a great extension and prolongation of formal schooling as education is recognized as a crucial investment for the exploitation of the new technology and as it rises ever higher in the order of public preferences for consumption goods; and secondly, the imposition of new tasks on the schools in connection with the process of social selection.

The pace of social change set by technological developments is ably described in the Crowther Report; its implications for the teacher are more obvious in America where these developments are much farther advanced than in this country; they are vividly rendered by Margaret Mead. Speaking of 'the fantastic rate of change of the world in which we live', she says:

'. . . children of five have already incorporated into their everyday thinking ideas that most of the elders will never fully assimilate . . . Teachers who had never heard a radio until they were grown up have to cope with children who have never known a world without television. Teachers who struggled in their childhood with a button-hook find it difficult to describe a buttonhook to a child bred up among zippers, to whom fastnesses are to be breached by zipping them open, rather than fumblingly feeling for mysterious buttons. From the most all-embracing world image to the smallest detail of daily life the world has changed at a rate which makes the five-year-old generations farther apart than world generations or even scores of generations were in our recent past then people whom we bear and rear and teach are not only unknown to us and unlike any children there have been in the world before, but also their degree of unlikeness itself alters from year to year.'

To this we must add that just at the time when the social and spiritual gulf between the generations is widening in this manner to chasm-like proportions the biological gap between them is narrowing as adolescents mature earlier and adults marry younger.

In these circumstances, on what can the teacher's moral authority rest? Certainly not on the old pretensions—not on the superiority of his culture and experience, the value of which is no longer at all self-evident. And as his moral authority dwindles, so that of the peer-group waxes, and pedagogical devices to establish his personal authority over his pupils are rendered both more necessary and more difficult to carry into effect as his institutional position weakens.

On the other hand, however, the affluent society endows teachers, if not with moral and intellectual authority, then at least with a new power over their pupils. Under conditions where the bond between occupation and schooling is very tight—where vocational qualifications are the modern 'means of production' (Geiger) and in scarce supply, the school becomes an important agency for the distribution of 'life-chances'. What has long been commonplace among parents is now being recognized by teachers—that the school is not only an agency of social promotion but also, in the Welfare State, one of the few remaining agencies of social demotion. So that, so far as parents are concerned, it is less a trusted collaborator in the task of educating their young according to their ability and aptitude than a resented bureaucratic or 'Official' arbiter of their children's social fate.

However, this extraneous power over pupils which is thrust on to the teacher in the affluent society is no simple substitute for his eroded moral authority. In so far as parents and pupils acknowledge and defer to this power (and this, as one knows, is very much a matter of social background) it tends to induce a utilitarian, more or less cynical attitude towards what the teacher has to offer—an unflattering preoccupation with his more commonplace intellectual capital of knowledge and skills, an emphasis on instruction and know-how and an unwillingness to be educated. Alternatively, pupils may react to the pressures of the new situation by withdrawal and flight into indifference to learning or into the active anti-intellectualism of the adolescent sub-culture. This is a phenomenon with which we are all familiar and which Professor Parsons touches on in his essay 'The School Class as a Social System'. It underlies the disturbing picture painted by Riesman of the lengths to which the deterioration in the teacher's traditional authority can go. He shows him entirely dependent for success in the classroom on a tenuous status with his pupils as 'opinion leader', under cloak of which he must manipulate and persuade them to the best of his ability in the light of personal values which are increasingly secular, neutral and imprecisely defined.

How far, we may ask, are we in this country along the road to this particular perdition? The same general social pressures are certainly to be felt over here; but in a radically different social and educational setting and at a lower level of affluence their impact has been more restrained. Thus, the progressive movement in education which deliberately underplays, even when it does not actually deny, the element of authority in the teacher's relationship with his pupils, and is thus both kin and accomplice of the processes we have been describing, cannot be said to have played itself out with us to the point of becoming positively disfunctional in the way that Riesman most plausibly suggests that it has in America. It still stands here for progress in the classroom—for a more humane and technically more skilful pedagogy and for the elimination of some of the occupational hazards to teachers' personalities. Its beneficial effects are most in evidence in our primary schools. But that there is an incipient crisis in the secondary teacher's role cannot be doubted.

Apart from the well-known fact that they are inadequately paid and consequently in very short supply, the striking fact about teachers—at least secondary teachers—is that they are, speaking generally, ill-equipped by their social and educational history to cope with the tasks confronting them in the schools. The majority of our secondary teachers are college-trained non-graduates, successors of the nineteenth-century teacher-missionaries with whom they retain close affinities. A small proportion of secondary teachers, serving mainly in the selective schools, descend from a different tradition—a tradition of being, not social missionaries, but guardians at the gateway into higher education and initiators into the national heritage of learning and culture. Neither group of teachers can be said, for different reasons in each case, to be adequately equipped to man the new national system of secondary schools the absence of which in this country makes one wonder whey we persist in using the term 'affluent society' so freely. If I may generalize wildly, I should say that at a time when all secondary schools must aim to provide for pupils likely to proceed to higher education, the college-trained non-graduate teacher is ill-prepared intellectually, having snatched his personal education from a crowded course of professional training; whilst the graduate teacher, trained or untrained, is ill-equipped to understand the social dimensions of his work even in the selective schools in which he mainly serves. Social factors play an increasingly important part in the work of these schools. They have an intake of pupils which is increasingly representative of the population at large and, like the non-selective ('modern') schools, are undergoing a subtle change of social function.

It seems that the college-trained secondary teacher needs to be more of an intellectual and the graduate teacher more of a social worker. The fact is that the intellectual qualifications for teaching are bound both to rise and to become more uniform throughout the profession in the affluent society, and I think that this should be encouraged.

The teacher-missionary in the nineteenth century needed less education than character, less of the trained intellect than of stamina nourished on firm religious (or sometimes, as in the case of France, secular philosophical) beliefs and principles. In the early history of the normal schools and colleges in which they received their education and training the authorities had frequently to rebuff candidates of superior ability or social standing who could not be expected to remain in the profession once they had received a little education; or to lower the academic quality of the college course in order to narrow the difference between the level of education acquired by teachers in training and the more modest equipment needed on the job in the schools. Fortunately, as we know, they were fighting a rear-guard action against the educational upthrust of the working class—an upthrust which is by no means yet spent—so that the teachers have always had among them a substantial number of able individuals of humble origin out to get an education otherwise inaccessible to them. Nevertheless, the effect of this social and educational history has been to cut the main body of secondary teachers off from the older professions based on the universities.

It is ironic that the Welfare State, in the ante-chamber of the affluent society so to speak, should have introduced measures of educational and social reform which, by democratizing secondary and higher education and widening the occupational horizons of school-leavers, have changed the social basis of recruitment to teaching and threatened its intellectual quality by removing the traditional supply at a discount of able working-class candidates just at the point when the universities were brought to a gesture of recognition (through the institutes of education) of their responsibilities for the education and training of teachers. It is even more ironic, however, to consider that the likely effect of the sluggish expansion of higher education in the next decade will be to drive back into the training colleges large numbers of able working-class boys and girls who will be unable to find places in universities under conditions of intense competition. They will get a better educational bargain than they might have hoped for with the introduction of the three-year course in the colleges, which through the Institutes of Education are in constitutional relationship with universities. But they will emerge nevertheless unnecessarily poorly prepared for the tasks they will confront in the schools.

The problems facing teachers in the affluent society, whether they work in the suburbs or in the slums, are formidable. We have seen how their traditional authority is undermined by social pressures over which neither they nor we can have much control, and how if they are to achieve the indispensable moral ascendancy over their pupils without which they cannot teach, they need to understand, in a way that has perhaps never before been necessary, the social dimensions of their work—the social determinants of the educability of their pupils, the hidden social tensions of the learning situation in contemporary schools, especially in secondary schools.

The case for reshaping the prevailing patterns of recruitment and education for teaching in the light of these considerations seems to me to be overwhelming. Riesman feels 'forced to take for granted the vested interests—the very vested existence—of the schools, and the prevailing patterns of career choice out of which teachers and scholars arise' and is accordingly pessimistic for the future social role of teachers in the United States. Our situation is more flexible and I think we should seize the modest chance offered by our position on the threshold of a period of expansion and re-construction in higher education to bring the recruitment and education of our teachers into line with the complex demands of the social situation in which they now have to work.

Peer Groups
D. Downes

Reprinted with permission from 'The Gang Myth', *The Listener*, April 14, 1966.

What research has been done in Britain implies a radically different group framework for delinquency to that portrayed in the American literature, though it is true that British work is limited to the mid-nineteen-fifties and after. In the most systematic study so far, Dr. Peter Scott, a psychiatrist at the Maudsley Hospital, interviewed 151 boys who were known to have committed group offences. The results were published in 1956—which was, after all, about the heyday of the teddy-boy movement, which was supposed to have been, according to T. R. Fyvel's vivid study, a gang phenomenon. Scott found that only 12 per cent of the boys could be described as mem-bers of 'gangs proper', and these were generally in the young-est age-group—between eight and thirteen. He defined the gang as a group with a leader, definite membership, persistence over time, and definitely delinquent purposes; and he showed that far from supplying the bulk, or even the hard core, of his subjects, gangs barely figured at all as a significant factor on the delinquency scene. Yet the boys he interviewed were in a remand home, and generally this means that they were fairly serious offenders. The majority of them—86 per cent—had offended in what Scott termed diffuse, or loosely structured, groups, whose usual activities were not delinquent, and which did not attempt to coerce any member into delinquent activity—a feature which is inconceivable in the 'gang proper'.

Nevertheless, delinquent gangs were probably much commoner in this country up to and even after the second world war than they are now. In his widely reported New Society article, 'Beat Killed the Gang', Colin Fletcher argued, on the basis of personal experience, that gangs were prevalent in Liverpool until the mid-nineteen-fifties. Then the growth of teenage culture and the great increase in adolescents' spending power diverted the energies and aspirations of 'the boys' into the legitimate fields of youth culture and away from the street-corner gang.

Fletcher's analysis makes sense in more ways than one: the gang seems to be very much a phenomenon of the urban slum, which collects together the most deprived and exploited members of society at a great social distance from the more respectable areas and strata. The effect of teenage culture, and re-housing, was simultaneously to break down the parochial focus of slum adolescents' horizons and to disperse them geographically. And both factors served to undermine the traditional gang framework. There is perhaps an even more fundamental reason why this should be so. The adolescent peer group is, in most societies, a normal and necessary framework for youth. It occupies the stage between childhood dependence on parents and the social responsibilities of adulthood. With their peers—that is, people of the same age, sex, and status—adolescents really experience for the first time relationships embodying equality and democracy.

The gang is a relatively authoritarian form of peer group, so that unless there are powerful reasons why they should take the gang form, adolescent peer groups are most likely to be fluid, democratic and egalitarian, rather than hierarchical and tightly knit. Hence, we often mistake 'peer groups' for 'gang', and infer a 'structure' and 'hierarchy' which their members would themselves regard as ludicrous simply because of barriers to communication between them and us when the groups are both working-class and occasionally delinquent.

Yet the gang myth survives, and it is resurrected at appropriate intervals. The mods' and rockers' riots, for instance, were reported as 'gang delinquency'. An earlier example was the Finchley affray, the incident in which a boy was stabbed in a Finchley youth club after being sought out for some insult said to have been inflicted on a member of the 'Mussies', a couple of dozen boys from Muswell Hill in London. This case was heralded as 'gang warfare' by the bench and the press alike.

The only exception was the *Observer* reporter, Christopher Brasher, who took the trouble to visit the cafes where the boys hung out, and critically examined the gang stereotype. He wrote:

The fight was reported as a 'gang feud' between the 'Mussies' and the 'Finchley mob' . . . The judge said: 'All of you have behaved in a way that would bring discredit on a pack of wolves . . . This gang warfare has to be stamped out.' Yet in north London, as the police will tell you, the 'gangs' are no more than social gatherings in dance-halls and cafes of bored youths from the same area. They have no organization, no accepted leader, and no real name—they are just referred to as 'the mob from Highbury' or 'the mob from the Angel'. They seldom get out of hand, and their fights are usually restricted to a bash on the nose to settle an argument. But the danger is that anyone like Ron Fletcher (the leader of the 'Mussies', who was imprisoned for five years, and who was two or three years older than the rest) anyone like him can quickly whip up a gang to 'turn over' any individual or group which has 'offended' him. Then the iron bars and the knives appear like magic.

From Brasher's account, it is clear that the 'Mussies' constituted a 'gang' for the duration of the offence only; they were assembled virtually overnight by Fletcher from sheer acquaintances; and they would probably have dispersed anyway even if the police had not intervened so successfully. The crucial distinction to be drawn here is that between the 'gang' and what an American sociologist, Lewis Yablonsky, has called the 'near-group'. The 'near-group' lacks persistence over time, and any consensus on membership; it is activated by a hard core of as few as two or three usually seriously disturbed boys, who manipulate a large periphery of short-term members; and it acts through spontaneous mobilization for a single 'flare up' rather than through protracted organization for gang conflict. Obviously, the Finchley affray, and the mods' and rockers' riots, are much closer to the 'near-group' conflict than the 'gang' warfare model.

This distinction may seem trifling if you are worried by delinquency but not by the niceties of how it happens. Given the fact of a messy conflict, who cares whether 'gangs' or 'near-groups' are involved.

In this country gangs are virtually non-existent, but mobilization of 'near-groups' is possible in extreme situations. In a study in Exeter, M. R. Farrant located just this pattern, of 'five groups (of a few members each) which were in fact leadership nuclei of larger "quasi-groups"'; and these quasi-groups were mobilized and fused into a gang-like solidarity only on very rare occasions of extreme stress.

If we accept Colin Fletcher's view that the disappearance of the gang framework has left the seriously disturbed delinquent isolated, it follows that sporadic outbreaks of 'near-group' conflict will be high-lighted much more than in the past—for the seriously disturbed individual was then assimilated into the relative normality of the traditional gang. This means that if we want to prevent delinquency we should concentrate on locating these seriously disturbed adolescents and attempt to get them referred for social psychiatric treatment, rather than adopt social group work techniques and try to re-socialize the 'near-group' as a unity through its so-called 'leader'. Obviously, this type of leader has emerged in a situation of conflict. If we divert the group's energies as a group into more conventional fields, we undermine his leadership and render his position even more desperate. To my mind, the most valuable function of the so-called 'detached workers' is not so much to organize delinquent groups and channel their energies as to find out what is going on and document the reality—to act, in fact, as a communication link.

But once we have disentangled the occasional 'near-group' outbreak from the delinquency pattern as a whole, we are left with the rather unspectacular reality of thousands of small cliques who are from time to time engaged in often quite serious forms of delinquency; but this is essentially a phase they will outgrow, and they do not appear to contain any more psychiatric abnormality than you would find in the normal population. These tend to be what Brasher called 'social gatherings . . . of bored youths'. But how does the gang myth help to distort our understanding of these adolescents, and why is it perpetuated in the face of all the evidence to the contrary?

First, the gang myth makes adolescents' occasional delinquencies appear much more purposeful and systematic than they in fact are, so that when we try to understand them we stress their differences from the more conventional members of society, almost to the point of abnormality, and we tend to overlook their similarities, in values, tastes, and aspirations. This means that we cannot accept that they drift into delinquency; rather we see them as being marauders, committed to law-breaking as a 'way of life'. Secondly, this conveniently deflects us from our real task, which is to tackle the roots of their fatalism; these lie in the poor job opportunities, the run-down slum schools, the social hypocrisy they sense when the rhetoric of equality in our society clashes blatantly with their sole experience of inequality.

On one point I would like to develop Fletcher's thesis a little further. If 'beat' has killed the gang (or at least delivered the final blow of a slow, long-term dissolution) it certainly has not killed delinquency. Perhaps this is because those adolescents who are most conspicuously successful in the world of teenage culture are not builders' labourers and van-boys, but those who would have been socially mobile and relatively successful anyway, ex-art-students, for example. If one adopts David Matza's idea that there are essentially three types of adolescent protest—delinquency, bohemianism, and radicalism—then the effect of teenage culture seems to have been an increase in bohemianism at the expense of radicalism, but not at the expense of delinquency. So it is nonsense to suggest that the values of teenage culture are intrinsically delinquent—or even 'delinquescent'—that is, potentially delinquent. They are no more delinquent in themselves than the values of an Oxford high table or a board room meeting.

But teenage culture does generate goals and aspirations, and the divergences between these unreal goals and the drabness of real life could periodically erupt into a search for 'kicks' —and lead to supposedly 'motiveless' delinquency. But bohemianism is just as likely a response, especially among middle-class adolescents. The two are far too often confused in adult minds—'beatniks' and 'mods and rockers' are not equally anti-social. But both are protest roles which are only intermittently played out by their incumbents, who most of the time act conventionally.

In conclusion, teenage culture provides yet another area of discontinuity in the experience of the lower-working-class boy; and it may have increased delinquency by creating a new hierarchy of success in leisure in which he is, as in work and education, at the 'bottom of the heap'. But we would not expect the gang to re-emerge as a result of these pressures. This would probably happen only if new slums are created for, in particular, the immigrant communities; or if mass unemployment returns to the adolescent job market. Instead, we would expect an intensification of delinquency, but in intermittent and mundane forms, with the occasional 'near-group' outbreak. By perpetuating the gang myth, we fail to see the direction in which delinquency is moving; and as a result we fail to see the lessons it can teach us about the quality and faults of our society as a whole.

Further Reading: **Socialization**

H. GERTH AND C. WRIGHT MILLS: *Character and Social Structure*, London, Routledge and Kegan Paul, 1956.

*† A. H. HALSEY, J. FLOUD AND C. ARNOLD ANDERSON (EDS.): *Education, Economy and Society*, A Reader in the Sociology of Education, New York, The Free Press, and London, Collier-Macmillan Ltd., 1961 (and 1965 paperback).

* D. RIESMAN ET AL: *The Lonely Crowd*, New York, Doubleday Anchor, 1953.

* M. CARTER: *Into Work*, London, Penguin Books, 1966.

* J. W. B. DOUGLAS: *The Home and the School*, London, MacGibbon and Kee, 1964 (and Panther Books, 1967).

* F. ELKIN: *The Child and Society, The Process of Socialization*, New York, Random House, 1960.

J. B. MAYS: *Growing Up in the City*, Liverpool, Liverpool University Press, 2nd Ed., 1964.

* M. MORSE: *The Unattached*, London, Penguin Books, 1965.

M. D. SHIPMAN: *The Sociology of the School*, London, Longmans, 1968.

J. SPENCER: *Stress and Release in an Urban Estate*, London, Tavistock, 1964.

W. TAYLOR: *The Secondary Modern School*, London, Faber & Faber, 1963.

* R. WILLIAMS: *Communications*, London, Chatto and Windus, 1966 (and Penguin Books).

* M. YOUNG: *The Rise of the Meritocracy*, 1870–2033, London, Thames and Hudson, 1958 (and Penguin Books).

* Available in paperback
† Reference

Chapter Four   Work

When we want to describe someone we characteristically do
it in terms of his occupation. Words like 'miner', 'chemist',
'shop-keeper', and so on are more than convenient labels;
they indicate and illustrate aspects of a whole way of
life. This is true, perhaps even more so in the negative,
for when we describe someone as 'out-of-work', 'retired',
'underage', and so on, we indicate that the person so
described is in some way out of the mainstream of social
life. Just as these shorthand descriptions of a person
illustrate the way 'jobs' are deeply woven into the language
we use to interpret everyday social events, so occupational
roles have significance for the whole social structure.

This chapter is necessarily highly selective from among the
vast number of occupations, industries, and organizations
implied by the term 'work'. We have placed most emphasis
on the subjective experience of work and its relation to the
rest of social life. We focus first on the processes of entry
to the world of work. Keil, Riddell and Green indicate how
attitudes and behaviour at the work-place may be rooted
in social experience in the family, community, and the
educational system. In a paper based on a survey of a
thousand young people in Leicester in the early 1960s, they
look at work from the point of view of the entrant to the
occupational system and provide a frame of reference for
assessing the significance of these 'background' factors in
the transition from home to school to work.

They point to the importance of social class differences,
resulting in divergent expectations of what school can offer
in the way of preparation for working life. Moreover, the
actual choice of jobs, in many cases, does not take place
after a rational and realistic assessment of alternatives,

but may be rather narrowly determined by the 'horizon of expectations' set by experience within the family, of interaction with others of similar age in 'peer groups', and by the job of the father. In leaving school and entering work, a crucial role, then, is played by the expectations of work and of what satisfactions may be legitimately anticipated from it.

The research on which the paper by Goldthorpe was based was carried out in Luton between 1962 and 1965 as part of a study of affluent workers. A more complete account is available in the book by Goldthorpe, Lockwood, Bechofer and Platt referred to in the list of Further Reading. To quote the authors, 'The main objective of this study was to test empirically the widely accepted thesis of working-class embourgeoisement: the thesis that, as manual workers and their families achieve relatively high incomes and living standards, they assume a way of life which is more characteristically "middle class" and become in fact progressively assimilated into middle-class society.' They interviewed over two hundred 'affluent' car-assemblers, machinists, setters, chemical process workers, and maintenance men. They show that these social meanings given to work, based on previous experience, can largely determine the *content* of experience within the factory itself, and play a more important role in developing work-place attitudes and behaviour than the organization of work or technological imperatives. In other words 'assembly-line man' may be largely a fiction, which obscures the extent to which the labour force attracted to and entering a specific field of employment may be 'pre-selected'.

This approach emphasizes the importance of subjective experience in 'creating' a work environment, within certain limits set by the production, technology, and the administrative structure of the organization through which the work activities of individual participants are controlled.

Lupton indicates the relevance of this approach to the problem of 'restriction of output'. He shows that what appears at first glance to be 'irrational' behaviour in economic terms on the part of workers, in fact makes good sense when considered as part of rational strategies of action developed to cope with *real* conflicts of interest between management and workers. Focussing on the problem of controls exercised by workers on output and earnings, he lists the various factors, some 'internal', some 'external' to the structure of the firm, which may be associated with differences in the behaviour of workers on the shop floor. This study compares two firms, one ('Wye's') in the rubber-proofed garment industry, the other ('Jay's') an electrical components manufacturer. Lupton did not use survey methods, but gathered his material by the intensive method of 'open participant observation', which involved his working in the two firms for a considerable period.

Lockwood analyses the work situation of the clerk, as it has developed from the nineteenth-century 'counting-house' to a more rationalized, large-scale type of office. Relying mainly on documentary and historical materials he traces increase in 'rationalization' and the growth in the average size of the office, during this period in this country. The ratio of non-manual to manual workers in manufacturing industries has increased, as has the proportion of workers in 'white-collar' industries generally. But the physical concentration of large numbers of 'black-coated workers' has been counterbalanced by an increase in specialization so that the actual working group remains rather small in size.

Lockwood discusses the forms of organization and conditions of work which are conducive to the development of class-consciousness. He argues that the chain of command between 'management' and 'clerical staff' is rooted in personal contact, which leads to cooperative social relationships and a tendency to perceive the aims and ends of management and clerks as essentially similar, so that no fundamental conflicts of interest are felt to be present.

The work situation of the coal miner described by Dennis, Henriques and Slaughter is different from that of the clerk in many ways, but in two which have particular relevance. While the clerk is in the mainstream of society, working in acceptable conditions, and only rarely involved in shift-working, or any major disruption of conventional working routine, the miner is a representative of an 'extreme' occupation. He works under conditions of unpleasantness and physical danger, and is isolated from society by the nature of the work he is engaged in and the social relations of the community he lives in. Moreover, he may typically perceive relations between management and workers in terms of a conflict of interest, rooted in the economic wage-nexus and reinforced by the historical experience of depression and deprivation. Here again, as in Lupton's study, participant observation was the major research method and two of the three research workers lived in the small Yorkshire town that was the subject of the study, for some time.

The study of *The Dock Worker* referred to in Further Reading illuminates this further. In this field as in much of sociology, a good deal of research has been undertaken into aspects of social behaviour which, taken in isolation, may appear to be unusual, abnormal, or irrational. However, analysis of the context in which such behaviour takes place, and of the typical explanations and justifications advanced for it, can enable us to interpret the apparently 'irrational' by elucidating its 'subjective rationality' in terms of the norms and values of the appropriate social groups, and its 'objective rationality' in terms of the networks of relationships which being a member of such a group involves.

Thus Tunstall explains the apparent irrational resentment felt by deck-hands on a deep-sea trawler for the radio-operator, which makes him a scapegoat for the crew, although he provides an essential function and role in the fish-catching team.

The radio operator 'is isolated from the deckhands by the nature and place of his work, by social origin and style of life, and by his closeness to the skipper'. Moreover, 'he does not do a physically demanding job', which conflicts with the deck-hands' conception of fishing as a job requiring a good deal of strength, toughness and physicality. A scapegoat is required to absorb the tensions produced by the demanding conditions of the job. 'Being an object for their combined hostility the sparks helps to cement the unity of the deckmen'. Hollowell's book examines the sub-culture of another group whose working conditions tend to isolate its members from 'conventional' society.

Another theme of general relevance is that caused by the need to set boundaries to analysis and explanation of aspects of social behaviour. Both Goldthorpe and Lupton stress the importance of features of the social situation 'external' to the work place for understanding behaviour that occurs *within* it. Dennis, Henriques, and Slaughter place their analysis of the work-place relations of coal miners in the context of the historical experience of the social class of wage-earners, who sell their labour power to owners of capital in return for the opportunity of utilizing the facilities of employment to earn a wage.

Within this broad context, there are important links between occupations and the family and community. The extent to which work is a 'central life interest' for a particular occupational group may largely determine patterns of leisure also. Thus Parker distinguishes between three types of occupational groups. Among miners and fishermen leisure is sharply demarcated from work and is seen as providing both physical recuperation and compensation for the rigours of a dangerous way of life to which their attitude is generally hostile. Social workers, on the other hand, and many other professional workers who are more involved in their work, may regard leisure as largely an extension of activities in which individuals pursue 'special interests' and projects as a means to the development of personality. Parker found that bank employees fell into neither of these two groups, but tended to adopt a more 'passive' attitude towards leisure which is associated with an 'indifferent' attitude to work.

Many of these themes are examined in the books mentioned as Further Reading. Possibly the best review of the field as a whole is contained in the article by Burns in *Society* edited by Welford, Argyle, Glass and Morris.

Entry Into the Occupational System
E. T. Keil, D. S. Riddell, B. S. R. Green

Reprinted with permission from 'Youth and Work: Problems and Perspectives', *Sociological Review*, Vol. 14, No. 2, New Series, July 1966, pp. 117–37.

It should not be forgotten that the provision of full-time education for the whole of the population of Great Britain is less than a hundred years old. While the period of compulsory school attendance has increased, the minimum age of leaving has been fifteen years only since 1947, and fourteen only since 1922. Six out of every ten boys and girls leave school at the minimum age. The same proportion complete their education at secondary modern schools. Of fifteen-year-old male leavers 60 per cent go into unskilled and semi-skilled work, and 35 per cent into apprenticeships. Proportions going into unskilled work decline steeply as the age of leaving increases, but even among seventeen-year-old leavers, about one out of four goes into unskilled work. Because of the large numbers in the age group (the 'bulge'), there has been a slight decrease in the proportion entering apprenticeships in the last year or two, although the total number of apprentice entrants has gone up.

The influence of the Home

The importance of the home environment in discussing the process of adjustment cannot be over-estimated. In general terms, the recent study by Douglas demonstrates the marked effects of different types of social background on the school performance and the socio-medical histories of individuals. This national sample is being followed through into working life. The work of Bernstein has shown that there is a relationship between the forms of language learning and thinking, and the different methods of upbringing of working and middle class groups, so that it is no surprise to find that the social class of parents influences the type and length of education open to and received by their children. It follows from this that, since education and occupation are linked, such characteristics as social class and economic level of the family will have a marked influence on the attitudes to and expectations about work, as well as on the type of job entered. It is more difficult to identify and describe the processes which result in such attitudes and expectations.

Carter gives the clearest picture of the way in which the process happens for some working-class children: visits to the father's place of work, the talk at home about wages and hours, the relief that the working day is over, all convey to the young person the way in which his parents, siblings and relatives—often the people he admires and relies upon most—regard the world of work. From this he will accumulate general impressions of 'good' and 'bad' jobs, and work which is appropriate for him when the time comes to leave school. Reynolds and Shister, in a study of adult workers, suggest that home and neighbourhood experiences make for the development of job 'horizons' beyond which few individuals look. As a result, actual job selection often seems casual; it is not an assessment of the market possibilities but an apparently unthinking acceptance of the suggestions and recommendations of relatives and friends.

This qualification apart, parental occupation has a general importance both for aspirations and for job entry. There is some evidence to suggest that before taking a job the occupational goals of many young people are higher than their father's occupational level, for example, more boys want skilled manual work than have fathers in skilled manual work, and fewer whose fathers are unskilled want unskilled work for themselves. These aspirations are still connected with parental occupation though; the more ambitious sons of semi-skilled or unskilled workers aspire, not to professional jobs, but to skilled trades.

The home background provides continuity when the young person enters work, and again the work of Carter, and of Ferguson and Cunnison, describes its influence.

The young persons' wages bring benefits to the family, but economic independence may also be a way of achieving emancipation from the authority of home and family. This may lead to more or less overt parent/child conflict, expressed in disputes about use of money and leisure time, conflict which some researchers suggest is more frequent in middle-class than working-class homes. But on the whole, even in financial terms, the changes in the home appear to be gradual. Where a home breaks up, however, the effect on working life may be very marked. Ferguson and Cunnison's study indicates a high correlation between broken homes and job change.

The influence of the school

While schools obviously differ from most work situations in their age composition, there may be other important respects in which they are not dissimilar. Current discussion of the educational system has tended to stress its importance as an avenue of social mobility and the barriers impeding the achievement of this. It is also necessary to consider schools as, in many cases, reinforcing the informal patterns of home and neighbourhood. Carter, studying Sheffield school leavers, relates the attitudes found in the five schools he investigated to the predominant attitudes of the populations from which they drew their pupils, a finding reinforced by Coleman's study in the Chicago area. This latter draws attention to the importance of the informal social groups which develop among school children. Webb, in an impressionistic study of his experiences in a British secondary modern school, argues that the classroom situation contains many elements of informal cooperation among the children, who are as a group in conflict with the teacher. This kind of school, usually in slum buildings in decaying city centres, with inadequate facilities and high teacher turnover, is still very common in this country. The dichotomous 'us'–'them' view of society characteristic of industrial workers is strengthened by such situations. In addition, both Carter and Webb stress that for this group of young people, which must make up a significant proportion of the urban population, the last year at school is seen as a waste of time, imposed by impersonal social forces, interfering with what the young people feel is the real continuity in their lives—moving from home to work.

The General Work Situation for the New Entrant

The multiplicity of training procedures, the variations in their standard, and their uneven availability are all potential sources of dissatisfaction. Many more can be postulated such as payment, hours worked, and relations with authority, but the above suffices to indicate the range of variables within the work situation. It is in the light of this discussion that some studies of adjustment to work should be considered. At first it seems working life is very attractive compared with school. Young people mention especially the lack of formal discipline and the fact of earning. The demands made by the job are not too arduous. There is a general feeling of satisfaction. In terms of the whole process of adjustment to working life, the negative attitudes of young people towards their last year at school assume importance as a possible explanation.

But for those whose aspirations are not fulfilled, or whose grasp of the demand their work will make is inaccurate, the feeling of satisfaction may be ephemeral. Also for some it may be that further experience gained at work induces consideration of a range of alternative occupations now closed to the young person because of the work he has entered. In confirmation of this, where there is dissatisfaction, it appears to increase with length of work experience. In Tenen's study of unskilled young workers:

'It soon became evident that the most prevalent attitude to work and the work authority among the adolescents in these factories was that of dissatisfaction, even resentment. Neither youth nor sex was found to be the decisive factor in shaping these attitudes. On the contrary, among both sexes the average number of complaints increased with age.'

In a Glasgow study of day-release apprentices, the Eppels also found that dissatisfaction as measured by dislike of jobs, and frequency of changes, increased with age.

It is clear then, that while there is no evidence that the transition between the institutions of school and work leads to any kind of sudden traumatic experience, some evidence exists that for a minority at least there is a delayed realization that work may have more frustrations than were expected by the school leaver. This only begins the explanation. It is essential to be able to specify which social groups and which work situations are in conflict and, equally importantly, which coincide.

Factory Work 1
J. H. Goldthorpe

Reprinted with permission from 'Attitudes and Behaviour of Car Assembly Workers: A Deviant Case and a Theoretical Critique', *British Journal of Sociology*, Vol. XVII, No. 3, September 1966, pp. 227–40.

In the literature of industrial sociology since World War II studies of workers in car assembly plants have almost certainly outnumbered those of any comparable industrial or occupational group. The essentials of the characterization are by now familiar. The car assembly line is 'the classic symbol of the subjection of man to the machine in our industrial age'; the assembler 'approaches the classic model of the self-estranged worker'; he is 'the blue-collar prototype of "the mass men in mass society"' and, often, he is 'the prototype of the militant worker as well'.

In this paper, our first aim is to present results obtained from a study of workers, in a British car assembly plant; results which, in certain respects, differ fairly clearly from the pattern which has emerged from previous investigations. The nature and extent of the differences are not such that they would lead us to challenge in any comprehensive way the 'image' of the car assembler which is generally accepted. However, the 'deviant' aspects of our findings do indicate certain *theoretical* weaknesses in the sociology of the assembly-line workers as this has so far progressed: specifically, they suggest that (a) too great a weight has been given to technology as a determinant of attitudes and behaviour in the work situation; and that (b) too little attention has been paid to the prior orientations which workers have towards employment, and which in turn influence their choice of job, the meaning they give to work and *their definition of* the work situation. The second objective of this paper is, thus, to substantiate this argument and to point to the theoretical developments which would appear to be necessary.

The study on which we report was based chiefly on interviews with workers in six assembly departments of the Luton plant of Vauxhall Motors Ltd. Our sample was a random one of men in these departments who were: (i) Grade I assemblers; (ii) between the ages of 21 and 46; (iii) married; and (iv) resident in the town of Luton itself. The number in the original sample was 127; and of these exactly 100 (79 per cent) agreed to be interviewed at work. In connection with the wider purposes of our research project, 86 of these men were then re-interviewed in their homes and together with their wives. The data from this study which we wish to consider here can be advanced under the following three heads: (1) the assembler and his job; (2) the assembler and the shop-floor group; (3) the assembler and the firm.

The Assembler and his Job

In this respect, our findings were closely comparable with those produced by earlier inquiries.

(i) Assemblers appeared to derive little intrinsic satisfaction from their jobs; rather, in performing their work-tasks they tended to experience various forms of deprivation: Primarily monotony (reported by 69 per cent), and to a lesser degree physical tiredness (48 per cent) and having to work at too fast a pace (30 per cent).

(ii) These deprivations were directly related to characteristic features of assembly-line jobs: the minute sub-division of tasks, repetitiveness, low skill requirements, predetermination of tools and techniques, and mechanically controlled rhythms and speeds of work. Of the men in our sample 63 per cent said that they would prefer some other shop-floor job to their present one; and of these men, 87 per cent said they would have liked to move off the 'track' altogether, chiefly into jobs such as inspection, maintenance, rectification and testing. Moreover, among the reasons given for favouring such a move, those relating to the content of work were paramount. Jobs off the 'track' were seen as offering more opportunity to exercise skill and responsibility, greater variety and challenge, and more freedom and autonomy.

(iii) Consequently, the workers we studied were for the most part attached to their present employment chiefly through the extrinsic economic rewards which it afforded them. 31 per cent stated that the level of pay was the *only* reason why they remained in their present work, and, in all, 74 per cent gave pay either as the sole reason for this or along with others. The reason next most frequently mentioned was that of 'security' (25 per cent), and this, it was clear, was thought of far more in relation to long-run income maximization than to the minimum requirement of having a job of some kind. On the other hand, in contrast to this emphasis on economic considerations, only 6 per cent of the sample said that they stayed with their present employer because they liked the actual work they performed. In other words, then, our assemblers defined their work in an essentially *instrumental* way; work was for them primarily a means to ends external to the work situation. More specifically, one could say that work was seen as a generally unsatisfying and stressful expenditure of time and effort which was necessary in order to achieve a valued standard and style of living in which work itself had no positive part.

These findings are, we repeat, in all respects markedly similar to those of other studies of car assembly workers. To this extent, thus, our results tend to confirm the idea that the responses of men to the work-tasks and roles of the car assembly line are likely to vary little more, from plant to plant, than does the technology itself.

However, to our last point above—concerning the assembler's instrumental view of work—we would wish to give an emphasis which differs rather significantly from that of most previous writers. Generally, the 'devaluation' of work which is implied here has been taken as perhaps the clearest symptom of the car assembler's alienated condition. For Blauner, for instance, this concentration on the purely extrinsic rewards of work is 'the essential meaning of self-estrangement'; and in Chinoy's view, the alienation of the auto worker basically results from the fact that this work has become, in the words of Marx, 'not the satisfaction of a need but only the means to satisfy the needs outside it'. It is not our aim here to dispute this interpretation. But, at the same time, we would wish to stress the following point: that, at least in the case of our sample, the predominantly instrumental orientation to work was not simply or even primarily a *consequence* of these men being car assemblers; rather, one could say that most had become car assemblers *because of* a desire, and an eventual decision, on their part to give priority to high-level economic returns from work at the expense, if necessary, of satisfactions of an intrinsic kind. In other words, their instrumental orientation had led to their present employment, rather than *vice versa*.

These data would suggest, then, that the workers we studied had for the most part been impelled, by their desire for higher incomes, into taking work which was in fact better paid than most other forms of employment available to them largely to compensate for its inherent strains and deprivations. If, therefore, these workers are to be considered as 'alienated', the roots of their alienation must be sought not merely in the technological character of the plants in which they are now employed but, more fundamentally, in those aspects of the wider society which generate their tremendous drive for economic advancement and their disregard for the costs of this through the impoverishment of their working lives.

Furthermore, it also follows that in seeking to explain the industrial attitudes and behaviour of these workers generally, one must always be prepared to treat their essentially instrumental orientation towards their employment as an *independent* variable relative to the work situation, rather than regarding this simply as a product of this situation.

The Assembler and the Shop-Floor Group

In most previous studies of car assembly workers, attention has been given to the way in which assembly-line technology inhibits the formation of cohesive work groups. Although the majority of men work in fairly close proximity to others, the fact that they tend to be strung out along the length of the 'track' means that the development of specifically *group* relations is usually impeded; that is to say, workers are prevented from sharing in *common* networks of social relationships, set off from others by more or less distinct boundaries.

Findings of this kind have, without exception, been interpreted as evidence of yet further deprivation in the working life of the car assembler.

The results of our study which relate to the shop-floor situation at Vauxhall go contrary to the findings, and perhaps still more to the interpretation, of previous studies of car assemblers in two main respects.

(i) It was apparent from observation in the assembly departments that the nature of technical organization did in fact largely rule out the possibility of the formation of cohesive work groups. Most workers were close enough to others to be able to exchange words fairly easily: 59 per cent of the men we interviewed said that they talked to their workmates 'a good deal', and 29 per cent 'now and then', as against 11 per cent saying 'hardly at all'. But there was little to indicate that shop-floor relations amounted to more than a generally superficial *camaraderie*. Thus far, our findings conformed entirely to the established pattern.

However, not only did we find no evidence of a high degree of group formation within the assembly department, but we were equally unable to find evidence that the majority of men in our sample were actually *concerned* with 'group-belongingness' in work, or felt deprived because this was not to be had. Rather, our data pointed to the opposite conclusion. For example, we asked our respondents: 'How would you feel if you were moved to another job in the factory more or less like the one you do now but away from the men who work near you? Would you feel very upset, fairly upset, not much bothered, not bothered at all?' The result was that only 4 per cent answered 'very upset' and 25 per cent 'fairly upset'. The remainder were almost equally divided between 'not much bothered' (34 per cent) and 'not bothered at all' (36 per cent). And those men who talked to their mates 'a good deal' were as likely to fall into the latter two categories as were the others. Moreover the further comments which repondents typically made on this question confirmed the obvious implication of these data: that maintaining stable relationships with workmates was not generally regarded as a very important aspect of the work situation.

Moreover, this interpretation is corroborated by further data we have on the extent to which, among the workers we studied, work relations formed the basis of friendships outside the plant. Like an earlier investigator of the Vauxhall labour force, we found that for most men, work and non-work were largely separate areas of their social life. When asked: 'How many of the men who work near to you would you call close friends?' 63 per cent of the sample did in fact claim at least one such friend. But the answers to further questions revealed that only in a small minority of cases (18 per cent of the total sample) were these workmate friends actually seen outside the factory in other than a more or less casual way; and that in fact 40 per cent of those claiming 'close friends' among their mates saw these men outside the factory either not at all or only by pure chance. These findings were subsequently confirmed by data from our 'home' interviews which showed that workmates made up only a relatively small proportion of the persons with whom our respondents spent most of their leisure time and whom they entertained in their homes.

Most studies so far made have in fact revealed that assemblers express a relatively high degree of dissatisfaction with their firms and tend to show hostility towards their policies and management. Furthermore, it is clear from statistical evidence that in Great Britain and the United States, at least, the car industry is among the most strike-prone of all and suffers in particular from a high rate of 'unofficial' disputes.

In choosing Vauxhall as the basis of our study, we virtually ensured that, so far as workers' relations with their firm were concerned, our findings would in some degree diverge from those that have come to be regarded as characteristic of car assembly plants. For, as is well known, Vauxhall is conspicuous among major car manufacturing firms in Great Britain for its success in maintaining an almost strike-free record. However, our findings would in fact indicate that Vauxhall's atypicality goes some way beyond this low incidence of overt conflict, and in ways which again give rise to significant theoretical issues.

Our data point, in fact, to the possibility that, given a prior orientation to work of a largely instrumental nature, car assemblers may well see their relationship with their firm in a generally positive way; that is, as centring on a bargain that provides, better than most others available to them, the high-level economic returns which, for the present at least, they wish to derive from their work. Thus, in spite of the deprivations which their jobs on the line may entail, these men will be disposed to maintain their relationship with their firm, and to define this more as one of reciprocity and interdependence rather than, say, as one of coercion and exploitation. And furthermore, if among these workers' wants and expectations from their employment such 'social' satisfactions as 'belongingness' and 'togetherness' do not have high priority, then the impersonality and anonymity of the car assembly plant are no longer likely to give rise to discontent and resentment of a generalized kind. In conclusion, then, the several specific criticisms which we have levelled at the theoretical basis of earlier studies of car assemblers may be summed up in a single more general argument. Most previous writers, we would suggest, have tended to oversimplify the problem of workers' response to the stresses and constraints of assembly-line technology (and have tended to assume greater uniformity in this respect than proves to be the case) because they have left out of account an important *variable*; that is, the orientations which men *bring* to their employment and which *mediate between* the objective features of the work situation and workers' actual experience of, and reaction to, this situation.

The approach which we have found necessary, in order to make intelligible the attitudes and behaviour of our Vauxhall assemblers, entails a 'social action' perspective. The starting point is not with assembly-line technology, but rather with the ordering of wants and expectations relative to work, and with the meaning thus given to work, which result in men taking up and retaining assembly-line jobs. And the key explanatory notion to which we have then referred is not that of the enterprise as a production system, but that of the definition of work and of the work situation, dominant among the assemblers we studied; that is, as we have shown, a definition of work as an essentially instrumental activity— as a means to ends external to the work situation, which is not itself regarded as a milieu in which any worthwhile satisfactions of an immediate kind are likely to be experienced. In this approach, therefore, technology and formal organization are treated not as the direct determinants of shop-floor attitudes and behaviour but rather as constituting a set of limiting factors, the psychological and social implications of which will *vary* with the significance which workers attach to them. In brief, we reject the idea that workers respond or react in any automatic way to features of their work situation, objectively considered; and we emphasize the extent to which the 'realities' of work are in fact created through workers' own subjective interpretations.

Factory Work 2
T. Lupton

Reprinted with permission from T. Lupton: *On the Shop Floor*, Oxford, Pergamon Press, 1963, pp. 187–8, 195–9.

The expression 'restriction of output' is commonly used to describe the behaviour of workers who set standards of output below those which management considers that it can reasonably expect from them. The question 'why do workers restrict output?' has produced various answers. The most widely accepted of these is that which stresses the incompatibility of the rationally contrived controls over workers' behaviour which are imposed by management, and the controls which are to be found in the spontaneous social relationships which workers enter into at work. According to this interpretation, management formulates an expected level of output which is based upon considerations of technical efficiency. The behaviour of workers is then directed towards the achievement of this level of output. The social groupings in the workshops, which are based upon sentiments of friendship and sociability, and which adhere to values which are traditionalistic rather than rational, develop their own norms of what constitutes a 'proper' level of output and impose their own controls upon behaviour. The workshop norm may be well below what management expects. This interpretation of 'restriction of output' is attractive because it does not imply laziness, malice, or deliberate planning by workers to defeat the purposes of management. Its widespread acceptance is due largely to the influence of the work of Elton Mayo and his followers. It suggests that workers do not restrict output deliberately so as to safeguard themselves from exploitation, but to protect what they believe to be their best interests.

There are at least three questionable assumptions implicit in this interpretation of 'restriction of output' which I have thus summarized. The first of these is that there exist methods, which allow of accurate prediction for assessing the expected performance of productive units. Secondly it is assumed that the main impediment to the fulfilment of management expectations lies in informal relationships in the workshops. It is not admitted that expectations may not be fulfilled because of lack of ability by management to translate plans into actual output. Thirdly, the possibility is ruled out that there may exist real conflicts of interest and viewpoint between managers and workers. If such conflicts could be shown to exist, then it would be entirely reasonable to explain fears of rate-cutting and the like in terms of a rational and realistic appraisal of their interests by the workers.

There is no doubt that the market for electrical transformers is much more stable, and that there are no severe seasonal depressions. It is also clear that competition between the firms in the industry is not intense: indeed there is a good deal of cartelization, and there are many collusive marketing arrangements. The firms are very much larger and certainly the amount of capital required to enter the industry would not encourage any worker to expect to become an owner.

Thus there is, in the electrical components industry, more stability and less downward pressure on wage rates. One does not hear from managers at Jay's the kind of remark we heard from a sales manager in the rubber-proofed garment industry: 'A halfpenny on the price might mean the difference between getting an order and losing it'. Neither does one hear in the garment industry the kind of remark heard from workers at Jay's: 'When you are sitting around waiting for work the firm just passes the cost on to the customer, and the consumer pays through the nose for the special jobs we do, so why should the firm worry'.

Trade Unionism is highly developed in heavy electrical engineering and its organization is highly effective at workshop level. Thus at the same time as the structure and the economics of the industry create the 'elbow room' for manipulation, the existence of Trade Union power in the workshops provides workers with one of the means to control their situation. Since management is not pressed by competition continually to seek the 'trim' piecework prices they can accept 'fiddling' as a reasonable way of adjusting their relationships with the workers and their Unions. And this is further made possible because labour cost is a much lower proportion of the total cost of the product than it is in the garment industry, 8–10 per cent as against 13–15 per cent. Thus, if market conditions are adverse, savings can more easily be effected elsewhere. It would seem that the hypotheses suggested by me in an article based upon the Wye study emphasizing the importance of 'external' factors is consistent with the material from Jay's.

The difference in behaviour which I observed between the two workshops would seem to be explained if it can be shown that both management and workers made a realistic appraisal of their situation, and then acted according to their interests as they saw them. The material suggests that they did this. This is not to say that everyone always behaved rationally in the light of his or her interests. Much of the behaviour we observed can be interpreted in terms of 'Mayoism'. But a great deal of the field material ceases to make sense unless one admits of a realistic appraisal of interests, and of discrepancy—even conflict—between the goals of workers and managers in many situations.

I do not claim of course, that all the workers in the workshops I studied were aware in detail of all the factors which affected their interests. Obviously they were not, although I was often struck by the extent and accuracy of their knowledge. Sometimes their behaviour appeared to be directed against their own best interests. But lack of knowledge does not necessarily imply lack of realism. One acts on the knowledge one has. This applies to management too. For all the techniques of modern management it is not possible to predict production targets exactly, or so I found. Nor are the controls which management exercises perfect in their application. And this is because management also acts on incomplete knowledge.

Although partly one of communications, the problem is greater than that. Knowledge which is in the nature of things incomplete, is communicated, and upon this knowledge people must act. It is in this area of incomplete knowledge and understanding that the social adjustments which I have described are made. I conclude that in Jay's, where there was security, and 'elbow room' to make adjustments, the 'fiddle' was a quite stable adjustment of the discrepant goals and interests of management and workers. In Wye, 'looking after No. 1' seemed a logical sensible policy in the circumstances.

I have checked my findings with previous work in the field, and I have enquired about the state of affairs in other parts of the electrical components industry. In Roy's work, which describes a 'fiddle' closely resembling that at Jay's, there is not much reference to what we have called 'external' factors. His study was carried out in the steel industry, and it is reasonable to suppose that the complex of external factors closely resembles that which I found at Jay's. Enquiries made at a large electrical firm in the same area as Jay's making a similar product, and with a similar wages structure, revealed that an almost exactly similar 'fiddle' operates. A manager there told us that this firm had lately taken on some foreign labour. The story is now being told in the firm that the first English phrase that the newcomers learned was 'one hundred per cent'.

My analysis has taken me some way towards a definition of the conditions under which restrictive and non-restrictive behaviour may be found. It is now possible to list the factors I have been discussing under the headings 'external' and 'internal' with the object of discerning whether any particular combination, or clustering of factors seems to be associated with certain kinds of worker behaviour in relation to controls over output and earnings.

When one compares the situation at Wye and at Jay's, it is seen that with regard to all the factors listed there are significant differences. And these differences are associated in each case with differences in the pattern of shop floor behaviour. Thus we may define the situation in each workshop in terms of a 'cluster' of the characteristics listed in Table 1, and state the hypothesis that when the cluster of characteristics in column A is found one will find behaviour in the workshops which resembles the behaviour which I found in the workshop at Wye, and that when the Jay's type of cluster is found, one would expect to find Jay's type behaviour. I would also

Table 1. 'External' and 'Internal' Factors

	A Situation at Wye	B Situation at Jay's
External		
Market:		
(a) Stability	Unstable	Stable
(b) Size	Small Differentiated	Large, Undifferentiated
Competition	Intense, lack of collusive arrangements	Weak, Collusion and pricing arrangements
Scale of Industry	Small with small firms predominating	Large, small numbers of large firms
Location of Industry	Concentrated in one area	Widely dispersed
Trade Unions	Local, weak in workshops, poorly developed Shop Steward system	Nationally organized Powerful. Strong in workshops. Well developed Shop Steward system.
Cost Ratio	High labour cost	Relatively low labour cost
Product	Consumer goods	Capital goods
Internal		
Method of Wage Payment	Straight piecework Simple	Bonus system Complicated
Productive system	Minute breakdown of operations. Batch Production. Individual as unit in work flow Short time span	No minute breakdown Batch Production Section as unit in work flow. Long time span
Sex of Workers	Women predominate	Men predominate
Workshop Social Structure	Sociable grouping not co-extensive with prod. groupings	Sociable groupings are also productive groupings. Collective attitude to output and earnings.
Management-Worker	Economic interests tend to converge. Personal relationship, but values divergent. Worker control has no part in adjustment.	"Comfortable." Stable. Worker control plays part in adjustment. Economic interests diverge but large area of value convergence.

suggest that these two kinds of cluster are those which would be most commonly found. For example, it is in industries with small firms and intense competition that one would probably find lack of mechanization, high labour cost, women workers and weak Trade Union workshop organization. In an industry with large firms and little competition one would probably find mechanization, low labour cost, men workers and strong Trade Union workshop organization. But these are obviously not the only possible clusters. For example, one might find an industry which is composed of a large number of small firms which are not locally concentrated but widely scattered, but with Trade Unions that are strong at workshop level in such an industry. Or one may find that Trade Unions are strong in the industry in one area and weak in another. Or one might find a competitive industry of small firms which is highly mechanized. It is also true that some items in any 'cluster' may be very influential in relation to other items in the cluster and to shop floor behaviour. I have myself suggested already in the Wye and Jay's cases, that some items seem to have more weight than others.

On the whole I consider that the Wye and Jay type of cluster will be commonly found, and one could consider them as lying at either end of a continuum, with all sorts of combinations making up the clusters in between, but with similar clusters themselves clustering at each end of the continuum. Those clusters at either end are in a sense definitions on the one hand of situations where there is much collective worker control over output and earnings, and on the other of those where there is little control of this kind.

The Clerk
D. Lockwood

Reprinted with permission from D. Lockwood: *The Black-Coated Worker*, London, Allen & Unwin, 1958, pp. 89–95.

In all these ways—physical distribution, organization of work-groups, occupational differentiation and status difference formally and informally established within the hierarchy of the office—the work situation of clerical labour forms a social context in which office workers tend to be separated from each other on the one hand and closely identified, as individuals, with the managerial and supervisory cadres of industry on the other. Some of these factors, of course, are also to be found in the work situation of factory labour, but it may safely be asserted that they operate more powerfully in the environment of the clerk than in that of the bench-hand.

The converse of the working cooperation of clerks and management is the social isolation of the office worker from the manual worker. The completeness of the separation of these two groups of workers is perhaps the most outstanding feature of industrial organization. Because of the rigid division between the 'office' and the 'works' it is no exaggeration to say that 'management', from the point of view of the manual worker, ends with the lowest grade of routine clerk. The office worker is associated with managerial authority, although he does not usually stand in an authoritarian relationship to the manual worker, the order governing the labour force being transmitted from management through the foreman rather than through the clerical staff. Naturally there are degrees of isolation and contact between clerks and manual workers. Groups such as warehouse, railway, docking and colliery clerks are obviously more likely to be brought into contact with manual workers than are banking, insurance and civil service clerks. Finally, the administrative separation of the office worker from the operative, which is based primarily on the conception of the secret and confidential nature of office work, is completed by the separation of the works canteen from the staff dining room.

Labour Market Bureaucracy

Above and beyond these features of office organization, however, there is another dimension of the work situation of the office worker which may be interpreted as a further influence making for his social isolation. This has to do with the nature of clerical work itself, and the degree to which it is peculiar to the individual enterprise.

There is a sense in which the 'market situation' of clerical labour is not really a market situation at all; at least for many clerks. The prime social characteristic of a labour market is its impersonal nature. Insofar as a labour market exists, there is a tendency for skills and remuneration to be standardized.

In this way, we can speak of a 'class' of operatives, such as fitters or turners. Labour power is thereby made homogeneous and comparable, and is divorced from the setting of a particular firm. A fitter means much the same thing in firm A as in firm B; he is a worker with recognizable skills and standard remuneration. Manual workers have thus been identified with one another through the emergence of a market for their labour and the concomitant growth of such common standards of skill and payment.

Well into the present century, and over wide areas of commercial employment, the typical clerk was not really in the market at all in this sense. His initial engagement was secured through the personal contact of relative, schoolmaster or friend. It contained the implication that he would stay with his employer and perhaps become a partner himself, or at least a chief clerk, in due course. Moreover, the highly individual nature of business methods introduced him to a routine peculiar to the firm in which he started his career. He definitely acquired skills, but it was difficult to say exactly what they were, or to compare them with those of other clerks. His maturing experience would be peculiar to his own firm, often highly valuable to his particular employer, but relatively worthless outside. Promotion was given and responsibility added, not by virtue of his progressive certification, but in accordance with his employer's estimation of his merit and worth—in other words, by the value of a particular clerk to a particular employer in a particular business routine. Needless to add, all this could, and often did, rebound to the clerk's disadvantage.

How far a real market for clerical labour is emerging at the present time is difficult to estimate. But there can be little doubt that hitherto the lack of universally acknowledged standards of grading office work has weakened common identification and solidarity among commercial and industrial clerks. This deficiency has been frequently noted by the Union concerned with their organization.

Insofar as common standards are not instituted in office work, then, the clerical work force is not only physically scattered, but also socially separated into isolated units, between which there is little comparability in terms of work, skill and remuneration.

In fields other than industry and commerce, notably in the civil service, in railways, banking and to a lesser extent in local government, large-scale organizations have emerged in which many thousands of clerks are employed. In such administrative units, the rationalization of the work situation has been achieved other than by the creation of a labour market for clerical work. Through the introduction of uniform scales of remuneration, through the rigid classification of jobs, through the establishment of explicit criteria of merit, through the articulation of the individual career with prescribed examinations and certificates, through the facilitation of mobility within the organization—in short, through bureaucratization—the equivalent of a market situation has been brought about. The market and the bureaucracy are alternative modes by which the labour relationship may be rationalized. But in both cases, the ensuing relationship has the same basic character; the individual worker is related to his fellows through uniform and impersonal standards.

Such a work situation possesses features which differ substantially from those to be found in less rationalized structures of administration. In a bureaucracy positions are defined as clearly as possible, and the amount of skill, responsibility, income, status and authority going with them is made transparent. Competition for advancement between clerks is regulated in an orderly fashion through seniority and merit systems which are explicit and do not admit of exceptions to the rules. Such a situation may be contrasted with that in which the job is tailored to fit the man, in which promotion is left to the discretion of the supervisor, in which office titles are proliferated indiscriminately to satisfy prestige cravings. Both types of system encourage individualism; but the one through impersonal, the other through personal, criteria.

These differences, to be sure, are relative. Some large industrial and commercial undertakings may be highly bureaucratic in their staff organization; on the other hand even the most formally established bureaucracy never works according to blueprint. Between the small-scale paternalistic administration of a private firm and the large-scale 'civil service' bureaucracy of a public organization come admixtures of both types. A quasi-bureaucratic form is to be found in banking for instance. The various large banking concerns form a system in which there is a high degree of comparability of administration as between one bank and another, but not complete identity. Strong loyalties on the part of the staffs of the rival houses are encouraged deliberately, and clerks are not allowed to move from one bank to another in the wider system. Within the banks, such features as incomplete grading of jobs and secret reports on office staffs cause their internal administration to fall short of the pure bureaucratic form. The practical result is to create a working environment in which the common identification of bank clerks, both between banks and inside banks, is less than it would be were their mobility unhindered and their position unambiguously defined.

The degree to which administrative relations take on a purely bureaucratic form, therefore, is a crucial factor in the work situation of the blackcoated worker. In principle there is no difference between the impersonal and standardized relationships of the bureaucracy and those of the factory. But in most areas of private industry the small size of the office work force relative to the total number of employees, and the very diversity of competitively related firms, set narrow limits on the establishment of highly bureaucratic forms of administration. It is in the public or quasi-public organization whose labour force is predominantly clerical that bureaucratic administration flourishes, and is indeed imperative.

Mechanization

Mechanization is a process affecting clerical work that is distinct from rationalization, although the two often go together. Thus machinery was first introduced to meet the rapidly growing demands that were being made on office staffs, and then extended with the aim of reducing the cost of clerical work. It is, however, fallacious to argue, as is so often done, that the mere introduction of 'machinery' into offices reduces the status of the clerk to that of a factory operative. The meaning of mechanization, the different types of office machinery, the relation between the organization of machinery and the administrative division of labour, and the actual extent of office mechanization—all have to be examined before we can determine the degree to which the work status of clerical employment has been affected by the introduction of office machinery.

One of the main changes in the division of labour has been the appearance of the specialized, semi-skilled office employee who is responsible for the 'processing' of data. The actual division of tasks very often preceded mechanization, but machinery has speeded up the trend by which a small group of executives, who make decisions about the selection and analysis of data, are separated from a mass of subordinates whose functions less and less justify their classification as brain workers. 'The nature of the work tends to isolate the machine worker, and affords little opportunity for her to gain a general knowledge of the undertaking in which she is employed, which might lead to promotion into other grades of work. Continuous employment over a period of years on one process tends to create a rigidity of outlook which militates against the assuming of responsibility. This is true of all monotonous employment but the additional danger as far as machine workers are concerned is the fact that their work isolates them and creates of them a class apart.' 'Office workers, therefore, are now divided into classes. The managerial staff is being more and more sharply distinguished from the subordinates, and the standardization of duties and the fixing of salaries within narrow limits have placed the latter category in a position similar to that of factory workers. Before mechanization, on the contrary, duties were not so exactly defined, and the level of earnings was not subject to any uniform scale; consequently office workers, whatever their duties, did not feel a sharp distinction from one another.' To the extent that mechanization of this kind has taken place in large undertakings, the sense of separation from management through the impersonal relations of the work situation, which as we have seen is one of the main factors in the growth of working-class consciousness, is reproduced in the work situation of the office worker. 'Another psychological consequence of new organization methods in offices is that the division of labour and specialization have meant the loss of the power to satisfy what *de Man* has called the instinctive desire for importance. In the old-fashioned office, even the office boy felt that he was somebody, simply by belonging to the undertaking; but the invoice clerk who now works a book-keeping machine all day is nothing but an impersonal unit. In workshop and yard there has always been a considerable number of nameless hands; but these are undoubtedly a new feature of office work.' Further, 'the development of methods of selection has undoubtedly contributed towards the present feeling of inferiority among subordinate staff. One of the reasons why the office-boy of the old days thought himself an important person was the fact that no impassable barrier separated the lower from the higher grades, and many cases of a rise from one to the other did occur. But in selecting staff by modern methods for well-defined mechanical duties, the employer runs the risk of eliminating those who have not the physical qualifications for the use of certain machines, but have on the other hand the gifts of intelligence and character which would permit them to reach the higher rungs of the ladder. The inverse is equally true: owing to such methods, the employee employed as a machine operator receives a strong impression that he is meant exclusively for this unimportant function and must remain his whole life in an inferior post.'

Such a division of labour affects also the age and sex composition of office staffs. 'Visits to big mechanized undertakings will suffice to show that young persons of either sex between sixteen and twenty-five are very commonly used to work and supervise machines'. In the civil service, the introduction of machinery was accompanied by a large increase in the proportion of women in the machine-operating grade. The same was true of banking and railway office staffs during the inter-war years. Since the war, this development has speeded up, so that the machine-operating grades are almost exclusively filled by young girls.

When the mechanization and rationalization of office work has proceeded to the extent that relatively large groups of semi-skilled employees are concentrated together, separated from managerial and supervisory staffs, performing continuous, routinized and disciplined work, often rewarded in accordance with physical output, with little chance of promotion—then clerical work becomes, in terms of social and physical environment, extremely like that of the factory operative. The sense of isolation, impersonality, the machine-dominated tempo of work, the destruction of the unitary nature of the product, are all reproduced in varying degrees.

Conclusion

Although the above account by no means exhausts the topic, it may safely be asserted that the rationalizing tendencies of modern office administration have by no means completely swept away the personal and particular relationships of the counting-house work environment. The following appear to be the main reasons why this is so.

(1) In most fields of blackcoated work the average size of the unit of administration, and the resulting physical concentration

of clerical workers, is still small relative to the unit of production.

(2) The division of labour inside the office normally tends to separate office workers from each other by department, job grade and status, and to distribute them in small working groups where they are in personal and co-operative contact with management.

(3) There is a relative lack of universally accepted criteria for the standardization of clerical skills and qualifications. In other words, the rationalizing influence of a labour market for clerical work has been but weakly developed, though in the case of certain large-scale organizations an alternative rationalization of the work situation has been produced, in varying degrees, by the growth of bureaucratic administration.

(4) The intensive mechanization of clerical tasks, though comparable in its most advanced form to factory mechanization, has not played a particularly important role in the rationalization of the work situation because its application has so far been narrowly limited by the size of the administrative unit and the nature of clerical work itself.

Managers and Computers
E. Mumford and T. Ward

Reprinted with permission from 'How the Computer Changes Management', *New Society*, 23 September, 1965.

At present the effects of computer installations are discussed almost wholly in terms of their impact on lower grade staff. We are told of vast armies of clerical workers about to be thrown out of employment while the work they do now is carried out by some fast, quasi-intelligent machine.

Whether this will happen we simply do not know. It depends on many factors such as the speed of introduction and the extent of office automation, together with the rate of expansion of the economy as a whole. In 1965 there were less than 1,000 computer installations in this country and few have caused any significant release of labour. But only the most progressive and expanding companies are as yet using computers and these are the most easily able to absorb labour displaced from computerized departments.

In fact, it seems likely that computers will have a more immediate effect on one unexpected area of organization, that of management structure and power.

Managerial Power

All these organizational changes must affect the firms' power structure. Some managers will gain power, others will lose it. Inevitably, while the organization is in a fluid state there will be struggles for power as different groups strive to strengthen or retain their position.

At the top, it is now possible for a small elite of senior managers, supplied with the necessary information by the computer, to be responsible for most major decision making. This presents its own problems; senior management now has an increased work load, a very heavy responsibility and a new communications language to master. (Data is presented by the computer in mathematical terms and not in written reports.)

In addition, senior management may be forced to take decisions in an area where it, as yet, has little experience or expertise. For example, the initial decisions on whether to install a computer, on which model to get, and on the use of the equipment must come from the very top of the management hierarchy. Senior management is here at the mercy of the new breeds of expert, the systems analysts, programmers and computer technologists generally.

Of course, some managers will gain from an extension of computer technology, and find that by being freed from many routine procedures they are able to pay more attention to the really fundamental parts of their jobs. The American shoe company finds that 'the trend is to take away statistical and record-keeping work from people in middle management jobs, and to leave them with what is really the essence of their management task. They used to spend a lot of time in record keeping and supervision of large clerical staffs, but that part of the job has disappeared.'

However, many managers will see themselves as losing both function and status from these developments, particularly when their subordinates are greatly reduced in number. Inevitably they will strive to preserve the status quo. But their fight to retain power will be hindered by their lack of under-standing of the new business techniques and by the unwilling-ness of the new computer specialists to take much account of their opinions.

The future role of many managers is likely to be directed much more at looking after the personal needs of their staff and sorting out human relations problems than on business procedure as such.

Perhaps the most interesting product of the use of computers is the group associated with their operation—the systems analysts, programmers and so on. These new groups often have great power—a withdrawal of their labour, for example, would bring a highly computerized firm to a halt—yet little responsibility. They are there to provide information without which the business cannot operate, but have no responsibility for the economic goals of the organization, and are remote from such things as profit and loss accounts. Their casual attitude to spending vast sums on equipment would frighten managers brought up in the old school.

As a group they show interesting and unusual characteristics. They are technical specialists identified with computer tech-nology rather than with the aims of the business. This means that their reference group will be systems analysts and programmers in other firms, not their firm's management group. They are often physically separated from the day-to-day operation of the business. Computers are frequently in separate buildings situated some distance from the firm itself. Compared with the rest of the clerical staff, their surroundings may be luxurious. Because they are associated with a machine which needs space, air conditioning and temperature control, they are often provided with a better physical environment than other office workers. To their colleagues outside the computer centre they represent a new privileged elite.

Rolling Stones

For this technical group William Whyte's concept of 'organi-zation man' has little or no meaning. They are likely to be transients, staying with a firm during the interesting phase of introducing a new system, then moving on when the system is in operation and the work routine. Many business firms using computers can only give their computer personnel a job, not a career. To progress they must move on for there is little chance of promotion within the walls of the computer centre and—as educated today—they may not be suitable material for management. An American computer manufacturer has said that 'there is nearly always a problem of communications between the manager of the computer installation and his own senior management'.

At present computer specialists are narrow in approach and, compared with other technical groups, relatively uneducated. Many systems analysts and programmers acquire their skills on the job with little or no formal training. Whereas the engineering apprentice will spend five years learning his trade, the systems analyst or programmer—who has far more power and influence—is not yet required to produce any certificates and diplomas to show his competence, yet will be engaged on work which can dramatically change the structure of the enterprise.

Management Succession

This organizational rearrangement and new distribution of power brings with it a number of difficult internal problems. One of these is management succession.

The weakening of the middle management function raises serious problems for the recruitment of top management. Traditionally experience gained in the various levels of management is regarded in business as a necessary preliminary to a higher management responsibility. The concentration of power at the top and in the new computer centre groups will reduce the possibility of internal training for top management in a situation where it is increasingly difficult to recruit from outside.

It might be argued that, in the future, top management should be recruited from computer technologists as it is these men who have the knowledge of modern business operation. But the direction of a firm requires breadth of vision, insight, sociological understanding and an ability to devise imaginative goals and policies. Computer specialists are not, at present, usually these kind of people.

Other problems stem from the importance one or two key personnel now assume in the firm—if the computer manager or senior programmer leaves, the business may be in trouble— and from the lack of flexibility of a computer system—once in operation it is extremely expensive to alter. If the computer breaks down the work of the firm may be seriously disrupted as there is no possibility of carrying on manually for a temporary period. A computer application implies an extremely tight system; in any traditional business operation there is normally some 'slack' in the organization of work. If there are delays these can be made up by working longer or more quickly. Once a computer is introduced office workers have to meet 'deadlines', work must go on to the computer at a certain time and there is no allowance for crises or holdups.

There are also major problems of communication and co-ordination, some of which have already been referred to. The development of integrated data processing implies the growth of other specialist groups besides computer staff. There will also be O. & M. specialists, operational research groups and statistical forecasters. All of these technologists bring with them new skills and techniques, and use the language of mathematics. If they are to be fully integrated into the organization, it is important to have some mechanism for coordinating their activities. The creation of centralized management service departments is one solution to this problem. The skills and knowledge of these new specialists can then be directed in a controlled way to the fulfilment of the organization's goals.

Finally these organizational changes bring with them broad ethical problems. Is industry taking us to a future of productive and satisfying work for the majority or to prosperity and idleness? A number of American writers have suggested that industry is moving away from narrow economic self-interest and becoming much more aware of its group and community responsibilities.

Whyte has said that the old protestant ethic of individual striving for success is being replaced by a new 'social ethic' which pays attention to the group rather than the individual.

Built-in ethic

Now the question is whether the new technology is diverting us from these ethical goals, without our realizing it. It seems that computer technology has its own built-in ethic, that of striving for a totally rational and efficient business system. The new power groups who control electronic data processing techniques are motivated by technical perfection and have no responsibility for, or understanding of, wider human needs.

Senior management, which has a responsibility both for commercial success and for looking after employee interests, does not yet seem aware that the new techniques, in accomplishing the former, may sacrifice the latter.

Management and society must together solve the problems we have been discussing. At the moment neither group seems aware how imminent they are.

An Extreme Occupation
N. Dennis, F. Henriques and C. Slaughter

Reprinted with permission from N. Dennis, F. Henriques and C. Slaughter: *Coal Is Our Life*, London, Eyre and Spottiswoode, 1956, pp. 38, 44–5, 73–4, 76–7, 79–80.

Although older miners insist on the increasingly easier nature of the collier's work today, it is invariably said by miners that pitwork can never be other than an unpleasant, dirty, dangerous, and difficult job. A description of the different types of work in the mines will be useful in a discussion of attitudes to work, and the relation between work and life; if broad differences emerge between the work today and past conditions, then we will expect these to be reflected in the lives and attitudes of the different generations of workers.

Mineworking in Ashton itself is fairly typical of British mining, the degree of mechanization not being exceptional in any way. Approximately 53% of all underground mineworkers in Britain are 'contract-workers', i.e. they are engaged on piece-work. This percentage includes all those working at the coal-face, and men engaged on development work, which is usually either the making of roads, i.e. tunnels in the rock, or the opening out of new coal-faces. Those at the coal-face consist of ' colliers' (the term varies for different parts of the country—hewers, fillers, etc.) 'machine-men', 'drawers-off'. 'rippers', 'pan-turners' (or panners), and a few others.

A very common phenomenon is for men to stick together through many different contracts for years on end, sometimes for a score of years and even a working lifetime. A whole team often moves from a worked-out face to a new one, and with a few changes may last as a team for a dozen years.

There tends to be a core around which the team is built, some of the additions staying on, others drifting to a new team, being rejected, or finding employment at another colliery. The strongest and most permanent alliances are between pairs of men, though sometimes three men will stick together for long periods. These groupings affect the day-to-day work. Friends will work next to each other, help each other out in filling and timbering, in certain conditions even work their stints jointly. There are occasions when the team for a new coal-face is made up of, say, two groups of three who are un-acquainted one with the other, with a few single additions to make up the team; whether or not a harmonious combination is built out of such elements depends on the extent to which the smaller groups are closed and on the personalities of the individuals concerned as much as on their skill. As a rule a good workman is accepted by the rest of the team, but if he does not also fit in socially it is doubtful if he will stay long in the team; he must be a good miner, and his workmates must feel they can trust him. In teams of colliers containing two or three different nuclei of close friends there exists either good-natured rivalry and chaffing ('kidding') between the groups or just tolerance so long as efficiency is maintained. Colliers cannot afford to allow such differences to develop into antagonisms.

The miner does a job in conditions which are still worse than those in any other British industry, though he can see that improvements are rapidly being made. Higher wages were the first step, and the miner sees this as a sign of his emergence from the lowest ranks of society. In addition, he is proud, as he ever was, that he does a difficult, arduous, and dangerous job which deserves greater appreciation than it ever gets. Miners constantly say that no non-miner can appreciate the nature of pitwork and few would challenge them. When they hear complaints of miners' high wages, they confidently offer an exchange of jobs, and this is enough for most public-house politicians. In the pit itself, among his workmates, the miner is proud of doing his job as a good man should, and to a great extent a man becomes identified with his particular job. Recognition that one job belongs to one man is recognition of that man's fitness and his control of that job. Men in Ashton will half-jokingly say when they have spent a shift deputizing for another man, 'I've been Joe Hill (or whoever it is) today.' On the morning after the retirement of a 65-year-old deputy, W. H., two men greeted his successor (whom they knew well), 'Is tha' Bill H. today then?'

Pride in work is a very important part of the miner's life. Old men delight in stories of their strength and skill in youth. A publican or a bookmaker will often joke about the number of tons 'filled off' each day in his establishment by the old men. Older men in the pit who go on to light work will confide that they can still 'go as well as the young 'uns' but they think they deserve a rest. Men of over sixty still working heavy contracts are visibly proud of themselves and resent any preferential treatment. Another influence may be discerned in this pride of miners in their work. For long, and they know this, mineworking has been looked down on; this is felt strongly, and a man's assertion of pride in being a miner is often partly an attempted self-assurance that he does not care what non-miners think of him.

The identification of a man with his work is reinforced, and reaches a higher level of social significance, by the impact of class relations on the carrying out of work. It has been remarked that one of the tactics of which the employers were suspected by the miners in earlier days was an attempt to provoke competition between workers as a safeguard against the growing of their solidarity and strength. This suspicion is by no means dead, and it recurs in situations where a workman is sent to replace another, or to do any job which is not his own. Before a market-man proceeds to his allotted task for the shift he will ask, 'Am I being sent to do somebody else's work?' He wonders whether there will be too many men on the job to ensure a good rate for the regular contractors, or he may suspect that the fact of a face not being filled-off is the result of a dispute, so that in effect he would be blacklegging. These suspicions lend strength to the identification of a man with work commensurate with his skill and status.

It is clear then that the work a miner does and the wage he receives both express concretely his status as a man and as a member of his profession.

Many years of hard toil and social conflict had given rise to a social structure and an ideology in mining which were fraught with dissensions, contradictions, and suspicions. The ideology of the days of private ownership, the days of depression, unemployment and bitter social strife, certainly is operative in everyday social relations in mining. It is more difficult to say whether those relations themselves have changed, and this problem cannot be fully treated until some analysis of trade unionism is put forward.

In his everyday work the miner has seen great improvement in the physical conditions of labour; the reward for his labour has been comparatively great since 1939; mining offers complete security of employment in the West Yorkshire and most other coalfields. Nationalization, a long-standing aim of the miners, has been achieved. The prestige of the miner in the working class is higher than it has ever been, and the miner knows this. Does all this mean that the miner has experienced a basic change in his status and in the society, a change which goes with a transformation of the relations between the miner and his work? In fact no such basic change has occurred. In the first place the actual changes have been absorbed into the miners' traditional ideology rather than transformed it. Secondly, changes within the mining industry, and the quantitative improvement of the miners' position in relation to other workers, have been unaccompanied by any profound modifications in the general economic framework of which mining is a part, or of the social structure within which miners exist. Most miners know, for example, that the first charge on the industry's profits is compensation to the old colliery companies. They know that representatives of those companies were among the many non-workers appointed to the executive and administrative staff of the nationalized industry. They saw no change in the local management of the mines when nationalization took place. In all these ways they see themselves opposed to the same forces as before nationalization. When they are told not to strike because of impeding the national effort, when they hear of economy drives and efficiency teams, they see no reason why they should regard such admonitions any differently from the pre-nationalization period.

The fact of common residence is naturally of more significance in a town of Ashton's size than for larger industrial communities. A man's workmates are known to him in a manifold series of activities and contracts, and often have shared the same upbringing.

The effect of a common set of persisting social relations, shared over a life-time by men working in the same industry and in the same collieries, is a very powerful one. In the main, this factor is responsible for the reinforcement and reaffirmation of those social bonds which have been shown to be a characteristic of present-day mineworking. Solidarity, despite the division into interest groups among the miners in a given pit, is a very strongly developed characteristic of social relations in mining; it is a characteristic engendered by the nature and organization of coalmining: it is a characteristic that has been given added strength as a result of the high degree of integration in mining villages. A miner's first loyalty is to his 'mates'. To break this code can have serious consequences in any industry, but for a miner his whole life, not only his work, can be affected by the actions and words of his fellows. The 'blackleg' miner must be made a social outcast in every way and not only at work. This is possible in any situation where the workers in an enterprise are living together in one community and form the majority of that community; naturally it does not apply only to coalminers.

Work and Leisure
S. R. Parker

Reprinted with permission from 'Work and Non-Work in Three Occupations', *Sociological Review*, March 1965, pp. 65, 70–75.

There is a growing literature tracing the ways in which the kind of work men do influences their pattern of life. Studies of leisure which have hitherto focussed on social class differences are now developing the theme that there are occupational differences within class and status groupings which play a large part in determining the style of leisure, family behaviour, political orientations, as well as more general values. The investigation reported below is of people in three occupations at broadly the same class/status level, but who differ substantially in the kind of work they do and the conditions under which they do it. An attempt is made to analyse some of the specific components of these varying work situations, to determine the role which work plays in the lives of the people concerned, and to see whether they have typical ways of relating work and leisure spheres. The findings on the last point are likely to be useful in dealing with the social problem of the use of increasing leisure time which the growth of automation is likely to bring.

In the summer of 1963 a pilot study was carried out consisting of interviews with two hundred men and women in ten occupations, half business and half service (mainly social work). The main hypothesis at this stage was that people in different occupations would vary not only in their degree of commitment to their present jobs, but also in the part that work plays in their lives as measured by the encroachment of work on leisure time, the function of leisure, the extent of colleague friendships, and the preferred life sphere (work, family or leisure) of involvement. Of the occupations studied, bank employees were found to be one of the least work-involved; for example, they tended significantly more often than the people in service occupations to experience lack of scope in their jobs, to see their jobs mainly as a means of earning a living, and to prefer to do another kind of work if financially free. At the other end of the scale, child care officers showed a highly work-oriented pattern, and these two occupations, together with a third group of youth employment officers, were chosen for more intensive study.

The Following Patterns Emerge

(1) The bank employees characteristically enjoy leisure because it is completely different from work, do not have much of their free time taken up by things connected with their work, and have their central life interest in the family sphere, with leisure second.

(2) The child care and youth employment officers characteristically enjoy leisure because it is satisfying in a different way from their work, have a lot or a little of their free time taken up by things connected with their work, and have their central life interest in the family sphere with work second.

Certain differences also emerged in the type of people who tended to be work or non-work-oriented. One in two of the single women in the youth employment and child care samples appeared to have work as a central life interest compared with one in four married men in those occupations. However, the fact that only one in ten of the single women in banking had work as a central life interest shows that sex and marital status are not decisive but contributory factors. The propensity to have work as a central life interest was found to be related (at better than the two per cent level of significance) to: wishing to continue present job or do something similar as opposed to wishing to do something different; being subject to a way of dealing with changes or difficult problems other than superiors deciding without consultation; and to believing that people get ahead in that kind of work by working and studying hard. Even reasons for enjoying leisure—because it is completely different from work or because it is satisfying in a different way from work—are related respectively to wishing to do something different if financially free and wishing to continue present job or do something similar. In all of these ways, the significance of work in the life pattern and the role of leisure can be shown to be deeply influenced by the way people work, and in particular by the social conditions under which they work.

From these particular survey results, and from the pilot interviews, it appears that people in such occupations as youth employment and child care tend to have a way of relating their work to their leisure which may be called extension: their leisure activities are often similar in content to their working activities, they make no sharp demarcation between work and leisure, they are 'work-involved', and the main function of leisure to them is to develop their personality. By contrast, people like miners and distant-water fishermen have been shown to have a pattern of opposition between work and leisure: their way of spending leisure is typically contrasted with the way they work, they sharply distinguish between what is work and what is leisure, their work is done chiefly to earn a living, and leisure functions for them as compensation for dangerous and damaging work.

The bank employees who took part in the survey reported here do not appear to fall into either of these categories, and may well be representative of a third pattern which could be called complementarity: as with the 'opposition' pattern, leisure activities are different from work and a demarcation is made between them—both, perhaps, to a lesser extent. But these people are neither so engrossed in their work that they want to carry it over into their spare time, nor so damaged by it that they become hostile or develop a love-hate relation to it—they are largely just indifferent to it and unmarked by it in their leisure hours. Similarly they are led neither towards 'spillover' leisure nor compensatory leisure, but rather towards a middling pattern of relaxation. Their comparatively high preference for agriculture as alternative work may partly reflect their need for complementing the mechanized paper world of banking with a quieter, more basically productive life on the land.

These three hypothetical modes of relating work to leisure may be summarized as follows:

Table 1

	Spheres	Demarcation	Attitude to work	Main function of leisure
Extension	Similar	Little	Involved	Development of personality
Complementarity	Somewhat different	Some	Indifferent	Relaxation
Opposition	Very different	A lot	Ambivalent or hostile	Recuperation

The probability of an individual approximating to any one of these patterns will vary with type of occupation and with work situation or work values held in that occupation. In the present study, type of work was the main variable, but the work-leisure pattern may discriminate among individuals within occupations. Thus research carried out at the Regent Street Polytechnic on scientists in industry suggests that scientists oriented to progress within the employing organization have an instrumental attachment to their jobs and a non-work central life interest which are equivalent to the pattern of complementarity outlined above; while scientists oriented to the values of science have an expressive attachment to their jobs and have work as their central life interest, which can be equated with 'extension'.

On the basis of studies carried out so far, it seems clear that the work-leisure relationship is more than a personal preference; it is conditioned by various factors associated with the way people work. Further research needs to be undertaken to test the validity of these three possible patterns and the types of work situation in which they typically apply. In particular, an attempt should be made to explore more fully the opposition pattern which some of the bank employees responding to the questionnaire showed to some extent, and which is probably more typical of occupations which have not so far been investigated specifically for this purpose.

Further Reading: **Work**

* W. BALDAMUS: *Efficiency and Effort*, London, Tavistock, 1961.

* T. BURNS AND G. STALKER: *The Management of Innovation*, London, Tavistock, 1961.

T. BURNS: 'The Sociology of Industry,' in *Society*, edited by A. J. Welford, M. Argyle, D. Glass and J. Morris, London, Routledge and Kegan Paul, 1963.

*† T. CAPLOW: *The Sociology of Work*, New York, McGraw Hill, 1964.

* G. FRIEDMANN: *Industrial Society*, London, Collier-Macmillan, 1955 (and paperback 1964).

* JOHN H. GOLDTHORPE, D. LOCKWOOD, F. BECHOFER AND J. PLATT: *The Affluent Worker, 1. Industrial Attitudes and Behaviour*, Cambridge University Press, 1968.

P. G. HOLLOWELL: *The Lorry Driver*, London, Routledge and Kegan Paul, 1968.

LIVERPOOL UNIVERSITY DEPARTMENT OF SOCIAL SCIENCE: *The Dock Worker*, Liverpool, The University Press, 1954.

T. AND P. MORRIS, Pentonville, *A Sociological Study of an English Prison*, London, Routledge, and Kegan Paul, 1963.

E. MUMFORD AND O. BANKS: *The Computer and the Clerk*, London, Routledge and Kegan Paul, 1967.

† S. NOSOW AND W. H. FORM: *Man, Work and Society*, New York, Basic Books, 1962.

*† S. R. PARKER, R. K. BROWN, J. CHILD AND M. A. SMITH: *The Sociology of Industry*, London, Allen and Unwin, 1967.

* Available in paperback
† Reference

Chapter Five   Class

Almost all societies are stratified in some way, divided that is into strata, for instance, 'castes', 'estates', 'classes', 'status groups', the members of which possess certain characteristics in common, which serve also to mark them off from members of other strata.

However, a stratification system is not an inevitable and unalterable feature of all societies, but is associated with the historical development of particular societies, and not therefore with underlying 'natural' or biological characteristics of the members of the strata. In fact a good deal of sociological research has been devoted to analysing the lack of concordance between distinctions of 'ability' or 'fitness' and the divisions of rank and reward which form part of the structure of society.

Thus while stratification of *some* sort is a nearly universal feature of all societies its particular forms vary from one society to another, and do not, therefore, guarantee any 'natural' or 'proper' division into ranks.

For Marx, social classes were rooted in the system of production, by the fact that different groups stood in different relations to the means of production, and had different interests in it. Thus economic factors were paramount in determining class membership and class interest. The two most clearly distinguished classes were the bourgeoisie and the proletariat. The former both owned and controlled the means of production, and had the opportunity to accumulate surplus wealth; the latter had only their labour power to sell.

Weber further distinguished stratification by social status, honour, and prestige, and treated political power as an independent influence on stratification, rather than as a mere product of the class system. But the core of Weber's reformulation was to widen the notion of the economic basis of class formation, to include any situation where a market for scarce resources operated. Dahrendorf points to the emergence of other bases of social conflict, in particular the distribution of authority within 'imperatively co-ordinated associations'. Within this broad framework a number of major themes have engaged the attention of sociologists.

Marx predicted that the class system would tend to polarize and the relative gap between bourgeoisie and proletariat would grow, leading to an exacerbation of class conflict and eventually to a revolutionary situation in which the ruling class would be overthrown. However, the last hundred years has seen the growth of many intermediate groups of salaried and professional workers, bureaucrats, managers, technicians, and office workers for instance, who are neither clearly bourgeois nor clearly proletarian, but represent a sort of 'new middle class'. Some of the possible consequences of this are examined by C. W. Mills in *White Collar*.

Again, although the wage levels and standards of living of manual workers have risen a good deal in absolute terms during this century, there is a good deal of doubt about how much of a redistribution of wealth from rich to poor there has been. A clear and succinct account of this debate is given by R. Blackburn.

The diffusion of property ownership, through shareholding, and the growth in size of many economic enterprises have provoked rethinking about the nature of the link between ownership and control. Burnham argued that the managers were destined to become a new ruling class because of their control of the means of production and their crucial position in governmental administrative organizations, but this notion is radically questioned by 'The Insiders' (see Chapter VI), which examines the interlinkages between shareholding and managerial power. The thesis that the 'logic of industrialism' inevitably produces a 'convergence' between the class structures of Communist and non-Communist societies at a similar stage of development is examined critically by Goldthorpe.

However, empirical analyses of the class structure depend on the availability of data relating for instance to the distribution of wealth or income. Rex indicates the kinds of questions which sociologists require to be able to ask of this sort of statistical data before it can *begin* to make sense. Although this reading is extracted from a review of a book published ten years ago, the criticisms are still very relevant.

Goldthorpe and Lockwood examine the consequences of the idea that the general improvements in the standard of living of manual workers, greater economic security and the underpinning provided by the welfare state may have tended to produce an 'embourgeoisement' of the working class. The suggested consequences of this are for instance that 'affluent manual workers' would aspire to middle-class status, and become assimilated to it, would adopt middle-class patterns of consumption and recreation, and would tend to vote Conservative rather than Labour. The authors distinguish between the 'economic', 'normative' and 'relational' levels of stratification, and indicate that it is fallacious to argue a point at one level with data drawn from another level. Their overall conclusion is that 'middle-class' and 'working-class' patterns of life are clearly distinguishable and it is thus premature, if not simply inaccurate, to talk of Britain being a 'middle-class' or 'one-class' society, or to argue that class is no longer a useful category for the sociological analysis of an affluent capitalist society.

Arie shows how class factors still operate to affect differential life chances, including the most basic chance of all, of being born alive, and staying alive. Nevertheless some of these problems are changing, and not always in the expected direction.

Douglas, in comparing class inequalities in mortality with those in educational opportunity, re-emphasizes the points made in Chapter III by Little and Westergaard, and Elder.

We also need to refer to Chapter III to the work of Bernstein, at this point, in order to consider the way in which class factors actually *work* in concrete social situations. By conditioning and modifying the style of language which children develop and use, whole modes of apprehension of the external world and ways of relating to it are in fact *determined*. Thus a working-class child, brought up in what Bernstein calls a 'public language' style, may have a much more limited range of possibilities of relating to social situations and other people, than a middle-class child, who is equally fluent in a language style which encourages abstractness, symbolization and analysis, rather than description and personalization. Thus Bernstein draws attention to the importance of language in the process of the definition of social situations, and as the medium for the maintenance of distinctive class cultures.

Social mobility is often seen as an important feature of industrialized societies, and particularly of capitalist ones, (although downward social mobility is only rarely studied). However, the majority of people at any point in time in contemporary British society remain throughout their careers in their class of origin. But changes in the occupational structure involving the expansion of professional, managerial, and white-collar occupations, and the decline of many traditional manual occupations have led to an increase in the number of people in non-manual jobs, many of whom have parents who were themselves in manual work.

Increasingly the crucial nexus in the process of social mobility is the educational system, and Turner shows in a comparative study of the U.S.A. and Britain, how differences in the definition of the 'organizing norms' concerning the way in which upward social mobility should take place, are related to other features of society, and may predetermine which categories of the population are 'eligible' for mobility.

Watson's analysis of managerial spiralists links the national and local levels of analysis. He argues that the conditions of modern industrial organization, the growth in size of enterprises, and the necessity for aspiring executives to move from place to place to obtain promotion, have produced a class of managers who are highly mobile geographically and socially. This has consequences for social and economic participation in local affairs as the 'spiralists' tend to withdraw from the local community, and to leave the local leadership to shopkeepers and small businessmen. Thus the systems of local political power, and economic dominance may tend not to mesh as closely as they appeared to do in the local class structure described by Williams.

Pahl examines the impact on a village in the rural-urban 'fringe' where a local community way of life had previously been established, of an influx of 'spiralists' of the kind described by Watson. The newcomers effectively introduce a two-class system, and cannot become assimilated to the 'rural way of life' because they have no means of suffering the deprivations which gave the village community its sense of isolation, and promoted strong internal bonds of social cohesion between the villagers.

Finally Littlejohn illustrates from a study of a rural parish in the south of Scotland, how the factors of economic class, language style, and opportunities for social power, operate in a concrete situation to produce a local class and status system. Although this system has several 'objective' features it remains flexible and open to definition in different ways by its members, so that no *single* value is seen as predominant, or fundamental. . . . 'A social class is neither a mere category arbitrarily defined by myself on the basis of one or two "characteristics" such as property ownership, nor is it a group in the strict sense of the term as implying clear cut boundaries and a constitution laying down a limited set of relationships among its members. A class is rather, for its members, one of the major horizons of all social experience—an area within which most experience is defined.' (Littlejohn p. 242).

The Changing National Class Structure 1
J. Rex

Reprinted with permission from *The Yorkshire Bulletin of Economic and Social Research*, Vol. II, No. 1, 1959.

Originally published as part of a review of *A Survey of Social Conditions in England and Wales as illustrated by Statistics*, A. M. Carr-Saunders, D. Caradog Jones and C. A. Moser, Clarendon Press, Oxford University Press, 1958.

Sociologists often exasperate their colleagues by their apparent concentration on theoretical speculation, and their failure to undertake what, to common sense, would appear to be the first task for a science of society, namely the accurate description and classification of contemporary societies. It has been pointed out with some justice that British sociologists know more about Trobriand or Andamanese society than they do about modern Britain. Yet there are better reasons for this state of affairs than the critics of sociology will allow. The methods of the anthropologist are not really relevant to the investigation of the larger social structures of an industrial society, and it is usually necessary to glean what information one can about them *by inference* from the available statistics. These statistics, however, will not have been collected necessarily with a view to describing society. For the most part, they are gathered in order to throw light on some administrative problem, or with a view to promoting social reform by throwing light on the inequalities of opportunity currently existing. If they are to be sociologically useful, then it is essential that the sociologist should confront each new compilation with the question which theoretical considerations suggest are of importance in the description of industrial societies.

There are four important sets of questions which must be answered if a useful description of contemporary British or any other industrial society is to be given. Each set may be grouped under a general question as follows:

1. What are the social relations which exist between the various roles in industrial production, and between the dependents of those who participate, as a result of their participation?
2. What are the processes whereby individuals are recruited, selected and trained for the fulfilment of key roles in the industrial system?

3. In what ways do members of the society behave in their leisure time?

4. What is the extent and the manner of deviance from the social norms assumed in the answers to questions 1, 2 and 3?

Our first question may now be broken down into six questions as follows:

1. What is the size of the labour force and what proportion of the total, the male and female, single and married population does it represent?

2. How is this labour force divided between industries and occupations?

3. What status differences exist between different occupational roles, and what is the size of the various status groups?

4. What income differences exist between different occupational and status groupings?

5. What are the differences in property ownership between the participants in the industrial systems and, in particular, who owns and controls the means of production?

6. What is the size of the various groups in industry, classified according to their relationship to the means of production?

When we pass beyond classification of the population by industry to classification by occupation and status, the significance of the statistics becomes less clear. In the census classification of the population by occupation, for example, the largest group consists of those in manufacturing occupations, but the use of another heading 'administrators, directors, managers, not elsewhere specified' indicates that there is some doubt as to whether the category headed 'manufacturing' is not really an 'industrial' rather than an 'occupational' one. In fact, it probably falls between the two. Perhaps, however, it can be agreed that the percentage of the population in manufacturing occupations remains the largest single group. Much clearer is the continued growth in the percentage of workers in clerical occupations. Less than 1% in 1850, their percentage rose to 6·8% by 1931 and no less than 10·5% by 1951.

The significance of such a growth in size of the clerical population clearly lies in its impact upon the status and class situation in industry. But the attempts of the Registrar-general to distinguish the various status groups in industry still seem unsatisfactory. Three separate classifications are quoted by Carr-Saunders and his colleagues. These we may state summarily as follows:

Table 1.

I. Industrial Status

	%
Employers	2·1
Managers	3·7
Operatives	86·9
Own account	5·3
Unemployed	2·0

II. Type of Income

		%
Salaries		22
Managerial	7	
Technical & Professional	6	
Clerical	9	
Wages		78
Industrial	65	
Non-industrial	8	
Agricultural	5	

III. Social Class

	%
Professional, Administrative, etc.	3
Intermediate	15
Skilled occupations	53
Partly skilled	16
Unskilled	13

It is figures like this which drive the theoretically oriented sociologist to something like despair. Is the classification of the population into status groups meant solely as a statistical exercise, or are these classifications meant to refer to groups who might act as groups, or who might be thought of by their fellows as sharing a common way of life and meriting a characteristic degree of esteem? Clearly there does seem to be some claim that these represent real groups rather than statistical classifications. The third table above is said to be a classification according to 'social class'. But the implications of this term are left open to be filled in by the reader according to his own ideological preconceptions. Surely it would be more valuable if statisticians, who continually claim to be using sociological concepts, were to find out what groupings were of real sociological importance and then seek to describe these, rather than the groupings which are of little importance, but which happen to be easily measurable.

One of the facts which we should like to know about a status group or a social class (terms which are carefully distinguished from each other by the major sociological theorists like Weber and Tönnies) is what the 'life-chances' (to use Weber's term) of its members are. In particular, we should like to know what their income level was. Unfortunately the statistics of income which we have are mainly collected for other purposes, and are, for the most part, classified in terms of arbitrary statistical levels. The one potentially useful table from the point of view of a sociologist is that which shows the distribution of income according to income type. Both pre-tax and post-tax income tables show 'rent, dividends and interest' to have lost ground to salaries and wages. Curiously, salaries appear to have improved their position since the war, but this is largely due to the definition of the salarist so as to include the salaries and even some fees of directors as well as the salaries of top management.

Comparison of the spread of incomes pre-war with those of 1956 suggests a considerable degree of equalization. After adjusting the groupings to take account of the changed value of money, the bottom group has shrunk from 88% in 1938 to 65–70% in 1956, while the top group has shrunk from about 0·5% to 0·25%. But there is one omission from these figures. They take no account of either expense allowances or capital gains. We do not know how large a difference incomes from this source would make, but we may reasonably conclude that if account were taken of them, the income figures would show a lesser degree of redistribution away from the highest group (if not, as many people believe on the basis of their own observations of continuing conspicuous consumption, showing them to be actually maintaining or improving their position), and a greater relative share of the burden falling on the middle income groups and on the lower orders among the salariat. It is perhaps unfortunate that the possible effect of these factors is not mentioned, for students reading the book might easily jump to too glib conclusions about the extent of equalization which has gone on in our society.

That the figures given for the distribution of incomes may be misleading can readily be seen by turning to the chapter on personal property. Before the war, 1% of the population owned 56% of total property. In the period 1946–50, 1½% owned 54%. At the other end of the scale, pre-war 75% owned 5%, post-war 62% owned 3%. This does not suggest a society in which there has been a dramatic and revolutionary change in property ownership. It shows that the property-owning classes have exhibited a remarkable resilience in the face of the egalitarian atmosphere of the post-war world.

The mere facts of unequal property distribution, however, do not tell the whole story, or provide the answer to significant sociological questions. The sociologist is interested not merely in who owns property in an economic sense. He wants to know what kind of property different groups hold, because one kind of property puts its owner into a different social setting from that which another does. At the bottom of the scale, estates consisted mainly of money savings, furniture and houses (one in five households owned their house, outright or with a mortgage), while industrial shares counted for nothing. In the £2,000–£3,000 range, shares still only accounted for 4% of estates, but in the £100,000–£500,000 they accounted for 50%. Land also became an increasingly important type of property among the highest groups.

These are the only figures which are given about the ownership of industrial property, and from a sociological point of view, the failure to analyse the nature of groups owning and controlling industry represents an unfortunate omission.

What I am appealing for here is the presentation of statistics of the industrial population in a new form. We should spend less time in trying to make classifications according to some highly elusive criterion of status and direct our attention to the description and measurement of those social groups who, because of the distinctive way in which their motivations are bound into the industrial system, do tend to behave, and to be regarded as groups.

The Changing National Class Structure 2
J. H. Goldthorpe and D. Lockwood

Reprinted with permission from 'Affluence and the British Class Structure', *Sociological Review*, Vol. 11, No. 2 New Series, July 1963, pp. 133–63.

Until relatively recently, most discussion of change in the British class structure has been carried on in terms of (i) shifts in the occupational distribution of the population, (ii) the reduction of extreme economic inequalities and (iii) the amount and rate of intergenerational social mobility.

(i) Writers such as Cole, for example, have documented the process whereby technological advance and economic growth have greatly increased the importance of clerical, administrative, managerial and professional employments, and it has often been noted how in this way the overall shape of the British class structure underwent significant modification from the mid-nineteenth century onwards. A broad range of 'intermediate' strata emerged to bridge the gap between the 'two nations', perceived alike by Engels and Disraeli, of the manual wage workers and the major property owning groups.

(ii) It has been shown how also from the mid-nineteenth century, and again largely in consequence of continuing material progress, the national distribution of income and wealth slowly became somewhat less skewed; and how, eventually, with the aid of developing social welfare services, the problem of mass poverty was overcome. In this way then, it may be said, the span of social stratification in Great Britain was reduced; in other words, the range of differentiation, in basic economic terms at least, became less extended.

(iii) It has been frequently pointed out that as a result of the growing diversification of the occupational structure, the educational system, rather than kinship or 'connection', has come to act as the key agency in allocating individuals to their occupational roles; and further, that if for no other reason than the need to utilize talent more efficiently, educational opportunity, in a formal sense at any rate, has been made less unequal. Consequently, the degree of intergenerational social mobility, in particular, has tended to increase and in this way the stability of social strata has been in some degree diminished.

On these lines, then, a picture has been built up—and it is one which would be generally accepted—of a system of stratification becoming increasingly fine in its gradations and at the same time somewhat less extreme and less rigid.

The chief sociological implications of the argument that the more prosperous of the country's manual wage workers are being assimilated into the middle class would appear to be as follows:

(a) That these workers and their families are acquiring a standard of living, in terms of income and material possessions, which puts them on a level with at least the lower strata within the middle class. Here one refers to certain of the specifically economic aspects of class stratification.

(b) That these same workers are also acquiring new social perspectives and new norms of behaviour which are more characteristic of middle class than of working class groups. Here one refers to what may be termed the normative aspect of class.

(c) That being essentially similar to many middle class persons in their economic position and their normative orientation, these manual workers are being accepted by the former on terms of social equality in both formal and informal social interaction. Here one refers to what may be called the relational aspect of class.

One would have thought it obvious that in any discussion of the thesis of embourgeoisement distinctions on these lines would have been regarded as indispensable. What is necessary, in our view, is that the economic, normative and relational aspects of the matter should each be studied as rigorously as possible, and that any conclusions concerning embourgeoisement should be formed on the basis of research specifically focused on the problem in this way, rather than being merely ad hoc generalizations drawn from a shapeless mass of data.

So far as income levels and the ownership of consumer durables are concerned, comparisons can be made with a fair degree of reliability between the more prosperous section of the working class and middle class groups. Such comparisons have in fact shown that in these respects many manual workers and their families have achieved economic parity, at least, with many members of the lower strata within the middle class. However, the point that we would stress here is that incomes and consumption patterns do not constitute the whole of the economic aspect of class stratification. Such factors as security and prospects for advancement are also relevant; and in this connection the evidence at present available indicates that broad differences remain between manual and non-manual employments. In relation to security, for example, the manual worker is still generally more liable than the non-manual worker to be dismissed at short notice; he is also less likely than the latter to enjoy various occupational fringe benefits, such as sickness pay and pension schemes. In relation to advancement, not only are the non-manual worker's chances of upward occupational mobility significantly greater than those of the manual worker, but in any case the former can often expect his income to rise by calculable increments throughout his working life, whereas the income of the latter is likely to rise very little once he reaches adulthood— save, of course, as a result of general improvements in wage rates gained through collective bargaining.

So far as promotion is concerned, the chances of the rank-and-file worker rising above supervisory level are, on all the evidence, clearly declining in modern industry. For those who leave non-selective secondary schools at the age of fifteen for a manual occupation, this kind of work is becoming more than ever before a life sentence. The same factors that are making for greater intergenerational mobility—technological progress, increasing specialization and the growing importance of education in occupational placement—are also operating to reduce the possibility of 'working up from the bottom' in industry, and are thus indirectly re-emphasizing the staff-worker dichotomy.

The treatment of the economic aspect of class in the thesis of embourgeoisement is then unconvincing because it is incomplete. In regard to what we have called the relational aspect of the problem, however, the neglect is more or less total. A variety of studies carried out in different parts of Britain over the last ten years or so have pointed to a marked degree of status segregation in housing, in informal neighbourhood relations, in friendship groups, in the membership of local clubs, societies and organizations and so on. And in all cases the division between manual and non-manual workers and their families has proved to be one of the most salient. It may, of course, be held that very recently and in certain particular contexts—say the New Towns or the sub-urban areas of newly developed industrial regions—the extent of this segregation has begun to decline. But the point is that so far no evidence of this has been brought forward and, further, that the basic importance of such evidence to the argument concerning embourgoisement has not, apparently, been recognized.

In fact, apart from the statistical data on incomes and consumption, it is on evidence of changes of an attitudinal and normative character that the thesis of working class embourgeoisement largely rests. This evidence, which we must now examine, is of two main kinds: (i) evidence provided by enquiries—some of them field studies—into the changing patterns of the family and community life of manual workers; and (ii) evidence provided by attitude and opinion surveys of manual workers, in particular those dealing with individuals' own estimations of their class position. We may say at the outset that in our view the arguments put forward on this basis are again generally unsatisfactory ones. The material in question, we believe, has been treated in a far too uncritical manner and does not adequately sustain many of the interpretations that have been placed upon it.

It is our view, then, that if questions of class identification and class norms are to be at all usefully investigated through interview techniques, the pollster's overriding concern with easily obtainable and easily quantifiable results must be abandoned and an effort made to do justice to the complexity of the issues involved. Research has in fact already been carried out which gives a promising lead in this respect. In particular, one would cite here the studies of Popitz in Germany, of Willener in Switzerland and of Bott in England, which, although conducted entirely independently of each other, are essentially comparable both in their approach and their findings. In each case it was in effect recognized that the problem of the 'meaning' of respondents' statements on class and cognate questions could only be overcome by interpreting these statements in relation to respondents' overall perception, or image, of their society. Thus, in all three studies the elucidation of these images became a central focus of interest. It was generally found that as an idea was built up of the way in which a respondent saw his society, and especially its class structure, the more clearly the rationale of his answers to particular questions would appear. One was dealing, in other words, with a Gestalt, not with a series of separate and unconnected responses. A close interrelationship was seen to prevail between the individuals' perception of his society, his general value system and (insofar as these were investigated) the attitudes he took towards more specific social issues. Furthermore, it was in each case revealed that among groups of individuals occupying comparable positions within the social hierarchy, a broadly similar 'social imagery' tended to occur, together with a more or less distinctive normative orientation.

In the findings of these studies we have in fact probably the clearest indications that are available of the basic differences in the social perspectives of working and middle class persons and, thus, an important guide to the core distinctions which would be relevant to any discussion of their respective lifestyles. For this reason it may be useful to set out here—if only in a very simplified way—certain of the major conclusions which were arrived at in all three investigations.

(a) The majority of people have a more or less clearly defined image of their society as being stratified in some way or other; that is to say, they are aware of inequalities in the distribution of wealth, prestige and power.

(b) One 'polar' type of image is that of society as being sharply divided into two contending sections, or classes, differentiated primarily in terms of the possession or non-possession of power (the 'dichotomous' or 'power' model). Contrasting with this is an image of society as comprising an extended hierarchy of relatively 'open' strata differentiated primarily in terms of prestige (the 'hierarchical' or 'prestige' model).

(c) The 'power' model is that most frequently approximated in the images of working class persons—that is, wage-earning, manual workers. The 'prestige model' on the other hand, is that most frequently approximated in the images of middle class persons—that is, salaried or independent non-manual workers.

(d) Those images, at least, which approach at all closely to one or other of the two polar types serve as the focus of distinctive complexes of social values and attitudes.

(e) The distinction between these two complexes is chiefly that between two basic themes which may be called the collectivistic and the individualistic (these being understood not as political ideologies, but rather as the raw materials of social consciousness which political ideologies may articulate).

The rationale of this linking of collectivistic and individualistic orientations to 'power' and 'prestige' models respectively is not difficult to appreciate. On the basis of the research in question, and of earlier studies of class values and attitudes, it may be illustrated in the following schematic and, we would stress, ideal-typical manner.

	Working class perspective	*Middle class perspective*
General beliefs	The social order is divided into 'us' and 'them': those who do not have authority and those who do. The division between 'us' and 'them' is virtually fixed, at least from the point of view of one man's life chances. What happens to you depends a lot on luck; otherwise you have to learn to put up with things.	The social order is a hierarchy of differentially rewarded positions: a ladder containing many rungs. It is possible for individuals to move from one level of the hierarchy to another. Those who have ability and initiative can overcome obstacles and create their own opportunities. Where a man ends up depends on what he makes of himself.
General values	'We' ought to stick together and get what we can as a group. You may as well enjoy yourself while you can instead of trying to make yourself 'a cut above the rest'.	Every man ought to make the most of his own capabilities and be responsible for his own welfare. You cannot expect to get anywhere in the world if you squander your time and money. 'Getting on' means making sacrifices.
Attitudes on more specific issues	(*on the best job for a son*) 'A trade in his hands'. 'A good steady job'.	'As good a start as you can give him'. 'A job that leads somewhere'.
	(*towards people needing social assistance*) 'They have been unlucky'.	'Many of them had the

'They never had a chance'.
'It could happen to any of us'.

same opportunities as others who have managed well enough'. ' They are a burden on those who are trying to help themselves'.

(*on Trade Unions*)
'Trade Unions are the only means workers have of protecting themselves and of improving their standard of living'.

'Trade Unions have too much power in the country'. 'The Unions put the interests of a section before the interests of the nation as a whole'.

One has here, thus, two sharply contrasting social perspectives, each of which comprises a set of internally consistent beliefs, values and attitudes. Whether the same degree of logic would be found in the case of any particular individual may well be doubted: so too may any exact correspondence between 'collectivism' and manual workers and 'individualism' and non-manual workers, especially in regard to occupational groups on the manual/non-manual frontier. However, in the light of the evidence available, it would seem likely that approximations to one or other of the ideal-type perspectives outlined do regularly occur among social groups with less ambiguous class and status positions.

In conclusion, we may attempt to pull together the threads of our argument by using the discussion of this paper as a basis for the following, necessarily tentative, views, concerning the probable effects so far of working class affluence on the British class structure.

(a) The change which would seem most probable is one which may be best understood as a process of normative convergence between certain sections of the working and middle classes; the focus of the convergence being on what we have termed 'instrumental collectivism' and 'family centredness'. There is as yet, at least, little basis for the more ambitious thesis of embourgeoisement in the sense of the large-scale assimilation of manual workers and their families to middle class life-styles and middle class society in general. In particular, there is no firm evidence either that manual workers are consciously aspiring to middle class society, or that this is becoming any more open to them.

(b) The groups which appear involved in normative convergence cannot be distinguished in terms of economic factors alone. Certainly, on the working class side, affluence is not to be regarded as sufficient in itself to bring about the attenuation of solidaristic collectivism. The process of convergence must rather be seen as closely linked to changes in the structure of social relationships in industrial, community and family life, which are in turn related not only to growing prosperity but also to advances in industrial organization and technology, to the process of urban development, to demographic trends, and to the evolution of mass communications and 'mass culture'.

(c) Even among the 'new' working class groups in which instrumental collectivism and family centredness are manifested, status goals seem much less in evidence than economic goals: in other words, the privatized worker would appear far more typical than the socially aspiring worker. The conditions under which status aspirations are generated may be regarded as still more special than those which are conducive to a more individualistic outlook. Thus, we return to the point that normative convergence has to be understood as implying as yet only a rather limited modification of the class frontier.

(d) Finally, it is consistent with the above views to believe further that the political consequences of working class influence are so far, at least, indeterminate.

Class Differences in Life Chances 1
T. Arie

Reprinted with permission from 'Class and Disease', *New Society*, 27 January, 1966.

Many of the health differences between the social classes are reflections of economic and educational disparities—in other words, are due to poverty and ignorance. But different patterns of behaviour (not in themselves due to such causes) are important too. These may, indeed, follow lines of demarcation different from those of social class, and we are not always able to say which are 'better' for particular aspects of health, and which are 'worse'. Child rearing practices show great variation and there is only partial agreement about their effect on future health and personality. While it is relatively easy to study simple areas of variation (weaning, potting, punishment and the like) some parameters of behaviour have not yet been defined with sufficient precision for it to be possible to study them at all, whereas others are surely not yet even identified.

In the case of some health practices the phenomenon of 'cultural lag' is apparent. Circumcision (today unpopular with doctors) was once fashionable in the prosperous classes, but is now much less practised among them: but the children of working-class families are now more likely to lose their foreskins than they used to be. There is little doubt that the effects on health of such different practices can be important; circumcision in men, for instance, is probably associated with a lower rate of cancer of the cervix in their wives, and the evening-out of circumcision rates between the classes may eventually have important results on the disease's class pattern.

It is largely due to differences of personal behaviour that we have different types of gradients of disease across the social classes: the familiar 'poverty' gradient, running to a peak in social class V, and, in contrast, gradients which either show no relation to social class, or which show highest rates in members of the upper social classes. The poverty pattern is characteristic of the 'old' diseases—chiefly bacterial infections, nutritional deficiencies and some cancers—which are associated with social and economic privation. The other patterns occur in the 'new' diseases and seem to be related to different (and often new) types of behaviour (cigarette smoking, barbiturate taking, motoring, lack of physical activity, and many less simply definable patterns), which may or may not be related to social class.

Let us now look at the figures for some diseases. Not surprisingly, it is among the 'old' diseases that social and medical advance have had their greatest impact, and there is no field in which this has been more dramatic than in reproductive loss.

Since the turn of the century mortality in the first year of life ('infant mortality') has fallen from well over 150 per 1,000 live births, to just under 20. Yet the relative disparity in infant mortality between the classes has, as Titmuss showed during the war, scarcely changed since 1911. Up-to-date figures are available only for Scotland; they give an indication of the size of persisting disparities. The stillbirth rate is two and a half times as high in the families of unskilled workers as in those of professional and businessmen, the neonatal rate (first four weeks of life) twice as high in the unskilled groups as in the skilled, and post-neonatal (four weeks to one year) almost six times as high. Similar disparities, manifest also in rates of prematurity, were shown to exist for the whole of Britain in the Perinatal Mortality Survey which was carried out in 1958. There has, however, been a progressive diminution of the proportion of the population which is in social class IV and V (36 per cent of males in 1931, 20 per cent in 1951, and surely even less now) which is due in part to reclassification of occupations, but is chiefly the result of real changes; and this mitigates a little the impact of these disparities.

How, then, are we to explain these disparities, which persist despite the free availability of health services, and despite the great improvements in nutrition, and housing which this generation has seen? It has been suggested, by Illsley in particular, and with impressive evidence, that the poorer reproductive performance of the lower social classes is due to a process of 'social selection' of the healthier and more intelligent women into the upper classes. But Morris has pointed out that the consistent differences in rates of reproductive casualty between particular occupations within the same class may argue against this, for they would imply an almost incredible tidiness in socio-biological relationships. Probably, despite increasing prosperity, persistent environmental and educational disparities are also responsible; there is an inevitable lag between the arrival of increased prosperity and its expression in better health.

In childhood, the Social Medicine Research Unit has shown, death rates between the classes have narrowed much more than in infancy. Death rates from all causes at one to two years of age showed an excess in 1930–32 of over 400 per cent between social class V and I: in 1950–51 this had fallen to 63 per cent (the beginning of this improvement was already detectable in the last three months of the first year of life). For rheumatic heart disease (previously an area of great discrepancy between the classes) death rates have fallen so near to zero that comparisons are meaningless. Morbidity in childhood, as measured in consultation rates by Logan and Cushion's General Practice Survey, shows class gradients in, among other things, measles, bronchitis, impetigo and injuries (which are commonest in social class V) and whooping cough, asthma, some upper respiratory infections, and unexplained febrile illnesses (commonest in class I). Douglas's 'cohort' survey found, by contrast, little social class difference in the proportion of children having the common childhood infections, but poorer children were more likely to be admitted to hospital, or to die, because of their disease.

In nutrition, the National Food Survey gives evidence of inadequacies in the diets of large poorer families. This is not to say that there is overt malnutrition but these figures probably represent 'sub-clinical' deficiency states and unrealized potential for growth: it is well established that school children from large families tend to be less tall than those who come from small ones. There is also a report by a paediatrician of the return of rickets in indigenous children in the slums of Glasgow. In 1957–58 the vitamin D content of welfare foods and supplements was reduced because it was shown that excess of the vitamin could be harmful, and Arneil believes that the reappearance of rickets is due chiefly to this reduction, and to the consequent inadequacy in very poor homes of the other fortified food sources of vitamin D which are necessary when the baby has been taken off dried milk. The 'heavy smoke pall' which lies between Glasgow children and the vitamin D-producing sunlight plays a part; but Arneil also blames television advertizing of proprietary vitamin C preparations, which many women do not realize are useless for preventing rickets. The mothers of his patients, he writes, 'do not go to clinics, disregard advice from health visitors, and seldom read. They do, however, watch television.'

Let us look now at the general mortality picture. The overall gradient has become much less steep during this century (as indeed have the gradients for most individual diseases).

Table 1. Mortality From All Causes

Men 20–64 standardized mortality ratios ('SMR')* Social class	1921–23	1930–32	1949–53†
I	82	90	100
II	94	94	90
III	95	97	101
IV	101	102	104
V	125	111	118

* The SMR expresses mortality as a percentage of the rate for all groups, standardized for the age composition of the particular group.
† Adjusted for changes in classification since 1931.

The higher mortality from coronary heart disease in professional and businessmen than in men of social class VI and V has been the subject of a great deal of study, for coronary heart disease is the main killer of middle-aged men today. More than twice as many men die of coronary heart disease in middle age as from lung cancer, which is the other great epidemic disease of our time (and not consistently related to social class). The certified death rate from coronary heart disease has leapt throughout this century from somewhere in the region of 20 per 100,000 men in the 55–64 age group in the 1920s to the present level of about 600 per 100,000, though changes in ability to recognize the disease and in fashions of diagnosis must be in part responsible for the leap.

The social class distribution of coronary heart disease has yielded important clues to its causes. There is now evidence that many different factors are involved—genetic, dietary, psychological, cigarette smoking—but not one of these is as consistently graded across the social classes as are death rates. Moreover, there is a difference between the pattern in middle-aged men and women; the former show a steep class gradient, the latter none. The implication is that an important causative factor may lie in the nature of the men's work, which distinguishes the experience not only of the social classes from each other, but of husbands from wives.

Analysis by Morris and his colleagues of mortality by occupation has shown that the social class gradient is largely due to the variation between the physical activity involved in different jobs. Thus the higher a man's social class, the less physically active his work is likely to be. If the Registrar General's mortality figures are analysed by the degree of physical activity in the occupations of the men who died, the social class gradient virtually disappears, becoming instead one of degree of physical activity; in other words, the apparent relationship with social class is masking a more significant one.

Coronary heart disease is one of the 'new' diseases. Lung cancer is another; the epidemic of motor-cycle deaths in teenagers is another. These 'new' diseases pose questions which are actively being investigated: for instance, since physical activity of work (which is often sustained and regular) protects against coronary disease, are active leisure pursuits (which are likely to be sporadic, and of short duration) protective too? Or again, having established that cigarette smoking is the main cause of lung cancer, how can people be persuaded to give up smoking—at least to the same extent as doctors (and Edinburgh University teachers), twice as large a proportion of whom as of laymen are non-smokers?

The relationship between health and 'social class' remains close though not always simple. Certainly, there are diseases of the rich as well as diseases of the poor, but the burden of the latter is still heavy in our prosperous society; in the crucial area of birth and infancy, some of the gaps between the classes have scarcely changed in our time. We know that many of the diseases of poverty can be effectively attacked by remedying the privations from which they arise. But the 'new diseases' pose problems which are vastly more complicated, being due apparently to a multiplicity of causes, rooted in many aspects of human life and running across our conventional lines of social stratification. A 'new hygiene' is needed to tackle these problems, which will have to be concerned not only with standard of living, but equally with style of living; not only with the physical and economic environment, but also with the study of the individual and of what in his personal and social behaviour (as well as in his constitution) makes him susceptible to particular diseases. As we have shown, this approach is already yielding results and it has given new insights into the strategy of attack on the 'old' as well as the 'new' diseases. It is very clear that in developing and applying the new hygiene, doctors and social scientists depend upon each other.

Class Differences in Life Chances 2
J. W. B. Douglas

Reprinted with permission from J. E. Meade and A. S. Parkes (Editors): *Biological Aspects of Social Problems*, London, Oliver & Boyd, 1965, p. 86.

The persisting social class differences in educational opportunity are comparable with the persisting social class differences in infant mortality, and a description of the latter may help us to understand some of the difficulties we are likely to meet in trying to provide equal educational opportunities for all social classes and in all parts of the country. During the last fifty years the maternal and child welfare services have been greatly expanded and improved and the chances of survival of infants have improved dramatically in each social class. However, the relative levels of the infant death rates in the social classes have been maintained; indeed the unskilled manual workers are relatively rather worse off to-day than they were in the past. Where services have been expanded or improved it seems that those who least need them have benefited most. For example, the considerable number of additional maternity beds provided during the last twenty years has been taken up largely by women with relatively small numbers of previous pregnancies, whereas those who are having their fourth or later baby—who are in fact a more risk laden group—are still as likely as they were twenty years ago to be delivered at home. The fact that services are improved or expanded does not necessarily mean that they will be available to those who need them most and, put in the educational context, one could imagine circumstances in which large sums of money might be spent on education without improving the opportunities of those sections of the community that are least well provided for to-day.

The very self-fertilizing nature of education, by which those who benefit in one generation see to it that their children benefit in the next, increases the danger of persisting inequalities of opportunity. There are wide regional differences, for example, in the provisions of grammar and technical school places which are historical and bear no relation to the ability of the children who sit the eleven-plus examinations. Since the pressure for educational reform is likely to be greatest in those areas which are already well supplied with grammar schools and least in those which are most deficient, there is a danger that priorities will shift from remedying the gross deficiencies of the worst areas to tinkering with the minor ones in the best.

The evidence of the National Survey is that there are still wide inequalities in educational opportunity in different parts of the country and in different types of family. There are two main reasons for this: first, during the early years at school social class differences in measured ability increase; second, in the secondary selection examinations children from the poorer homes appear to be at a disadvantage, even when those of similar ability are compared.

Social Mobility 1
R. H. Turner

Reprinted with permission from 'Modes of Social Ascent Through Education: Sponsored and Contest Mobility and the School System', *American Sociological Review*, Vol. XXV, 1960, No. 5, pp. 855–67.

The object of this paper is to suggest a framework for relating certain differences between American and English systems of education to the prevailing norms of upward mobility in each country. Others have noted the tendency for educational systems to support prevailing schemes of stratification, but this statement will dwell specifically on the manner in which the *accepted mode of upward mobility* shapes the school system directly and indirectly through its effects on the values that implement social control. The task will be carried out by describing two ideal-typical normative patterns of upward mobility and suggesting their logical ramifications in the general character of stratification and social control. In addition to showing relationships among a number of differences between American and English schooling, the ideal-types have broader implications than those developed in this paper. First, they suggest a major dimension of stratification, which might profitably be incorporated into a variety of studies on social class. Second, they can be readily applied in further comparisons, between countries other than the United States and England.

The Nature of Organizing Norms

Many investigators have concerned themselves with rates of upward mobility in specific countries or internationally, and with the manner in which school systems facilitate or impede such mobility. Preoccupation with *extent* of mobility has precluded equal attention to the predominant *mode* of mobility in each country. The central assumption underlying this paper is that within a formally open class system providing mass education the organizing folk norm that defines the accepted mode of upward mobility is a crucial factor in shaping the school system, and may be even more crucial than is the extent of upward mobility. In England and the United States there appear to be different organizing folk norms, which may be labelled *sponsored mobility* and *contest mobility* respectively.

Contest mobility is a system in which elite status is the prize in an open contest and is taken by the aspirants' own efforts. While the 'contest' is governed by some rules of fair play, the contestants have wide latitude in the strategies they may employ. Since the 'prize' of successful upward mobility is not in the hands of the established elite to give out, the latter are not in a position to determine who shall attain it and who shall not. Under *sponsored* mobility, elite recruits are chosen by the established elite or their agents, and elite status is *given* on the basis of some criterion of supposed merit and cannot be *taken* by any amount of effort or strategy. Upward mobility is like entry into a private club, where each candidate must be 'sponsored' by one or more of the members. Ultimately, the members grant or deny upward mobility on the basis of whether they judge the candidate to have the qualities that they wish to see in fellow members.

Contest mobility is like a sporting event in which many compete for a few recognized prizes. The contest is judged to be fair only if all the players compete on an equal footing. Victory must be won solely by one's own efforts. The most satisfactory outcome is not necessarily a victory of the most able, but of the most deserving.

Sponsored mobility, on the other hand, rejects the pattern of the contest and substitutes a controlled selection process. In this process the elite or their agents, who are best qualified to judge merit, *call* those individuals to elite status who have the appropriate qualities. Individuals do not win or seize elite status, but mobility is rather a process of sponsored induction into the elite following selection.

The governing objective of contest mobility is to give elite status to those who earn it, while the goal of sponsored mobility is to make the best use of the talents in society by sorting each person into his proper niche. In different societies the conditions of competitive struggle may reward quite different attributes, and sponsored mobility may select on the basis of such diverse qualities as intelligence or visionary capability, but the difference in principle remains the same.

Under the contest system, society at large establishes and interprets the criteria of elite status. If one wishes to have his high status recognized he must display certain credentials that identify his class to those about him. The credentials must be highly visible and require no special skill for their assessment, since credentials are presented to the masses. Material possession and mass popularity are perfect credentials in this respect, and any special skill that produces a tangible product easily assessed by the untrained will do. The nature of sponsored mobility precludes this type of operation but assigns to credentials instead the function of identifying the elite to one another. Accordingly, the ideal credentials are special skills requiring the trained discrimination of the elite for their recognition. Intellectual, literary, or artistic excellences, which can only be appraised by those trained to appreciate them, are perfect credentials in this respect. Concentration on such skills lessens the likelihood that an interloper will succeed in claiming the right to elite membership on grounds of the popular evaluation of his competence.

Contest mobility tends to delay the final award as long as practicable, to permit a fair race; sponsored mobility tends to place the selection point as early in life as practicable, to insure control over selection and training.

A system of sponsored mobility develops most readily in a society with but a single elite or with a recognized elite hierarchy. When multiple elites compete among themselves, the mobility process tends to take the contest pattern, since no group is able to command control of recruitment. Sponsored mobility further depends upon a societal structure fostering monopoly of elite credentials. Lack of such monopoly undercuts sponsorship and control of the recruitment process. Monopoly of elite credentials is in turn typically a product of a society with a well-entrenched traditional aristocracy, employing such intrinsically monopolizable credentials as family line and bestowable title, or of a society organized along large-scale bureaucratic lines, permitting centralized control of movement up the hierarchy of success.

English society has been described as the juxtaposition of two systems of stratification, the urban-industrial class system and the surviving aristocratic system. While the sponsored-mobility pattern reflects the logic of the latter, our impression is that it pervades popular thinking rather than merely coexisting with the logic of industrial stratification. Students of cultural change note that patterns imported into an established culture tend to be reshaped into coherence with the established culture as they are assimilated. Thus, it may be that the changes in stratification attendant upon industrialization have led to many alterations in the rates, the specific means, and the rules of mobility, but that these changes have taken place within the unchallenged organizing norm of sponsored mobility.

The most obvious application of the distinction between sponsored and contest mobility norms is to afford a partial explanation for the different policies of student selection in the English and American secondary schools. Although American high-school students take different courses of study and sometimes even attend specialized high schools, a major preoccupation has been to avoid any sharp social separation between the superior and inferior students and to keep the channels of movement between courses of study as open as possible. Even recent criticisms of the way in which superior students may be thereby held back in their development usually are qualified by insistence that these students must not, however, be withdrawn from the mainstream of student life. Any such segregation offends the sense of fairness implicit in the contest norm and also arouses the fear that the elite and future elite will lose their sense of fellow-feeling with the masses. Perhaps the most important point, however, is that schooling is presented as an opportunity, and the principal burden of making use of the opportunity depends on the student's own initiative and enterprise.

The English system has undergone a succession of liberalizing changes during this century, but all of them have remained within the pattern of attempting early in the educational program to sort out the promising from the unpromising, so that the former may be segregated and given a special form of training to fit them for higher standing in their adult years. Under the Education Act of 1944, a minority of students have been selected each year by means of a battery of examinations popularly known as 'eleven plus', supplemented to varying degrees by grade-school record and personal interview impressions, for admission to grammar schools. The remaining students attend secondary modern or technical schools, in which the opportunities to prepare for college or train for the better occupations are minimal. The grammar schools supply what, by comparative standards, is a high quality of college preparatory education. Such a scheme embodies well the logic of sponsorship, with early selection of those destined for middle-class and better occupations, and specialized training to suit each group for the class in which they are destined to hold membership. The plan facilitates considerable mobility, and recent research reveals surprisingly little bias against the child from a manual-labouring family in the selection for grammar school, when related to measured intelligence. It is altogether possible that adequate comparative research would show a closer correlation of school success with measured intelligence and a lesser correlation between school success and family background in England than in the United States. While selection of superior students for mobility opportunity is probably more efficient under such a system, the obstacles to a person not so selected 'making the grade' on the basis of his own initiative or enterprise are probably correspondingly greater.

In the foregoing statement, two ideal-typical organizing norms concerning the manner in which mobility should properly take place have been outlined. On the one hand, mobility may be viewed as most appropriately a *contest* in which many contestants strive, by whatever combinations of strategy, enterprise, perseverance, and ability they can marshal, restricted only by a minimum set of rules defining fair play and minimizing special advantage to those who get ahead early in the game, to take possession of a limited number of prizes. On the other hand, it may be thought best that the upwardly mobile person be *sponsored*, like one who joins a private club upon invitation of the membership, selected because the club members feel that he has qualities desirable in a club member, and then subjected to careful training and initiation into the guiding ethic and lore of the club before being accorded full membership.

Upward mobility actually takes place to a considerable degree by both the contest pattern and the sponsorship pattern in every society. But it has been suggested that in England the sponsorship norm is ascendant and has been so for a century or more, and that in the United States the contest norm has been ascendant for a comparable period. A norm is ascendant in the sense that there is a constant 'strain' to bring the relevant features of the class system, the pattern of social control, and the educational system into consistency with the norm, and that patterns consistent with the ascendant norm seem more 'natural' and 'right' to the articulate segments of the population.

Social Mobility 2
W. Watson

Reprinted with permission from 'The Managerial Spiralist', *The Twentieth Century*, May 1960.

Two distinguished American sociologists recently expressed their surprise at discovering that rates of social mobility in Britain were much the same as in America. So down goes the hoary myth that America is an 'open society' while Britain is 'closed'. The trend of industrial organization in both countries is to develop along similar lines, and opportunities for persons from lower social classes to reach higher classes arise from the nature of this organization.

These changes are nowhere more evident than in the social consequences that have followed the rapid expansion in the size and scale of our industry. We are shifting over from small-scale to large-scale organization of production. Many firms now operate on a national or even international scale, and present conditions appear to favour the continuance of this process. In private industry, large firms with 10,000 or more people on the pay-roll already employ more than 20 per cent of all workers. Nationalization too has encouraged large-scale organization, and the public sector of industry alone now employs more than two million workers. Such organizations are also exploiting a new complexity of techniques through the application of scientific discovery and method. One consequence of this complexity is the emergence of many new professional and technical skills, and a great increase in the number of persons in professional and technical occupations increased by 84 per cent, against an increase of 19 per cent in the occupied population as a whole.

In effect, this is an increase in the number and function of the category of persons usually designated 'managers'. The exact definition of a 'manager' is still subject of debate, for the word embraces a wide range of occupations.

Some people have taken a gloomy view of this on the grounds that managers may become an elite perpetuating themselves through the exercise of political as well as industrial power, and that their influence will produce a 'managerial society'. But managers differ so much in function and origin that such speculations must be regarded as premature, although not without foundation. However, the needs of large-scale organizations are tending both to standardize the kind of recruits they seek and to impress a homogeneous character on their staff.

Large organizations, whether they are privately or publicly owned, usually have a similar bureaucratic structure consisting of hierarchies of executives, technicians, supervisors, accountants, administrators, and so on, all of them in various positions of superiority and inferiority to one another. These bureaucracies form a system of ranking wherein men are promoted from below. At the lower levels, promotion is bound up with the exercise of professional skills. But at the higher levels, other qualities and a more general ability are needed and the professional qualification becomes relatively less important. Promotion to this level depends on imponderable factors not susceptible to customary processes of selection by examination, such as 'administrative ability', 'drive', 'qualities of leadership', 'personality', 'judgment', and so on. Hence the general manager in industry may have begun his career in any one of the specialized departments, for all specialists are eligible to compete for the highest executive positions.

A successful career enforces residential movement on the ambitious managers in a large firm, because of the scale of operations. Workshops and offices may be spread through many places in Britain or even abroad. The successful executive may have to live in half a dozen counties during his way to the top. Each move takes him through another community, where his position in relation to his colleagues and to other people may differ considerably. Some firms facilitate this process by providing company houses, furniture, and cars for their managers, so that speedy moves need not be hindered by attachment to private property.

This combination of mobility in residence, career, and social standing, is characteristic of managers in the largest concerns, a form of social mobility we may sum up as spiralism. Its essential quality lies in the necessity of residential movement. What is perhaps new about it is the wide extension to industry and business generally, and the effects of this extension on our social life, particularly on community life.

The popular image of British communities as self-contained, venerable places where the members of all social classes have deep local roots, and with a social life dominated by tradition, is one that may be useful in tourist advertisements, but does not conform with present reality. The changes and expansion of our industry has helped to alter both the symbols of social class and the lines of cleavage between classes, as well as recruitment to them. The changes in clothing, food habits, leisure pursuits, and social services, that have followed mass production and consumption and the intervention of the State into social affairs, have produced a greater exterior uniformity. The expansion of education too has made it easier for more children from the lower social classes to move up the social scale, especially as the concomitant expansion of industry and State services has provided opportunities for careers as spiralists.

Social and economic leadership in local affairs has altered accordingly. The main gap left to be filled from beneath was caused by the withdrawal of the occupants of the 'big house'. These people often had strong attachments to the towns they dominated, and adopted paternalistic attitudes towards the locals, who were often dependent on them for both work and leisure facilities. A recent study of one Lancashire town showed that the competition of two such families, opposed in both religion and politics, helped to ameliorate the harsh environmental conditions that their industrial activities had created. One family gave the town a public park, the other riposted with a library, and their competition in benefactions in fact provided quite elaborate amenities. In the process both families were ennobled, thus following the line of social mobility of their time.

On the whole, their successors in local affairs have been the small shopkeepers and local businessmen whose economic and social interests are still wholly bounded by the local community. Because of this bias, they tend to be more limited in outlook, although perhaps in closer touch with the classes beneath them, whose local culture they share. The spiralists, who include the new industrial managers and administrators, might have been expected to take over, but they tend to take a very small part in local affairs. Although they share similar economic and housing standards with the small businessmen, and in that sense are of the same social class, they are differentiated clearly from them by function and education, and experience. Their education, through either grammar school or public school to a university, equips them with a generic culture with international standards of value, and through this and their occupational experience, their interests are wider and more varied and less easily satisfied locally. The young business executive in Wigan is likely to have more interests and friends in Manchester and London, or even in New York, than he has in Wigan. Indeed, he may not even live in Wigan, but drive in from a suburb where his neighbours are people like himself. Their mobility, real and potential, together with their culture and residential segregation, all help to keep the spiralists apart from the locals, of all classes. Whether or not some actually do take part in local affairs will depend largely on their social origins and on the particular rung of the ladder they have reached. A young spiralist who is still on his way up has his eyes fixed on targets outside the local community. He has to maintain contacts, work on his career, and be prepared to move. He is unlikely to have social connections within the community, outside his colleagues and his peers in other concerns. An older man, on the other hand, who reckons he has reached the last stage he can reasonably expect to achieve, is more likely to turn his interest to the community in which he now finds himself living. Although blocked for further promotion, he may be senior enough to be called on to participate in local affairs. Both of them may be affected by company policy, in that some firms encourage local leadership while others feel that this is a dissipation of interest and energy. In any case, they are unlikely to be local people, and will lack the intimate acquaintance with the quirks and subtleties that still mark British regional cultures. In their professional and social life they tend to judge themselves and others by the frame of reference of their spiralist culture and experience.

The higher levels of large organizations are usually concentrated in cities, towns or in conurbations, and it is here that concentrations of managers are to be found. Such large communities usually have socially distinct and segregated residential areas, so that there are whole suburbs composed of business and professional people with similar incomes and interests, who commute to their offices. Where place of residence and place of work are so clearly demarcated and distant from one another, relations between persons of different social class must be affected, and must differ from those in smaller communities where contact is easier and more likely to occur. The concentration of populations in a few great conurbations and their segregation by social class has also happened elsewhere, and the social and political outcome of this development is still obscure.

In a world where large-scale organization of production and services has become characteristic, the sphere of interest of managers is bound to be extensive and their outlook cannot be parochial. Although they still form a minority of the educated British middle-class, they are growing in number and influence, and the impact of their industrial power and system of values will have a lasting effect on our political and social institutions.

Local Class Structures 1
W. M. Williams

Reprinted with permission from W. M. Williams: *The Sociology of an English Village:* Gosforth, London, Routledge and Kegan Paul, 1956, pp. 86-9, 103, 104-5, 107-20.

It was soon obvious from the behaviour and conversation of the people of Gosforth that, apart from personal likes and dislikes, their attitudes towards certain parishioners, both as individuals and groups, tend to vary along well-defined lines. In a chance encounter—on the village street, or at an auction sale—the behaviour of any two or more people will depend largely on whether they think themselves members of the same group or not; in the latter case it will depend further on what is locally regarded as the 'correct' relationship between the specific groups involved. This division of the parish into groups of people became more apparent with time. There were men who were 'a different type from the village' and others were 'people who won't acknowledge you'. There were 'better class folk who make you feel awkward' and 'people who are different because of the way they carry on'. These groups or classes are also believed to possess qualities which make them 'better' or 'higher' than another class. Gosforth has its 'Upper Ten' or 'Top Class' and there are 'people you look up to' and 'people you look down on'.

Since the same people were always mentioned in connection with a particular class, and never as belonging to another class, it became possible to divide the parish up into a number of classes, each with a comparatively fixed membership, and arranged in a graded series. Two methods were used to determine the nature and membership of each class and the results showed that the people of Gosforth believed themselves to be split up into seven social classes.

Each class is thought by members of other classes to have special attributes and modes of behaviour. The seven classes will be described in turn, as more or less separate entities. Although this is in keeping with the local belief that a class has definite limits and a social reality of its own, it must however be borne in mind throughout this chapter that each class has position only in relation to other classes, and that the characteristics of any one class become meaningless when divorced from the total system.

The fact that everyone is expected to act according to a prescribed code of social behaviour, dependent on individual rank, is of enormous importance as a controlling factor in everyday life. On occasions far too numerous to count, a person's actions in a specific situation were explained as having taken place because 'He (she) was afraid people would think he (she) was a snob'.

When a person fails to behave 'properly' and ignores the comments and criticisms of neighbours, then he or she ceases to be regarded as a living member of Gosforth society to all intents and purposes. There were several people in the village, surrounded on all sides by neighbours, who had 'no friends or visitors'.

When the socially maladjusted person is a stranger the isolation is even more marked. The family with no kinship ties coming to live in the parish for the first time is soon assigned a position in the class system, and is thereafter expected to live in the same way as other families of equal rank. When this does not happen, the newcomers find themselves living in a social vacuum. There are three such families in the parish who have lived there two, five and seven years respectively. The first of these is known by name to most people in Gosforth, but no one admitted to knowing the family personally or could think of anyone who did. The names of the other two families were known only to their immediate neighbours, and people living less than half a mile away from them stated that they had never heard of them. This was often demonstrably untrue, but it was undeniable that as a social fact their existence was, and would probably remain, unrecognized.

It will be clear from what has been written in this section that since the 'social perspective' varies from class to class (compare, for example, the respective attitudes of the 'Upper Ten' and the lower class to a stranger) each class will have its own conception of the other classes and behave towards them accordingly. Since there are seven classes, even representative attitudes cannot be considered fully, let alone deviations from the norms; but some conception of the more important differences may be gained from the following 'class perspectives'.

(i) *Upper-Upper class:*

Upper-Upper class	'Our social level.' 'Better class.'
Lower-Upper class	'Social climbers.' 'Not quite our class.' 'He *tries* to behave like a gentleman, but . . .'
Intermediate	'Neither here nor there. More intelligent than the normal run of people around here.' 'Quite well educated and very handy when you have about a dozen village organizations to see to.'
Upper-Medial	'Social climbers in the village.'
Medial and Lower Medial	'Villagers and farmers.' 'Decent lower class people.' 'The country people.'
Lower class	'The immoral element in the village.' 'The worst kind of countryman.' 'The worst of the lower orders.'

(ii) *Lower-Upper class:*

Upper-Upper	'The Upper Ten.' 'The people who have more breeding than sense.' 'They have no money, but because they talk like a B.B.C. announcer and their great-grandfather was a tuppeny-ha'penny baronet, they think they own the place.'
Lower-Upper	'Ambitious people.' 'Go-ahead people.'
Intermediate	'In between.'
Upper-Medial	'The village aristocracy. They try their best to get ahead, but everything is against them.'
Medial	'Farmers and small professionals.' 'Farmers and village tradesmen.'
Lower-Medial	'The village.'
Lower class	'Dirty people. I can't understand them. Some of them are quite well off, but you'd never think it to look at them.'

(iii) *Intermediate class:*

Upper-Upper	'The Nibs.' 'The usual well-off people you find in the countryside these days. Mostly retired people; very few of them are old established.'
Lower-Upper	'The money-maker class. They have ambitions of climbing, but they don't seem to have much luck.'
Intermediate	'We are in a class of our own.' 'Our position is not a very easy one to understand.'
Upper-Medial	'The kind of people who don't mix with their neighbours. Usually they are social climbers.'
Medial	'The majority of ordinary people with good jobs—including farmers, of course.'
Lower-Medial	'The average villager.'
Lower class	'An unfortunate minority. You can tell them by the way they live. Most of them are dirty.'

(iv) *Upper-Medial class:*

Upper-Upper	'The sort of people you can really look up to.' 'The proper gentry.' 'The better class people.'
Lower-Upper	'They are not Upper Ten but they like to think they are. They are not all that different from us, except for their money.'
Intermediate	'School teachers and that sort.' 'I think folks make far too much fuss about them.'
Upper-Medial	'People who keep themselves to themselves.' 'Decent people who try to get on.' 'The sort of people who try to improve themselves a bit.'
Medial	'Farmers and such.'
Lower-Medial	'Village people.' 'The ordinary working class people.'
Lower class	'People who don't try to lift themselves.' 'Dirty people who have no self-respect.'

(v) *Medial and Lower Medial:*

Upper-Upper	'People who are higher class than we are.'
Lower-Upper	'Folks like X who have plenty of money and plenty of cheek. They want to get on in t'world.'

Intermediate	'In-between because of education.'
Upper-Medial	'Snobs.' 'Stuck-up folk.'
Medial and Lower-Medial	'Ordinary Gosfer' folk.'
Lower class	'Folk who don't care what they look like.'

(vi) *Lower class:*

Upper-Upper	'Them posh folks living in the big houses.' 'They won't acknowledge you and the way some of them behaves you'd think you was some mak o' animal.'
Lower-Upper	'The folk with brass who acts like they was big nobs.' 'Bloody snobs.'
Intermediate	'Don't know much about them. A lot o' bloody barrack room lawyers if tha ask me.'
Upper-Medial	'A lot o' **** **** **** snobs.'
Medial and Lower-Medial	'Village folk like us, but some on 'em is very high and mighty.'
Lower class	'Decent folk.' 'Folks that like to do what they wants to.'

Some mention must also be made of the concept of 'the old standards' in relation to the social classes. The people to whom 'the old standards' are ascribed are generally those whose families have lived in Gosforth for generations, even centuries. While they are not confined to one social level, they are to be found mainly in the Medial and Lower-Medial classes, and never in the Lower-Upper class. Being of the 'old standards' implies high rank within a class, but at the same time there is a strong suggestion that these families are in some way outside the normal working of the class system. People would often remark that 'Such and such a family isn't in the same class (as "A", "B" etc.) but they are the real old standards you know' or 'That mak o' folk is different from the rest of us.'

In the same way, life-long bachelorhood and marriage of first cousins both of which are more typical of families belonging to the 'old standards' than of others, are considered 'natural' to the former and very abnormal otherwise.

Life in the village is greatly influenced by two important facts. Firstly, that the people live close together, and secondly, in part as a result of this, that they see much more of each other and of strangers. Consequently there is ample scope for the development of devices to increase personal status, the maintenance of which occupies much of the villager's time and energy. As one villager remarked, 'You can't blow your nose in Gosfer' without ivverybody knows about it; and half on 'em knows about it afore you does it.'

Local Class Structures 2
R. E. Pahl

Reprinted with permission from 'The Two Class Village', *New Society*, 27 February, 1964.

I have been concerned in an examination of the postwar social changes in three contrasting villages in Hertfordshire. 'Dormersdell', which I have chosen to describe here, is admittedly a rather extreme example, but served to highlight some of the problems in which I was interested. I wanted to know, for example, more of the reasons people give for living in the country and the way the newcomers react on the established village community. To what extent does the more mobile, cosmopolitan middle class manager and his wife make any sort of contact with the villagers and how do village organizations change or respond to the new situation?

Dormersdell has a population of just over 1,000 and a 50 per cent household sample was taken in the spring of 1961. Of the 144 households interviewed, 90 of the heads of households were classified as middle class, on a scale derived from the Registrar General's Classification of Occupations (1960). The remainder were classified as working class, apart from twelve heads engaged in agriculture, who were exempt from this stage of the analysis, and a further five for whom no information was obtainable. About 60 per cent of the middle class group is concentrated in an area of woodland about a mile from the centre of the village. This area, known simply as the Wood, became synonymous with both the middle class and new-comers.

Some 29 per cent of all chief earners work in London or the Greater London conurbation and 53 per cent work in the surrounding Hertfordshire towns; only 18 per cent work in the parish or the neighbouring parish. However, it was not so much the place of work which seemed to be important but rather the class, as defined by occupation and the place of residence in the parish, the two going together. The community was not only polarized spatially but also socially. The two worlds of the working class (the old established villagers) and the middle class (the immigrant professional and managerial people) could hardly have been further apart.

Commuters and Joiners

Many middle class people move out to a village in order to be a member of a 'real' community, which, in practice, means joining things. It might be thought, however, that the length of the journey to work would make it difficult for commuters to get home in time to participate in local organizations in the evening and that the women might be housebound on account of their children during the day. Discussion has often centred on the lack of participation in local activities by middle class commuters, while it has long been widely known that it is not part of the working class culture to join formal social organizations. The working class men may be members of the local darts team or football club but their wives would not be expected to join a dramatic society or discussion group.

In fact Dormersdell is renowned for the wealth of activities which flourish there. The joiners and organizers of most village activities are middle class commuters' wives. It is true, of course, that the middle class considerably outnumber the working class, but it appears that in the working class it is only some of the wives of commuters who take any part in village activities. It is interesting that among the middle class there is some indication that commuting is not a disincentive for some of the men to take active part in local organizations, and the proportion of the joiners who work in London is about the same as of those who work locally in nearby towns. When considering office holders, the contrast between the classes is striking. As well as taking a large part in running the village, the middle class men are also very likely to hold office in organizations meeting outside the village. This is further evidence of the urban, mobile and outward-looking middle class living in a wider, regional sphere of action.

Although it first appeared that middle class people are well integrated into village social organizations and indeed appear to run most of them, this is in fact a rather false picture of middle class dominance, although one the working class seem happy to hold. Certainly this is the case in the Women's Institute, which has, as already described, been taken over by the middle class. The Badminton Club is also entirely run for and by young middle class men and women. However, this is no great loss to the working class villagers: the younger ones monopolize the Youth Club and the Football Club and have good representation in the Cricket Club: the old age pensioners go to the Greenleaves Club (that is the women do—the men go to the pub) and a few older middle class people in fact enjoy to go and serve tea or act as treasurer without the indignity of becoming a member! Perhaps the only club where the village and the Wood meet on anything like equal terms is the Village Horticultural Society.

Sport is, of course, also a potential mediator between the classes but there are few young people in their teens and twenties living in the Wood since most of the immigrant newcomers arrive in their thirties. The Church also provides some common meeting ground for the two worlds. Here the respectable, conservative working class is matched with a similar proportion of middle class people. To summarize the interaction of the middle and working class in the social sphere, it would appear that by and large the working class people are not deprived of any activity by the middle class immigrants (if we accept the Young Wives' Club as a substitute for the Women's Institute), despite many activities taking place in which they are not represented. Because of this lack of contact each group accuses the other unfairly.

The wider, national class divisions in society are here played out in the local scene in Dormersdell. The contact between the classes becomes less, since however much the newcomers may try to be a middle class squirearchy, the radical working class resent it, and the conservative working class find it no real substitute for the Gentry. How much the change is due to physical contact with the outside world in surrounding towns and how much it is due to the influence of the new middle class is difficult to say. My own view is that change in the village community has not taken place as rapidly as might be expected. To give an example, there are two pubs in the village. One is almost entirely devoted to the middle class, developing the atmosphere of a private party at which most people know each other. The other pub has tried to follow suit and certainly in the saloon bar has achieved some success. However, the public bar of the pub nearest to the village contains little sophistication. Talk centres around local events, neighbouring villages, football or cricket.

Generally the villagers were not effusive about Dormersdell. 'It's quite nice in summer but a bit dreary in winter' summed up many people's feelings.

The whole working class situation was a highly complex structure of definite roles, relationships and behaviour, far too delicate to be able to generalize about. The broad distinctions between the middle and working class were so enormous that quite crude methods could be used to portray them. But within the classes much greater study in depth is required than was possible with a sample of this size. Not only has there been little contact between the worlds but the main way of breaking down these barriers—by the children of the two groups going to the same schools—seems less likely to take place.

A Process of Polarization

The different patterns of life which have been described are based on two main differences. The middle class have greater mobility owing to the use of private transport, particularly by the wives, often driving a second car. The changeover from the hierarchical social structure, which was functionally suited to the village as a community, to the polarized two-class division may be the chief cause of the working class people's resentment. The more traditional working class element is resentful, partly because it has lost its clear position in the hierarchy and the reflected status of the gentry for whom it worked, and partly because it now finds itself lumped with what it would feel to be the less respectable working class. This traditional group would like to be given respect and position in society, but gets neither. The non-traditional working class see the segregated middle class world as a symptom of the inequalities in society, and condemn all middle class people as snobs and nouveaux riches without basing this on individual knowledge and experience.

The middle class people come into rural areas in search of a meaningful community and by their presence help to destroy whatever community was there. Part of the basis of the local village community was the sharing of the deprivations due to the isolation of country life and the sharing of the limited

world of the families within the village. The middle class
people try to get the cosiness of village life, without suffering
any of the deprivations, and while maintaining a whole range
of contacts outside.

New middle class people are unprepared for what they find.
Determined to move out of suburbia and influenced by the
pastoral vision portrayed by everything from the Scott Report
to the popular novel, many do expect to become the squire's
successor. Indeed many of the women have the sense of
service to others, sometimes found in the squire's wife. On the
other hand, to the working class they might just as well not be
there. The main exception to this is the advantage which many
working class women gain in the way of untaxed extra income
from those middle class housewives who employ them to
clean their homes. This is probably the most direct form of
social contact. Some firm friendships between Wood and
Village exist at this level, but this does not extend to a more
normal social relationship. National class divisions come into
sharper focus in the local setting of such metropolitan villages
as Dormersdell.

Local Class Structures 3
J. Littlejohn

Reprinted with permission from J. Littlejohn: *Westrigg, The Sociology
of a Cheviot Parish*, London, Routledge and Kegan Paul, 1963, pp. 1, 2,
7–9, 81–4, 90, 111–12, 117–21, 223–9.

Westrigg is an upland parish in a mainly rural county in the
south of Scotland.

Settlement is of the dispersed type. There is no village in the
parish, no shops or pubs; dwellings and the few public buildings are scattered along the valley floors with here and there
a small cluster, the two most compact being forestry settlements. The two nearest towns are fifteen and seventeen miles
away. Near the junction in the parish of the two roads from
these towns are a post office, school and smiddy. This, the
centre of communication, is thought of by parishioners as the
centre of the parish, though the geographical centre is two
miles north from it. By common agreement a Public Hall was
erected at the geographical centre in 1922.

The scattered settlement pattern is partly due to the requirements of large-scale sheep farming. Almost every cottage is tied, i.e., is part of the property of a farm (or the Forestry Commission now) and can be rented only if one is employed by the farmer (or Forestry Commission).

However, the settlement pattern cannot be explained simply by reference to the environment and the requirements of sheep farming. The present pattern took shape under an organization of the farm in which the farm worker and his family belonged to the farm in a more strict sense than is the case now.

In everyday conversation parishioners categorize each other into three classes by using the terms 'gentleman farmer', 'working farmer' and 'working folk'. There are differences in the frequencies with which persons of these categories employ the terms; those designated 'working farmers' and 'working folk' use all three terms much oftener than those designated 'gentleman farmer'. The 'gentleman farmers' rarely use the term to refer to themselves, and do not often speak of 'working farmers' either, preferring the term 'small farmer'.

The local terms, gentlemen and working farmers, and working folk, obviously imply a classification of the agricultural population and of forestry labourers.

That the classes are viewed as superior and inferior to each other is soon apparent in conversation. When identifying a third party for me informants would say, e.g. 'he's not a working farmer, he's *only* a working man' or 'he's not a gentleman farmer, just a working farmer.' An upper-middle class man once remarked of agricultural labourers 'of course some of these people are hardly better than animals in intelligence and way of living.' Sometimes irritation at one provokes sweeping condemnation of the class as when a farmer exclaimed *a propos* some minor lapse on the part of a shepherd, 'they're all alike these people, they just can't think.' A lower middle class woman remarked of a working-class neighbour, 'you can see the lower element coming out even in her.' A view of the working class widely held among both the middle classes is that they are 'childish'. Direct remarks like these are not very common: more common is the indirect and quite unmalicious reference like this by a farmer, 'This morning a stranger passed by the field where I was working and said "good morning" to me as if I were just a labourer. I was quite pleased, in fact a lifelong ambition of mine has been to be treated as if I were nobody.'

Employers of labour obviously wield power in the sense of being in the position to hire and fire, and in addition a farmer's power of influencing a workman's chances of employment in a district are by no means negligible. Farmers in any one district are in an informal compact as over against workmen, shown in this farmer's description of hiring, 'You advertise in the papers and wait and hope someone will answer. Then when you get an answer you ring up his employer and ask "are you finished with this man"—"yes"—"is he any good?"— "wouldn't touch him with a barge pole"—"all right, thank you". Eventually you meet a man and tell him the conditions he'll work under . . .' When a workman leaves a job he is given a written testimonial containing no adverse judgements, which he knows to be worthless. A shepherd said, 'You only ask for the testimonial because if you didn't get one your neighbours would think there was something far wrong. But the bosses talk about you on the telephone to each other. That's where they have you.' Several workmen cited cases of alleged victimization, in which a farmer prevented an employee he had sacked from finding another job.

The sociological problem of determining how class status is allocated cannot be solved solely by pointing to so many factors, all of which are already known, or by an arbitrary decision that one or other is 'fundamental'. What is important is that at different points in the system different factors become of crucial importance in the allocation of status. This again was clear from comments of informants while making class placements. An area where there was much hesitation in judgement (among informants of all classes) was the distinction between craftsmen and the smaller working farmers. A craftsman may own no more property than a bag of tools and a motor car, yet his income can be as sizeable as a small farmer's. A craftsman may be in a position of authority over an apprentice or may hire a young assistant, and though in such a relationship the teacher/pupil note will often sound, the craftsman has ultimate sanctions at his disposal not greatly different from those a small farmer has *vis-a-vis* an employee. In this area too it is often difficult to make a distinction between craftsman and farmer on the basis of 'standard of living' or style of life. Yet all informants eventually did draw a distinction solely on the basis of the sheer fact of land ownership (it being understood that 'land' meant a holding large enough to be an independent business enterprise). 'After all,' they would say, 'he does own a farm, and (X the craftsman) doesn't.'

Higher up the system neither the sheer fact of property ownership nor its amount distinguishes between one class and another, the professional people having none and several upper-middle class farmers having holdings as small as those of lower-middle class farmers. The point in land-values where factors other than size of farm come into play (in this community) seems to be at about 2,000 acres. Above this size farmers are all of the upper-middle class, and sheer size is an important qualification; of one farmer a class peer remarked 'he gets in (to our class) of course just because his farm's so big.' Below this size the farmer may be of either class. The other factors brought to bear on status judgements at this point with regard to both farmers and professionals are education and 'background', 'style of life' and estimate of relative income. Though I call these 'factors' as if they were four clearly distinguishable variables, informants did not in fact separately specify them as such. None used the actual term 'style of life', though women informants obviously meant this when they stressed the importance of good manners, eating customs and size of house as determinants of status.

It is implicit in the data presented above that the class system of the parish cannot be represented as three distinct groups sharply demarcated one from another so that boundaries are clearly apparent between adjoining classes. There is obviously a certain indefiniteness about it—a feature of class systems in industrial society which has often been commented upon. The area of indefiniteness in the system calls for some explanation but first it must be described. Briefly, the position is that while the upper-middle class is sharply distinguished from the lower-middle class there is not the same clarity of boundary between the latter and the working class. Taking the criterion of association this means that while members of the upper-middle class do not associate with members of the other two classes, some members of the lower-middle sometimes associate with some members of the working class.

This feature of the system is closely connected with another already discussed, namely that the class status of a person or a family is not necessarily determined by reference to one single value; and since the values used in allocating status are hardly commensurable on a single scale, in the area described status can be allocated or claimed on the basis of several values.

All informants agreed that speech and accent were the most trustworthy symbols in placing a stranger, with clothes and manners a fairly reliable second. That all these function as symbols of status is clearly seen in the treatment meted out to persons who attempt to display one of these traits as it is displayed by a class higher than the one they are known to belong to. They are ridiculed in a way which shows that they are held to be trying to claim a class status they are not entitled to. For example, recently some working youths bought a suit of clothing of the expensive sort worn in the upper-middle class. They were jeered at by their class peers and each given a nickname showing he was regarded as claiming illegitimate status—'Lord Westrigg', 'Sir X', and so on. Similarly there is one working-class family whose speech is more like the middle classes than like the rest of the working class. The lower-middle class regarded this family with approval saying they did not speak so 'Scotch' as the others and were not 'rough' in manner, etc. To the rest of the working class the family is 'affected', accused of 'putting on airs' and 'thinking itself above us'.

The culture of the higher classes is officially defined as better than that of the lower. In the local school the language and manners taught are those of the middle classes. Though the majority of the children are of the working class they are discouraged from using their own normal speech. During one lesson, for example, the children were asked to name various sorts of buildings shown to them in pictures, of which one was a kennel. Asked to name it one of the boys replied correctly in dialect 'a dughoose'. He was somewhat chagrined to be told he was 'wrong'. In short the children are being trained to believe that their normal way of speaking is wrong and to imitate the dialect of the middle classes. The same applies to manners; the children are taught to address and refer to adults as 'Mr.' and 'Mrs.', to use handkerchiefs and to be circumspect in interaction with others. These are middle-class customs. Working-class men in particular demand of each other an immediate solidarity in interaction which seems to render middle-class manners superfluous.

This brief sketch of class cultures I hope justifies the use of the term 'social milieu' to describe the nature of social class. A social class is neither a mere category arbitrarily defined by myself on the basis of one or two 'characteristics' such as property ownership, nor is it a group in the strict sense of the term as implying clear cut boundaries and a constitution laying down a limited set of relationships among its members. A class is rather, for its members, one of the major horizons of all social experience, an area within which most experience is defined. Encompassing so much, it is rarely conceptualized.

This does not mean that the concept of a local class system is a sociologist's myth; it only means that individuals, when asked about it, answer in terms of their own experience of it. That there is a system is I think shown by the fact that no informant placed him or herself wrongly, no one claimed a status higher or lower than that accorded by the majority of fellow parishioners. Each person knows his or her place in the system, can place accurately other people he has the requisite information about, but has no need to turn his experience of the system into a conceptual scheme.

The classes differ in the range and frequency of their association outside the parish. The norm here is that the higher a class the wider and more frequent are its contacts outside the parish; or to adopt the network image, the higher the class the more dispersed is the network of relationships in which it is involved, the lower the class the more contained is its network. The basis of the difference in scale is the former's relative freedom from having to work to a routine timetable, and ownership of private means of transport and communication, as opposed to the latter's being tied to a daily job and dependent on public transport.

At this point it may be asked whether in fact the middle classes have lost power in the parish over the last fifty years. The data suggests that the more frequent contacts, both formal and informal, of the upper-middle class outside the parish serve to maintain their position of dominance within the parish.

It is the family and not the individual that is the unit of social class. By family in this context I mean those members of a family living together in the same household. It is necessary to state this because an individual can alter his class status in his own lifetime; the child can come to occupy a different status from his parents, the sibling from the sibling. In such cases persons of different status do not live together as members of the same household. That the family, in this sense, is the unit was clear both from informants, class placements and their comments while making them.

Since a family begins with a marriage, and since a class system restricts association among the population stratified, a full account of the connections between family and class must deal with the process known as assortative mating. Social barriers of any sort limit the possibilities of random contact among people, and tend to foster marriages between persons with similar social characteristics. Social class barriers are among the most important in this process. Where a class system prevails there are three possible combinations of class status of the spouses. The two can be of equal status, the man higher than the woman or the woman higher than the man. The first combination is the normal one; of all marriages in the parish only eight were not of this sort. The second combination is much more frequent than the third, the ratio here being seven to one.

It may be asked why any sort of marriage across class lines is relatively rare. Numerous reasons can be adduced which, however, are merely implicit in the class system itself.

These 'reasons' are however only aspects of the class system itself. Perhaps a more cogent explanation is to be found in the incompatibility between kinship norms and those governing relations between classes. There is a warm and friendly relationship between grandparents and children, and between parents' siblings and siblings' children. In cross-class marriage the children are in a different class from the parents and siblings of one of the spouses. People of different classes do not associate in warm and friendly relations. It seems likely that if marriage between members of different classes became general either the kinship system or the class system would have to alter very much from their present form. While I have no data to prove this, it is clear that in the community there is incompatibility between the two sets of norms and that where they conflict class norms take precedence. Relations with kinsfolk of a lower class are either severed or become characterized by a certain reserve. In either case accusations of snobbery are made by the lower against the higher. For example, one lower-middle class man has an uncle in the parish who is a farm worker, but the two never associate. The former and his wife regard the latter as a tiresome old man, though he is highly respected among the working class. The uncle and members of his household sometimes express resentment against the nephew and his household.

That too frequent marriage across class lines might destroy the present class system is suggested by the fact that marriage of a woman of higher status to a man of lower is very much rarer than the opposite. It is regarded as a more serious breach of the norm. Association outside of work relationships is not merely a sociologist's index of equality of status; it is what equality of status means in everyday behaviour in the community itself.

Further Reading :   **Class**

* P. ANDERSON AND R. BLACKBURN (EDS.): *Towards Socialism*, London, Fontana, 1965.

C. BELL: *Middle Class Families*, London, Routledge and Kegan Paul, 1968

† R. BENDIX AND S. M. LIPSET: *Class, Status, and Power*, London, Routledge and Kegan Paul, 1966.

R. BLACKBURN: 'Inequality and Exploitation', *New Left Review*, No. 42, March, 1967.

* ALSO IN R. BLACKBURN AND A. COCKBURN (EDS.): *The Incompatibles*, London, Penguin Books, 1967.

*† T. B. BOTTOMORE: *Classes in Modern Society*, London, Allen and Unwin, 1965.

* J. BURNHAM: *The Managerial Revolution*, London, Penguin Books, 1962.

R. DAHRENDORF: *Class and Class Conflict in Industrial Society*, London, Routledge and Kegan Paul, 1965.

* J. GOLDTHORPE: 'Social Stratification in Industrial Societies', *Sociological Review*, Monograph No. 8, 1964.

* JOHN H. GOLDTHORPE, D. LOCKWOOD F. BECHOFER AND J. PLATT: *The Affluent Worker in the Class Structure*, Cambridge University Press, 1969.

* C. W. MILLS: *White Collar*, New York, Oxford University Press, 1951.

W. G. RUNCIMAN: *Relative Deprivation and Social Justice*, London, Routledge and Kegan Paul, 1964.

* Available in paperback
† Reference

Chapter Six   Power

In many ways this chapter develops and forms a counterpoint to the themes which emerged in the section on class while some selections take up topics which were raised in the section on community.

One crucial dimension is lacking, not because it is considered unimportant, but because few sociologists have been able or have wished to undertake research in this area. There is very little which helps to explain the actual dynamics of power, how power operates in specific situations, how it is handled by the various interest- and pressure-groups involved, and what the outcomes of decision-making are. It would have been possible to include some impressionistic accounts of the experience of being involved with power and politics at first hand, but it was felt that these would not have been in tune with the remainder of this book.

In the first selection Worsley indicates in what ways a sociological analysis of politics involves a much broader definition of what is 'political' than does the conventional account in terms of 'what governments do'. He examines the reasons for the subordination of the power of the military and religious sectors of society to the political 'state', and for the close association between the political and the economics in Britain. Of crucial importance is the mechanism by which the ruling groups 'legitimate' their possession and exercise of power, by manipulating the symbols of authority. Clearly even an analysis in the simplest terms of 'who governs' involves explanations in terms of 'why, and how are they allowed to govern?'—'why is it felt appropriate, and by whom is it felt appropriate that they should govern?' Thus political sociology needs to go much

further than the mere examination of the correlates of
specific types of voting behaviour, into an analysis of the
formation of political culture.

This involves a consideration of political socialization, of
how certain symbols come to be regarded as legitimate and
their possession vested in representatives of particular classes
and interest groups—a theme which links this chapter to
those on education, social class and the family.

A concern with the ruling elite and how it maintains its
hegemony underlies Miliband's book and also the analysis
of 'The Insiders' which examines the thesis of the separation
of ownership and control. By a careful and detailed
examination of the records of public companies the authors
illustrate the phenomenon of the 'interlocking directorate'. In
this milieu a powerful role is played by large institutional
investors, the banks, insurance companies and holding
companies, whose representatives hold key positions on
boards of directors. Often their presence represents a latent
source of power, unused during the normal contingencies of
business operations, and activated only in critical situations.

Guttsman provides the essential background material on
the composition of the political elite, over the past fifty
years, while Rogow and Shore illustrate how the power of
finance and industry was turned against the 1945–51 Labour
Government.

Still focusing on power at the national level, Finer,
Berrington and Bartholomew analyse the social background
of Labour backbenchers in the House of Commons, during
the last Conservative government. They demonstrate that
there are three rather separate, and in fact disparate, groups
of members, some of whom may, in terms of background
attitudes and orientations, have as much in common with
some of their political opponents as with their own
colleagues. Moreover although each major political party is
class-based, neither is exclusively a class-party, evidenced
by the thirty per cent of manual workers who habitually
vote Conservative. Mackenzie argues that despite the
apparent differences in the organizational structure of the
Conservative and Labour parties, they are in fact more alike
and more oligarchical than democratic.

The background to an event of significance in national
politics, the Bank Rate tribunal of 1958, is examined by
Lupton and Wilson. They apply the techniques and approach

of the social anthropologist to examine the extent to which individual power-holders are members of a network, linked to others by relations of kinship, background, and common association. This notion of network can be a pervasive and important one in the analysis of social structure.

There are several excellent studies of various aspects of political life at the level of the local community. In a study of Newcastle under Lyme, Bealey, Blondel, and McCann analyse the variation between the three major political parties in terms of the relative influence and social standing of key persons. Another important study is that of Banbury, an extract from which appears in Chapter II.

A dimension that is often neglected is that of the personal and psychological attributes of those who wield power, and how these attributes are related to the motivation to succeed. Presthus indicates, on the basis of a comparative study of British and American executives, and the way in which they accommodate to the demands of authority, that there is a strong relationship between organizational mobility and political conservatism, though this is not uniform between Britain and the U.S.A. This theme is, of course, taken further in W. H. Whyte's *The Organization Man*.

The final article by Hill is itself a summary of the many studies that have been undertaken in Britain since the war into voting behaviour. As well as illustrating the importance of factors like age, sex, 'objective social class', and religion, in affecting voting behaviour, the author casts a sideways kick at the notions of the 'floating voter' and the myth of the importance of the election campaign itself. The study by Lockwood, Goldthorpe, Bechofer and Platt is again concerned with the effects of 'affluence', in this case with the possibility that the 'class' support for the Labour Party may have been eroded.

The Analysis of Power and Politics
P. M. Worsley

Reprinted with permission from 'The Distribution of Power in Industrial Society', *Sociological Review Monograph 8, The Development of Industrial Societies*, 1964, pp. 16–17, 20–26.

Insofar as people's behaviour takes account of the existence of others, and is affected by expectations about others, we call it 'social'. Some of this behaviour is specifically purposive; it aims to produce effects. But not all of it is, and not all behaviour of interest to the social scientist is 'social', in Weber's sense of the term. Weber himself, indeed, emphasized that 'sociology is by no means confined to the study of "social action"; that is only . . . its central subject matter . . .' Causally determined action, as well as 'meaningfully' determined action, is part of the sociologist's subject-matter. So, although 'meaningfully' behaviour may be 'non-social', causally it can never be without social consequences.

Restricting ourselves, however, to 'social' action, we can be said to act politically whenever we exercise constraint on others to behave as we want them to. The allocation of resources to further these ends is an economic allocation. The overall assertion of values entailed is an operation of political economy.

These conceptual departure-points imply a very wide conception of politics, what we may call Politics I. By this definition, the exercise of constraint in any relationship is political. All kinds of pressure, from mass warfare and organized torture to implicit values informing inter-personal conversation, make up the political dimension. Looked at this way, there is no such thing as a special kind of behaviour called 'political'; there is only a political dimension to behaviour. Yet the vulgar (and often academic) use of the term 'politics'—what we shall call 'Politics II'—restricts the term to the specialized machinery of government, together with the administrative apparatus of state and party organization. To follow the implications of this usage through, strictly, would involve us in denying to simple undifferentiated societies the privilege of having a political system at all. Moreover, we also recognize that extra-governmental organizations within advanced societies dispose of power, and have their own constellations of power: we speak of 'university politics'. By this, we do not mean, merely and obviously that organizations like universities or trade unions, either continuously or inter- mittently, bring pressure to bear upon government, and are thereby behaving 'politically'—and only on such occasions. Nor do we mean that party politics emerges from and intrudes into sub-cultures. We mean, rather, that these sub-cultural groups are, latently and constantly, organized power-group- ings. They have an internal system through which this power is deployed; externally, their mere existence is a fact which governments, even the most authoritarian, have to take account of. Normally, too, such power-groupings make sure governments do take account of their interests; they are not merely passive.

Power does not exist 'in itself': it flows between people. And everybody has some of it, some area of choice, of ability to affect things his way. It may only be the power to be negative, to 'vote with one's feet'; in the extreme, only to choose death—but that is a choice, and, as the study of martyrology alone shows us, one which is by no means without social consequences. But some people have overwhelming and decisive power. Power is not randomly distributed, but institutionalized.

The identification of the rulers, therefore, must involve an examination of the distribution of power generally within civil society. In British society, there are only two institutional orders, however, within which very great power is concen- trated: the political order and the economic order. This is not true for all societies. In some, for example, those in control of the means of violence are specially important. In the U.S.A., organized religion is a far more potent force than in this country, especially at the community level. The identification of the power elite, the delineation of the distribution of power, are matters for empirical investigation. But a simplistic kind of political behaviourism does not carry us very far. It is commonly assumed, for example, that the role of the military in the U.S.A. is very much more considerable than in the U.K.

Only in wartime has the military successfully and seriously obtruded itself into the formation of public policy—or even tried to—but at such times, military policy is the central issue in public policy. Viscount Montgomery's public pronounce- ments are striking in their atypicality—and are self-consciously 'deviant' and outrageous into the bargain.

The British military, then, has never become a caste—it is too closely woven into the culture of the ruling classes. It is no longer, however, one of the major magnetic power-centres attracting the enterprising and the ambitious, probably because, increasingly, it no longer makes the key military decisions. These are made abroad, and the military machine which once coped with the Indian sub-continent, to mention no other area, finds itself stretched in dealing with Cyprus and other backwaters of the world.

Many of these features are reproduced in another formerly central institution of British society, the Church of England, which has been recently described as 'by far and away the most important social institution in the land', and 'by far and away the largest organizer of youth in the country'. Yet, in quantitative terms alone, it now exercises direct and regular influence over less than three million adult members, plus a further 1,161,000 Sunday school children aged between 3 and 14. By contrast, the Daily Mirror had a readership of nearly thirteen million people in 1954—one third of the population aged 16 and over and 'Granadaland' alone embraces some eight million adults.

The Army, the Church, and the Law are not what they were. But ordination still does not mean alienation: four Oxbridge colleges produced nearly one quarter of the Church of England bishops between 1860 and 1960, and the public schools and older universities still dominate recruitment. The class connections of the lower clergy, however, have become less specifically tied to the upper classes (and 22% of contemporary ordinands attended secondary modern and similar schools). Like the Army, as the Church has become less attractive to the upper classes, it increasingly finds its new recruits from formerly excluded social strata, and its senior leaders from within specifically churchly families. If the Church is no longer 'the Conservative Party at prayer', it is also still a long way from being 'that nation on Sunday'. Paradoxically, its democratization, which might well be a future source of religious strength, reflects its diminished social position. It no longer attracts those in search of decisive power; prelates have less to be proud about: education has long slipped from their grasp; morals are increasingly becoming the bailiwick of the B.M.A., and ideology of the mass media.

As serious centres of power, then, we are concerned predominantly with the political and economic orders. It is significant that Dahrendorf, who emphasizes, pluralistically, that all institutions carry their quantum of power, in fact only singles out economic and political power for special analysis. For Britain, the close association between the two elites at the apex of these institutional orders—the governing elite and the coalesced property-owning landed aristocracy and industrial bourgeoisie—has recently been very closely documented by Guttsman, together with the entry of 'new men' into the ranks of the governing elite (largely via the mechanisms for upward mobility presented by the Labour Movement and an extended educational system).

The uninterrupted, albeit modified, dominance, of the property-owning classes, in a society which has long been the most highly 'proletarianized' in the world, is surely one of the most striking phenomena of modern times.

The answer does not lie in the possession of machine-guns by the ruling class. In this century, only in 1926 has armed force ever been in sight. The challenge of the masses—who created a whole series of instruments of self-expression and self-assertion, from the co-operatives and the trade unions to the Labour Party—has never been a revolutionary one.

The exploration of this continuity and stability involves examination of the modification of both the ruling class and of the ruled. The former were able to accede to the demands of the masses for the vote flexibly and gradually; in the economic sphere, concessions to the 'welfare' demands of the newly-vocal enfranchized masses were also made skilfully and gradually. In the process, the theory and practice of laissez faire had to be thrown overboard. Gradually, the State assumed more and more responsibility for more and more areas of social life. In an age when the nationalized sector of the economy is responsible for half the investment spending, a third of the employment income, and a quarter of the national product, Herbert Spencer's resistance to state interference, whether in the shape of the Post Office, the public mint, poor relief, 'social' legislation, colonization, organized sanitation, or state education, seems remote indeed.

The extensions of the franchise in 1832, 1867, and 1884, were the crucial steps, politically. Yet the beginnings of reform produced no sharp polarization of forces. In the crucial period 1832–68, 'the classes were represented in almost the same proportions in each of the two parliamentary groupings' —'left centre' (Liberal) and 'right-centre' (Conservative). After 1867, the new middle classes gradually crept onto the governmental scene (normally holding offices of lower prestige and 'administrative' content). Not until 1923 did a non-aristocrat hold the office of Foreign Secretary, and not until 1929 was a British government elected on full adult suffrage.

The entry of the middle classes into the centres of political power was thus a long-drawn-out process; the emerging proletariat, in its turn, only very gradually distinguished itself from the party of the middle classes.

Much more was involved in the diffcult enterprise of modernization than political changes alone. On their own these might well have led to the rule of the masses so feared by sections of the elite. The modernization of British society was a much more many-sided process, the rationalization and stabilization of a whole 'political culture'. This enculturation was not accomplished by some undifferentiated 'ruling class': more specifically, many of the crucial reorganizations were the achievement of the Liberal Party, and bore the stamp of liberalism, even though that party, theoretically the repository of anti-bigness, anti-statism, and the cult of the individual, nevertheless had quite determinedly reorganized itself as a centralized, hierarchical machine, modelled on Chamberlain's Birmingham caucus system, and as a political party with a mass, extra-Parliamentary base. Self-rationalization was the climax to a long series of rationalizations of the wider society in the third quarter of the nineteenth century, a watershed between the society symbolized by Palmerston and modern mass democracy: reform of the Civil Service (the Northcote-Trevelyan reforms), of the Army (Cardwell's reforms, 1868–71), and of education, both for the elite (the development of public schools on the Rugby pattern) and for the masses (the development of primary education, 1870–80). For the newly-literate, a special literature industry was founded. Via education, a proportion of the working-class could find its way into the middle classes. Convinced by their personal experience of the reality of upwards social mobility, they constituted, and constitute, an important reservoir of believers in the notion of la carriere ouverte aux talents; their consciousness is structured by their own experience of mobility in the 'middle levels of power', to use Mills' phrase, and generalized into a theory applicable to the society as a whole.

The persistence of patterns of deference and traditionalistic loyalty among other large segments of the lower strata cannot be documented here, nor has it yet been adequately documented anywhere. 'Deference', however, only explains part of the mass vote which the Conservative Party has been able to mobilize since modern politics began in the 1870s.

This solidarity, was far more complex than any crude label like 'feudal', 'deference-pattern', or even 'traditionalism' would imply. The imperialist note, indeed, was strikingly untraditional, and was resisted for a long time in both Conservative and Liberal circles, as well as Labour. As Guttsman has pointed out, the feudal heritage was, in fact, a distant one (and had been profoundly challenged and modified via Civil War and industrialization): 'English romantic thought accepted the basic tenets of the Enlightenment: freedom of thought, equality before the law, but it reacted against the libertarian and egalitarian views of the French revolution'. The latter tradition was taken up and developed by the working-class; it could not easily form a part of the self-legitimation of the ruling class.

Simple, 'objective' classification of occupations, then, or of the distribution of power, does not take us very far in explaining the success of British conservatism in attracting one-third of the trade union vote even to this day. Counting heads is essential in order to establish some primary facts about who people are, but even in order to know what to count at this level, we operate with (often implicit) theoretical assumptions. To get any further, to explore deeper levels of behaviour, we have to move beyond this kind of classificatory activity into the field of 'political culture'. Of course, crude classification and correlation is analytically easier (if technically, perhaps, complicated enough) than more sophisticated exploration; it is also less controversial. The difficulties entailed in exploration arise intrinsically from the fact that human consciousness is involved, for we are dealing with attitudes, shaped by many variables. But the really fertile fields for sociological investigation lie precisely in the exploration of the interplay between the subjective and the objective. Class does not, metaphysically, mean anything 'in itself'. It is always acted upon, interpreted, mediated, by somebody, and it is the social agencies which inject meaning into class, and transmit these meanings to people, that must increasingly concern us. They concern us increasingly, both because this

is the needed development in intellectual and analytical
terms, and because, empirically, the mechanisms by which
consciousness is manipulated are of growing importance in
modern society.

The National Decision-Makers 1
S. Hall, R. Samuel, P. Sedgwick and C. Taylor

Reprinted with permission from 'The Insiders', *Universities and Left
Review*, Vol. I, No. 3, July 1957.

'Minority Owners Control'

It is true that the general body of shareholders is now so
fragmented and dispersed that they cannot provide 'effective
control' of the giant firms. The very spread of small and
middle-sized holdings, and the 'absentee ownership' attitude
on the part of many smaller shareholders, make it possible
for 'effective control' to fall into the hands of a relatively small
group consisting of the large shareholders owning a relatively
small percentage of voting capital.

The Pattern of Oligarchy

The twenty largest shareholders are rarely single persons. This
does not mean that a large bloc of shares or a directorship
is not an indication of great personal wealth. The scale of
corporate enterprise is such that only the very wealthy could
own more than 1% of voting capital. In addition there is,
to an increasing extent, the policy of a spread of holdings by
the very wealthy through the large companies, though in the
major corporations large holdings tend to be relatively more
concentrated than in the middle-size firms.

But to a remarkable degree, the large shareholders are
'corporate' persons. This fact reflects both the scale of
economic activity and the pattern of behaviour in institutions
which tend towards oligarchic group control. In some companies the classical entrepreneur or family owner-manager
is 'simply reclothed in corporate garments.' More often the
large shareholders are themselves corporate institutions, or

financial concerns (banks, insurance companies, investment trusts, etc.). These financial institutions buttress a corporate economic system.

The complicated patterns of ownership are drawn together in many cases by an elaborate network of 'interlocking directorships'. C. Wright Mills, in his book on the American economy, *The Power Elite*, remarks: '"interlocking directorate" is no mere phrase; it points to a solid feature of the facts of business life, and to a sociological anchor of the community of interest, the unification of outlook and policy, that prevails among the propertied class. Any detailed analysis of any major piece of business comes upon this fact, especially when the business involves politics. As a minimum inference, it must be said that such arrangements permit an exchange of views in a convenient and more or less formal way among those who share the interests of the corporate rich.'

'The Managerial Revolution'?

But the top managerial executives are themselves, often, members of the board of directors. They provide the pivot between general policy and its detailed administration. As such, they are another group whose interests are protected and whose power is exercised through the corporate oligarchy or power elite which we have been describing.

Interests and Motives in a Corporate Economy

The analysis which we have outlined above suggests that, to a remarkable degree, private wealth in a capitalist economy has been incorporated and the motivations of private enterprise have been institutionalized with the corporate structure. These joint stock firms, and the financial institutions which serve them, are now the organized centres of the private property system in modern capitalist states. The corporate economy has outgrown the personal shareholder and the robber baron. In the modern state, the old-style capitalists have made themselves over in the image of the giant firm: they must combine together—in a multitude of formal and informal ways—in order to secure their interests and wield their power. The ownership and control of these concentrations of industrial property can now be exercised only through a series of loosely organized but tightly knit oligarchic groups.

The groups may represent several interests—financial, mana-gerial, industrial: but, as in any true oligarchy, the 'natural competitiveness' of these elites of power has been subsumed into their greater interests—the mutual care of corporate property. Acting together, they constitute a group of economic and social interests more powerful, and more remote from the control of the community, than the capitalist world has ever known.

As C. Wright Mills has remarked: 'Under the owners of property a huge and complex bureaucracy of business and industry has come into existence. But the right to this chain of command, the legitimate access to the position of authority from which these bureaucracies are directed, is the right of private ownership.'

The men who constitute these new elites of corporate power—both those who manage and those who own—are the executors of private property. The incorporation of wealth and the institutionalization of economic motive means, in fact, that directors, large shareholders and managerial execu-tives all stand in more or less the same relationship to private property. Their personal wealth and power is intimately related to the power, stability and success of modern business enterprise. These oligarchic groups can no longer think only of their own personal wealth: they must think of this by thinking of the concerns through which wealth accrues. They cannot seek the quick maximization of private wealth, for the scale and complexity of enterprise is now too great. This goal has been institutionalized in our economy—but it remains the driving power of the whole system. The wealth and power of the large shareholder or director is derived either through dividends or through concealed profits—in the form of capital gains or capital appreciation. The non-owning manager derives his power and status through immense salaries, expense accounts and bonuses—which, like dividends and capital gains—can only be derived through the profits of corporate enterprise. Quick profits have to be considered in conjunction with other motives which are not opposed but complementary to the driving motives of wealth and power. These must be safeguarded by the taking into consideration of such new features of institutional property as long-term growth and expansion, the level of investment and innovation necessary to keep the corporation ahead, the dove-tailing of pricing and product policies, the pressure for increased wages on the part of organized labour. But the salaries and perquisites of the managers and executives are merely new concealed forms of capital appreciation. 'Stability' and 'growth' are, after all, motivations which each of the groups can well afford, particularly when they lead to the increasing control over the supply of goods, and when, through appreciation, they ensure the long-term maximization of wealth and status on an unprecedented level.

The Unity of the Propertied Class

The very oligarchic nature of economic power in the new capitalist economies makes for a solidarity of the propertied classes. Into this social stratum, the chief managerial executives have been drawn. They are the most recent recruits of the corporate revolution.

But economic power, derived and concentrated in this fashion, is also social power. Since the price and supply of goods, the size of dividends and salaries, and the nature of their 'higher emoluments' are, to an increasing extent, the result of decisions which they themselves can consciously take, the men who compose this power elite are as wealthy as they choose. The only limitation to wealth and power is the success of the corporate enterprise which they serve. This is true, whether they choose to show their wealth by consumption, or grow wealthy in secret. The personal fortunes of the wealthy and powerful are coincidental with the 'stability' and 'scale' of their enterprises. This fact serves to draw together into a single social elite the different oligarchic interests which are represented in joint stock enterprise. The success of enterprise generates consumption power of immense proportions—and thus makes possible a style of life which is commonly enjoyed.

The National Decision-Makers 2
S. E. Finer, H. B. Berrington, and D. J. Bartholomew

Reprinted with permission from S. E. Finer, H. B. Berrington, and D. J. Bartholomew: *Backbench Opinion in the House of Commons 1955-59*, London, Pergamon Press, 1961, pp. 62-5, 74-5.

The Labour Party is, broadly speaking, polarized on ideological matters between the left-wing Miscellaneous Occupations and the right-wing Workers, with the Professions mainly taking the middle view: and on material matters between the left-wing Workers, and the right-wing Professions and Miscellaneous Occupations.

It is easier to say 'how', than 'why'. The sociology of British classes has hardly been developed in this country. Furthermore, we are dealing with classes as they were in the twenties and thirties which was the period in which most of the Members acquired their formative occupation.

The Workers—who are largely identical with the Trades Union sponsored Members—are perhaps the least difficult to understand. There is little to add to the perceptive sketch of Mr. J. P. W. Mallalieu, M.P., the Parliamentary correspondent of *The New Statesman*. In an article entitled 'The Trade Union M.P.', he observed:

'From the earliest days, there have been some suspicion and lack of understanding between the middle-class and working-class sections of the Parliamentary Party. This arises only partly from differences in background and social habits. Far more important is a difference in the approach to politics. The "working-class" member has tended to be concerned with immediate objectives, with immediate if small improvements in the living standards of his fellow workers. So long as the party continued an effective instrument for achieving that he was acquiescent though not necessarily satisfied. Hence for fear that the party might be diverted from immediate needs, he suspected middle-class members who, less conscious of hardship in their own surroundings, tried to widen the party's horizons. He could be relied upon to help the leadership at any time, either by pulling such high fliers down to earth, or, failing that, blasting them off the earth altogether. This difference in approach was accentuated by an uneasiness which some trade union members felt in trying to work with men whose upbringing provided them with a fluency which sometimes sounded like glibness and an assurance which often seemed like arrogance . . .'

It is more difficult to account for the contrast between the Professions and the Miscellaneous Occupations. Education may be a factor. Nearly all the Professional Members received a university education and half of them a very protracted one—viz., the doctors and the barristers. Only one-third of the Miscellaneous Occupations had proceeded beyond the secondary level. There was a marked divergence of viewpoint between university and secondary school types, as far as ideological issues were concerned and so the relatively high proportion of secondary school Members in the Miscellaneous group and of university people in the Professions must play some role in determining attitudes. The subject studied may also have had its importance. Left-wing radicalism in the thirties made its greatest inroads in the arts and sciences; medicine and the law seem to have been resistant. Most of the Professions are doctors and lawyers.

On the other hand, the family background of Members, especially in respect to wealth, might have been a factor. For the twenties and thirties, the type of school attended offers a rough index of family income: public school, secondary grammar school, elementary school spelt affluence, a very moderate income, poverty, in that order. As the following table shows, the proportions coming in each case, from affluent ('public school') families were not widely different, but the proportion from elementary and elementary/secondary + were very divergent.

Table 1. School Background of Members of the Professional and Miscellaneous Occupation Groups

	Elementary; elementary/ secondary+		Grammar Secondary		Public school		Not known	
Miscellaneous Occupations	19	31%	21	34%	17	28%	4	7%
Professions	6	8%	37	49%	26	24%	4	9%

Perhaps the decisive factor, however, lies in the character of the work which Members of these two groupings performed. The Professions were principally lawyers (32), doctors and dentists (8) and schoolteachers (19); with three university teachers and four established adult education teachers. For lawyers, even attending the House is a part-time occupation: and all—lawyers, teachers and doctors—have an established profession into which they can slip back if at any time they quit the Commons. For them—in a word—becoming an M.P. is exchanging one profession for another. (Of course, this is less true of the schoolteachers.) Again, in their professional dealings lawyers and doctors, pre-eminently, are acting on *behalf* of other people, and must take full responsibility for them; added to which, the nature of their tasks demands great sobriety in judgement. In short, in their professional dealings, neither doctors nor lawyers 'may answer for themselves'. They are under restraints.

The Miscellaneous group pursue quite different occupations. One-third of them were in minor professions or white-collar avocations:—housewives, professional politicians, welfare workers, personnel officers, local government officers, insurance agents and the like. Two-thirds of them were journalists and publicists. Five were established professional journalists; seven were party publicists and journalists (e.g., 'former editor *New Leader*' or 'former editor of a . . . Socialist weekly journal') and fourteen pursued a variety of tasks, often simultaneously, but were all part-time journalists. Finally, another fourteen were publicists, party organizers and party research workers. 'Became a lecturer', runs the biography of one: 'has been teacher, freelance journalist, labourer and insurance official', runs another. Two were organizers for the Co-operative party. Three were research officers of the Labour party or the Co-operative party.

For the great majority of this group, politics was the great obsession, and once a seat has been obtained, the great profession. The occupations pursued were, for most, the means of preparing for the profession of politics or ways of making a living to support such a profession. Furthermore, very few of these occupations entail bearing a personal responsibility for a client, nor do they—like medicine and the law—demand controlled judgements. This group is, at once, highly politicized and highly subjectivist. It largely corresponds to Leon Epstein's characterization of the Labour 'intellectuals'. 'This category', he said, 'did include some of the university teachers (and former teachers) who were active in the post-war Labour party, but "left-wing intellectuals" were also, by definition, a more heterogeneous collection of white-collar socialists who customarily earned their living by journalism, lecturing, politicking, or any one of a large number of other journalistic activities. Although most of them were respectable participants in the life of the community they were rarely the holders of organizational responsibility either in government, business corporations, or trade unions.'

British socialism is a syndrome of attitudes, some idealistic, some materialistic. Two of the attitudes, egalitarianism and public ownership, do not figure in this analysis. Both, incidentally, have an ideological as well as a materialistic aspect. In the light of the story so far, it would not be surprising if on these issues the two chief occupational blocs, the Miscellaneous Occupations and the Trades Union cum Worker bloc, joined hands.

Leaving aside egalitarianism and public control, however, on which we have no information, it is possible to discern the balance of forces in the party.

On the knife and fork questions, the impulsions came from the Trades Unionists, the Workers, the elementary and elementary/secondary+ groups. If all these are conflated together, they total 120 members—one-half of the backbenchers. But this represents the outside limit of this bloc. Its hard core consists of only those who were, simultaneously, Workers and Trades Unionists with elementary or elementary/secondary+ education. This hard core amounts to 55 Members.

On the ideological side, this bloc of 55 Members represented the right-wing force in the party. It opposed and was opposed by the Miscellaneous Occupations, the Co-operators and to some extent the secondary school group and Members who had proceeded from secondary school to provincial universities. The size of this group, when all are conflated, is 85 Members. Here the attitude of the Professions has proved decisive: sometimes siding with the working-class bloc (as with unilateralism), sometimes against it (as with anti-colonialism).

Thus the various parts of the party key into one another. Miscellaneous Occupations, Co-operators, and the secondary schools form the ideological vanguard: the Trades Unionist cum working-class cum elementary school Members hold them back. The latter bloc form the materialistic vanguard: the Miscellaneous Occupations, the Professions and the university graduates constitute the inertia.

Now, in the usual way, one would expect the two extremes to cancel. But these forces are part of a parliamentary party, whose effectiveness, in opposition no less than in power, depends exclusively upon its solidarity. The extremes, in such a case, do not cancel out: they add up. Following its Trades Unionist and elementary schooled colleagues, the whole party presses for improved material standards for the workers. Following the lead of its ideologically inclined Miscellaneous Occupations, its Co-operative group, its secondary, and secondary-cum-provincial university Members, the whole party plunges towards pacificism, humanitarianism and anti-colonialism.

And all of this takes place in the context of Members' age and year of election. The younger Members and the more recent Members are at one with their elders and seniors on the welfare services. They are ahead of them on the ideological issues of pacificism, humanitarianism and anti-colonialism. Irrespective of the occupational or educational balance or the balance of sponsored membership, as old Members drop out and seniors decline to stand again, so the ideological tone will move leftwards. The failure of the Labour party to win the 1959 election only checked the replacement of the old and the senior by the young and newly elected; it happened more slowly than in the conquering party—but, to an extent, it did occur.

Furthermore, as it occurs, so will changes in the educational system influence the party. The occupational balance is at large—nobody can predict what will happen here. The balance of sponsorship looks as though it will remain steady for some time to come since both Co-operators and Trades Unions are loath to retreat from their present proportion of Members. But the educational balance is bound to change. The elementary school and the elementary/secondary+ types belong to a past age. They will be increasingly replaced by secondary school, and university Members: and this will reinforce the ideological drive to the left.

The National Decision-Makers 3
T. Lupton and C. S. Wilson

Reprinted with permission from 'The Social Background and Connection of "Top Decision Makers"', *Manchester School of Economic and Social Studies*, Vol. XXVII: 1, 1959.

Our interests as sociologists have led us to make use of the Parker Tribunal evidence as a convenient starting point for the analysis of some social connections between persons prominent in banking, insurance, politics, and public administration. Our choice of persons and categories was influenced by our starting point, and our enquiries were limited by considerations of time and space, and by gaps in the published sources of data. For these reasons our results are not statistically significant. But they will be of interest to sociologists, as representing the beginnings of an analysis of the social origins and interconnections of what we shall call the 'top decision makers' in British society. To us, as sociologists, and as members of a Department of Social Anthropology, it was a natural first step to enquire whether the persons whose names appeared in the Tribunal evidence were linked to each other by relationships of friendship, kinship, affinity, common membership of associations, and so on. And the descriptions of behaviour given by witnesses in evidence revealed that some persons were so related. Reference to published sources revealed many more such relationships.

In attempting to interpret the behaviour they observe, sociologists look first at these 'networks' of relationships, and at the kind of training people receive to occupy positions within them. It seemed to us likely that there would be a 'structural' explanation for some of the behaviour described by witnesses at the Tribunal. This article is an attempt to map out some parts of the social structure of 'top decision makers'.

The evidence of Lord Kindersley and others revealed that some important decisions were taken and others accepted because colleagues knew about, and relied upon each other's beliefs and special aptitudes. Lengthy analyses were not a necessary prelude to decision making. This is not surprising. When decisions have to be made quickly most persons have to act according to precedent and 'hunch' and not in the light of detailed analysis of the current situation. The consequences of this process for economic decisions such as those which were described by Tribunal witnesses are the concern of the economist. As sociologists we were particularly interested *inter alia* in the influence of custom and precedent in defining roles and activities in the decision-making process. That influences of this kind were at work was indicated by persons appearing before the Tribunal.

In addition to the influence of custom and precedent in decision making, informality in relationships between decision makers came out clearly in the evidence. A good example of this came out during the examination of Lord Kindersley by the Attorney General. The Attorney General was asking Lord Kindersley why he, and not Mr. Cobbold, had gone to see Lord Bicester about the possible effect of the Bank Rate rise on the Vickers issue and on relations between the 'city' and the Bank of England. Lord Kindersley replied:

'I consider it perfectly natural that I should be allowed to go and talk to a colleague on the Bank of England . . . I do not think that Lord Bicester would find it in the least surprising that I should come to him and say to him: "Look here, Rufie, is it too late to stop this business or not?"';
    and:
'I have discussed this with Jim—with the Governor and I am coming to see you.'

The same kind of informality was seen in the activities of directors of some City merchant houses as described before the Tribunal.

The basis of informality in social relationships is often a shared social background, which promotes shared beliefs and confidence in customary procedures. It was this evidence of informality and custom which led us to look for common social background, and links between persons other than those arising from the formal needs of business life. There were pointers in the evidence itself and elsewhere that we might find connections of kinship and of affinity. Ties of friendship and common interest were revealed by the description of a shooting party at which members of the Keswick family were joined by Mr. Nigel Birch and others; and by the meetings of Messrs. J. M. Stevens and D. McLachlan.

Since it was clear that many of the "top decision makers" whom the evidence mentioned were interlinked in sets of relationships other than those directly arising out of business arrangements, we wondered whether the same kind of affiliations would be found in a wider sample of such persons, i.e., whether such affiliations tended to be typical of the social milieu of this particular set of 'top decision makers'. Our choice of a wider sample was influenced by our starting point, and the reader will find that it is biased. But we have included enough persons to make our findings of some sociological, if not statistical, significance. . . .

Our study must be regarded, then, mainly as a contribution to the 'ethnography' of finance, politics, and administration. But we cannot conclude without attempting briefly to relate what we have said to one aspect of social structure which is of particular interest to us.

We have referred to the tradition of intermarriage between banking families. Also by tradition, some merchant bankers become directors of the Bank of England. It is not surprising then that kinship diagrams show connections between directors of merchant banks, and between merchant banks and directors of the Bank of England. Nor is it surprising that we find that positions in certain firms are occupied by adjacent generations of the same family. The positions of chairman of Lazard Bros. and director of the Bank of England, for example, are now occupied by Lord Kindersley and were once occupied by his father.

What might seem surprising is that kinship connections of this kind have persisted through many changes in the scale and functions of banking, in the organization of industry, and in the complexity of politics. Bagehot, referring to the family basis of private banking at the end of last century, argued that it was inappropriate for modern large scale organization. Weber has also argued that bureaucratic 'civil-service-type' structures, in which recruitment and promotion are based on specific technical qualifications, and in which authority rests in the office and not in the person, is the most appropriate to modern conditions, while traditional structures are unsuitable from the point of view of effectiveness. But Weber also argues that, for effectiveness' sake, decision making and execution ought to be separate. And he notes that: '. . . administrative structures based on different principles intersect with bureaucratic organization.'

Some of the organizations to which we have referred seem to have the separation of decision making and executive functions to which Weber refers. Possibly they incorporate both traditionalistic and bureaucratic structure. They have both directors and the managers, generally different sets of persons, possibly of different social background and training. While there have been studies of the influence of kinship as a mode of succession amongst managers, we are not aware of any study which has extended to boards of directors.

Weber's point about the intersection of different structural principles has not been followed up by empirical research in the area covered in this article. Gouldner's examination of some hypotheses derived from Weber in the light of facts about factory social structure could be taken as a model for such work.

The intersection of different social principles has another, individual aspect, that of role conflict. Our evidence shows that many people occupy several social roles. For example, a person may have one role in a kinship system, be a member of one or more boards of directors, and a member of various clubs and associations.

The evidence at the Parker Tribunal referred in many places to this problem, but especially as it related to the dual roles of director of a merchant bank and of the Bank of England, which were occupied by Lord Kindersley and Mr. W. J. Keswick. Commenting generally on this kind of problem, Mr. Cobbold addressed the Parker Tribunal as follows:

'It seems to me that a similar position often arises both in business matters and, more generally, in other walks of life, where an honest man must often divorce one set of interests from another . . . The position arises almost every day in banking, where a banker is not expected to use, for his bank's profit, secret information about a customer's affairs';

and:

'. . . the existence of the problem (even if it arises infrequently) must pose the question whether the present arrangement is on balance best suited to the national interest. I am most strongly of the opinion that it is.'

Mr. Cobbold seemed aware that there were disadvantages in a situation where individuals were faced, as a consequence of discrepancy between structural principles, with conflicts of loyalty or allegiance. But he was personally convinced that these were outweighed by the advantages. This raises a general problem of comparative social structure. The field we have ourselves surveyed provides extensive data relevant to this problem. These data suggest that 'top decision makers' as well as being linked by kinship, business interests and similar background, are also divided by competing, even conflicting interests. Indeed kinship itself, in certain circumstances, may act as a divisive as well as a uniting force.

To carry out the research into the problems we have briefly outlined would require investigation of a wider field than we have surveyed, and the use of techniques other than those we have used. Interviews, direct observations of behaviour, complete quantitative analysis of such items as leisure time activities, as well as the construction of complete kinship diagrams would be necessary. This latter technique would close many gaps in knowledge of British social structure. Sociologists, including ourselves, have tended to concentrate on the study of working-class groups or small local communities where there is much knowledge of the operation of kinship in social life. For our 'top decision makers' we have only biographical material, inspired comment, and little more. It is possible that sociologists have avoided the problem of kinship in 'higher circles' because of the formidable problems presented for empirical field research. We can see that there may be many problems of this kind but there is no reason why the published sources of data should not be fully used.

Local Political Systems
F. Bealey, J. Blondel and W. P. McCann

Reprinted with permission from F. Bealey, J. Blondel, and W. P. McCann: *Constituency Politics. A study of Newcastle under Lyme*, London, Faber and Faber, 1965, pp. 390–400.

Decisions made by the active party workers do not make a regular or heavy impact on the man in the street. Only at election times do the militants come into contact with the voters. Moreover, the sort of choice in which the most powerful of the party workers are likely to exert an influence on the eventual decision is seldom more important than 'Shall we fight this ward or that?' or 'Shall we canvass tonight or tomorrow night?' Occasionally it is true, Parliamentary candidates have to be selected, but the Conservative and Liberal militants have not, since 1918, chosen one who has subsequently been returned to Westminster. Nor are the

Labour Party's militants always in command of their own household, as the events of 1951 demonstrated. Then the most active party workers were unable to get their favourite chosen as Labour candidate because the trade-union delegates, usually absent from party meetings, turned up in order to obtain the nomination of a different aspirant.

Thus there are few rewards for party workers and control passes into the hands of those members who have the enthusiasm to bear the brunt of the work. These few are the nucleus of the party leadership: they hold the power (such as it is) for it is difficult for the members who attend irregularly or not at all to have much say in the direction of the party organizations. As in all voluntary bodies the dedicated few call the tune.

How small the minority can be that runs the parties is shown in Table I which analyses the attendance at the Executives of the Constituency and Borough Labour Parties

Table 1. Attendance at Executives of the Constituency and Borough Labour Parties and at the Liberal Party Executive

		Constituency Labour Party		Borough Labour Party		Liberal Party	
Percentage of attendance		1949–51	1960–62	1948–50	1960–62	1956–58	1960–62
'Stalwarts'	80–100%	1	3	—	1	3	4
	50–79%	6	2	6	3	4	6
	25–49%	14	7	9	6	9	8
Less than 25%*		26	12	11	15	36	41

* Does not include those who attended no meetings.

and of the Liberal Association. In the case of the Labour Party we were able to compare the pattern of attendance at executive meetings for two periods of three years—the era of great Labour activity in the late 1940's and the last three years. With the Liberals we were not able to take the same early period, but 1956–8 was before the Liberal 'revival' and the comparison with the present thus shows, in contrast with the Labour Party, an increase in the number of members attending half or more of the meetings. These last we shall describe as 'stalwarts'.

Few 'stalwarts' participate in both the Constituency and Borough Labour Parties. Only one person, and he in the later period, has been simultaneously a 'stalwart' in both. It is also noteworthy that there is only one person who is in both periods, and he has moved from the Borough to the Constituency Party. Most apparent is the difference between the 'stalwarts' in the days of buoyancy and in the present. Today five out of the eight Labour 'stalwarts' are non-manual workers or their wives as against only three out of thirteen in the late 1940's. But the overall impression is of Labour Party leadership springing from a variety of backgrounds with a sprinkling of railwaymen and rather more than a sprinkling of Co-operators, the result of the strength of 'the Co-op' in the area and its willingness to allow its employees time to serve.

The type of analysis we are able to make with the Labour and Liberal Parties is not possible with the Conservative Party. In the absence of data about attendance of Executive Council meetings for the purpose of comparison we were forced to make the assumption that the direction of the Conservative Association was vested in the ten people on all the three important committees. We are only able to present this group of interlocking committee men for the present day. Such information as we have, however, suggests that though people of similar social background ran the Conservative Party ten or twelve years ago, very few of them have survived and the bulk of these ten cited below have come comparatively recently to constituency politics.

Some features of this list are not dissimilar from those discovered in the cases of the other two parties. For example, there is a preponderance—eight out of ten—of officers of the party. There is also some connection with Borough and Rural District politics, though any direct participation is in the past. At the present moment none of the ten are council members in spite of the fact that eight of them are members of the Local Elections Committee. Finally, in one way this hierarchy is reminiscent of the Labour Party's. Only two of the ten are women, in spite of the fact that the latter provide twenty-seven of the fifty-nine members of the Executive Council.

The social standing of the Conservative Association's leadership is from 'higher' social groups than that of the other parties. Though there is perhaps not quite the wealth of professional training there is in the Liberal Party, there is a good deal more commercial and industrial substance, and among the six from the countryside three are J.P.s. There is a notable and expected absence of manual workers while possibly the nearest thing to a clerical worker among them is a bank manager!

The four men among these ten who are residents of the Borough are younger than the others and of less social standing. Though they may play their part in the affairs of the constituency Association, they have no influence in the decision-making processes of Newcastle Borough. In fact, because the Conservative council members are so little involved with the Association's affairs, the Association has little or no impact as a corporate body in Borough politics. For the very opposite reason the Liberal Party has behaved much more vigorously in the municipal field. It remains to be seen whether a large contingent of Conservatives on the Borough Council would provide any leaders for the Conservative Association.

Many of the important decisions affecting Newcastle's citizens that are not made in Stafford or Whitehall are not made in the party Executives either: they are reached by the two local government authorities. It is their decisions that, as we have seen, can make thousands of people angry.

Observation and discussion with many council members of all parties make it clear that there are four members of the Labour majority who hold most sway over the activities of the Borough Council. Three of these are Committee chairmen. One of them is a 'Co-op' manager. Another is a schoolteacher who has been on the Council since 1945. He was chairman of the Education Committee for eight years and has been chairman of the Finance Committee for six out of the last seven years. The third, a bank official, who has been on the Council since 1951, was treasurer of the Borough Labour Party for four years and, except for the few months of Independent control in 1958, has been chairman of the Housing Committee since 1957. His predecessor in this position had held it for ten years and during that time had become the acknowledged leader of the Labour Party in the Borough. In a Borough rightly proud of its extensive housing programme, the chairman of the Housing Committee has become the Council's main 'trouble-shooter'. We have already seen how the present chairman has dealt with the anger of both council tenants and ratepayers and made himself pre-eminently conspicuous in the process. The fourth of these 'men of power' is the only one who is not a chairman of a committee; but as secretary of both the Constituency and Borough Labour Parties he naturally has considerable influence in the Labour Group, especially over the more recently elected councillors with whom he will have become acquainted in the nominating process.

Except for the last-named, the four most important members of the Labour Group are not among the 'stalwarts' in the Borough or Constituency Parties. In fact the demands that council chairmanships make on a man's time are such that tenure of them is hardly compatible with organization work in the wards. Thus three out of the four most important figures in the Labour Group are not closely in touch with the 'doorstep' workers and two of these, being aldermen, do not have to present themselves trienially to the voters. Furthermore, none of the four are manual workers, the class that makes up the majority of Labour councillors, Labour Party members and Labour voters. They are all, in fact, men who through their occupations have acquired skills such as commercial management, financial expertise, public speaking and dialectical disputation that stand one in good stead in local council work.

Finally it should be noted that political leadership does not often coincide with the leadership of other associations. None of the Conservative 'stalwarts' serve on the committees of other Newcastle organizations, though one of the Liberal 'stalwarts' is a member of the Workers' Educational Association Committee. Two of the Labour 'stalwarts' are members of both the Silverdale Co-operative committees and one of these two is also treasurer of the Newcastle Trades Council. One of the Labour Group's quadrumvirates is the president of this latter body while another of these four is both a committee member of a workingmen's club and president of an old age pensioners' association. The Labour leadership has thus rather more contact with Newcastle's associational life. Even so, eight of the Labour 'stalwarts' and two of the Labour Group's four 'men of power' have no such connections.

It thus becomes apparent that leadership in Newcastle is widely diffused. There is most connection between social and economic leadership, that is, between the highest social status and business ownership or management. Even in this case, however, there were only eight out of 143 social leaders who were also economic leaders. On the other hand there is no connection between economic and political leadership. The withdrawal from local politics of the large-scale employers began, as we have seen, before the First World War and those Conservative 'stalwarts' who are employers are resident in Newcastle constituency but in business elsewhere. Doubtless there is embarrassment in carrying on a business in a Labour-dominated constituency while being a Conservative leader there.

Between social and political leadership the connection is slight and entirely on the side of the Conservatives and Liberals. The three Conservatives and the one Liberal who are social leaders are not so by virtue of being Rotarians or members of the Round Table but by virtue of being J.P.s; and, as we have noted, there is a sense in which the appointment of magistrates is a 'political' act. Moreover, all four of the magisterial 'stalwarts' live in the countryside: none of them are resident in the Borough. Consequently there is no coincidence of social and political leadership in the Borough. None of the Labour 'stalwarts' and none of the Labour quadrumvirate on the Labour Group are social and economic leaders; but neither are any of the Conservative or Liberal 'stalwarts' who live in Newcastle Borough. Political control in Newcastle Borough is independent of high status and economic hegemony.

Leadership by the leaders of the Labour Party has not brought about, however, rule by manual workers. Only two out of the eight Labour 'stalwarts' and none of Labour's municipal leaders work with their hands. Thus after the early post-war years of Labour domination, leadership of the Borough Council again became vested in the middle classes. But with a difference; shopkeepers and small businessmen are no longer supreme, and in command one finds members of the professional, managerial and clerical classes.

Power in Organizations
R. Presthus

Reprinted with permission from R. Presthus: *Behavioural Research on British Executives*, University of Alabama Press, 1965, pp. 105–7, 111–12, 133-4.

The ability to handle authority gracefully is assumed to be critical in organizations because they are essentially, as C. Wright Mills has said, 'systems of hierarchical roles graded by authority'. Perhaps the major currency in the bureaucratic interpersonal market, authority may rest upon skill, seniority, status, or empathy, or some combination of these. Any given actor must interact daily with subordinates, superiors, and equals; the behavioural dynamics of each situation differ. This demands a certain versatility, not only in a superficial 'professional mask' context, but in a deeper sense which engages personality, that is, one's learned ways of handling interpersonal situations.

Individuals who can play a graceful and controlled authority role only by violating their basic personal needs must, it follows, experience considerable tension in such roles. Indeed, I do not believe that any executive can long play such a role if it is contrary to his personality structure. He will gradually adopt stereotyped authority relations that are natural to him. This accommodation may be conscious, or it may be subconscious, in the sense that he is obliged to adopt it even though it complicates his authority relations.

A further hypothesis is that the bases of such accommodations are mainly acquired in childhood.

An opportunity occurred for me to test some of the propositions, using a sample of British executives in two large corporations, British European Airways (BEA) and British Industrials, Ltd. (BIL).

Broadly speaking, it was more difficult to gain access and carry out the research than expected on the basis of similar experience in the United States. For example, even though I approached eight major corporations, and had fairly good sponsorship, I gained access into only two firms. Partly, no doubt, this was because my research was of an attitudinal kind which could not promise any useful results in exchange for the time required on the corporation's part. Yet my own conclusion is that the main problem was one of opposition to the principle of such research, which runs against dominant British themes of amateurism, humanism, and resistance to the values associated with American industrial research and management practices. Another factor was the understandable reluctance of the executives to reveal to an outsider their private views and group affiliations. (I am quite sure that this reluctance is also related to conditions of life on a very crowded island where privacy can only be insured by systematic and symbolic effort, which includes building walls around every yard, a great deal of reserve in interpersonal relations, the emphasis upon private clubs, schools, and the like. It may be that these behaviours are inspired less by social class considerations, as often assumed, than by the simple effort to retain privacy.) Indeed, I am convinced that I was able to secure data on religion, income, and political affiliations only because the executives concluded that, being a foreigner, I just didn't understand that one doesn't ask such questions, and that perhaps it would do no great harm to humour me.

Table 1. Organizational Mobility and Authoritarianism*

| | Mobility | | |
	High (138)	Medium (109)	Low (161)
Authoritarianism: High	57%	54%	44%

* Authoritarianism is measured by a scale comprising the following items: 'People should be more careful with their money and save it instead of spending it all'; 'No decent man can respect a woman who had had sex relations before marriage'; 'We should fight an all-out war to stop world communism before it gets any stronger than it is.'

Although the differences are not always statistically significant, the data generally support the hypothesis. Executives who have experienced the greatest organizational mobility also rank highest on authoritarianism (fifty-seven per cent). There is, moreover, a significant difference between them and the least successful executives ranking high on authoritarianism (forty-four per cent). This positive relation suggests that some of the values typically associated with authoritarianism are indeed functional in large-scale organizations. The finding, in effect, supports one of the main theoretical propositions of *The Organizational Society*, which held that the upward-mobile types who found the bureaucratic situation congenial would be likely to possess certain authoritarian values including conventionality, aggressiveness, respect for power and authority, personal disciplines, and so on. The relationship is impressive when one considers that highly successful executives are disproportionately recruited from upper-class and upper middle class groups, members of which have usually been found to rank low on authoritarianism compared with those from other class strata.

Attitudes toward authority were next analyzed along the dimension of organizational expectations, using the following indicators: 'I believe it is proper for my organization to be concerned with, (1) whether or not I use its products, (2) my own attitude toward sexual morality, (3) the tidiness of my office, (4) the number of drinks (if any) I have at lunch.' The rationale here is that responses will indicate the extent to which an executive legitimates the authority of the organization in a highly generalized context. Thus a high level of acceptance can be regarded as a valid indicator of a generally positive attitude toward organizational authority.

A difficulty here, pointed out by some respondents, is that such items are not always perceived in an authority context, but instead they may be viewed as expressions of a perfectly normal loyalty to an organization in which one has chosen to spend a good deal of his life. British conceptions of work and the work-place do indeed stress loyalty and long service to a greater extent than in the United States. The philosophy is similar to that reported of Japan, where the employer apparently assumes a protective, familial relationship with his employees rather than the strictly contractual nexus often found in our society. On the other hand, it does seem that loyalty to the organization is very much like our conception of authority as a positive acceptance of the organization's policies.

Given the British executive's apparent lack of familiarity with current organization-man themes in the United States, it is interesting to compare their responses on four of these items with an American sample. Table 2 gives the distributions.

Along a scale ranging from plus one-hundred to minus one-hundred, the relative scale position of each item is similar in both groups. In effect, their zone of indifference on these discrete manifestations of organizational authority is similar. In each case, however, the British executives are far less willing

Table 2. Comparative executive attitudes on selected authority variables

	American (391)	British (409)
'I believe it is proper for my organization to be concerned with the tidiness of my office'	88	53
'I believe it is proper for my organization to be concerned with how many drinks (if any) I have at lunch'	77	28
'I believe it is proper for my organization to be concerned about whether or not I use its products.'	21	1·5
'I believe it is proper for my organization to be concerned with my own attitude toward sexual morality'	15	−68

to grant the organization's right to influence their behaviour. One of the strongest relationships found in this preliminary analysis is between organizational mobility and political conservatism. The stability, consistency, and respect for established authority that characterize political conservatives are apparently well-suited to the bureaucratic situation. Organizations of most kinds, including universities, one suspects, prefer steady men who will fit into the ongoing web of custom, power, and authority. Most organizations moreover, spend most of their time carrying out rather stereotyped activities, which seldom require, and indeed are inapposite to, individuals who retain some spontaneity and the belief that change is the law of life. Organizations, in effect, require Stalins rather than Lenins, for their role is usually to make good some past revolution. It is not surprising, therefore, to find a strong positive association between conservatism and bureaucratic success. Of those who are high on organizational mobility, thirty-seven per cent are high on conservatism, a level which declines significantly as one moves across the lower levels of mobility.

Although not shown here, a noteworthy difference between the two samples exists at the very highest level of mobility where the proportion of British Industrials' executives ranking high on conservatism was fully one-third larger than in BEA.

Since BEA is a government-owned corporation, while BIL is private, this difference is probably not surprising.

Regarding the comparative findings, British managers seem significantly more liberal politically than the American group, but they are more alienated concerning the meaningfulness of human existence and the kinds of behaviour required to get ahead. They are much less alienated, however, in their assumed ability to influence political affairs and in their opinion that government is effective in solving vital national and international problems. Finally, as a group, the British managers are much less inclined to accept the organization's influence in peripheral areas of work such as the use of the company's products and their off-the-job behaviour.

Voters and Their Characteristics
M. Hill

Reprinted with permission from 'The English Voter', *New Society*, 17 September, 1964 and 24 September, 1964.

In the history of voting studies it was the development of the sample survey which started the ball rolling in Britain, because as long as the sample was representative enough, generalizations could be made with a reasonable degree of confidence about voting behaviour in the total population. At first there were strong criticisms of the sample method, but these have grown less as the findings of surveys have consistently if by no means invariably coincided. A glance at the dozen or so election studies in England shows that they do in fact agree on certain broad fundamentals, and not always mere commonsense projections. The purpose of this article is to draw together the common findings, qualifications and particular findings of several studies in order to gain some idea of the way in which 'the English voter' behaves.

Objective Social Class

At first this seems to be a matter of commonsense and if you were to ask the first person you met in the street (assuming for the moment that you don't live at Clapham or travel by bus) he would probably say that the middle class votes Conservative and the working class Labour. As a broad majority generalization this would not be far from the truth. But if, as Bonham calculates, the middle class vote totals 30.4 per cent and the manual wage vote 64.6 per cent, there is then the tricky problem of explaining how the Conservative party ever manages to get into power. What all the election studies have found is that as they go down the social scale they reveal more Labour voters and fewer Conservative voters, but regardless of which criteria for social class assessment they use they have always found a sizable proportion of Conservative voters among the working class electors: one third of the working class votes Conservative and this makes up half the total Conservative vote.

On the Hall-Jones scale, the 1950 Greenwich study by Benney, Gray, and Pear found the following political allegiances:

Social Class % voting	1,2,3	4	5	6,7
Conservative	66	80	28	17
Labour	23	16	66	80
Liberal	11	4	6	3
number	52	57	263	237

Here the general trend is clearly observable, but with one notable difference which is found in some studies but not all. This is the comparatively high percentage of Conservative voters in group 4 (even higher than the proportion in the first three groups in this case), which by the Hall-Jones scale is translatable as lower middle class white collar workers. On the one side it is possible to argue that this high proportion is merely the result of a biased sample; but it is equally plausible that this white collar group, being that most threatened economically by the working class, sets a higher premium on maintaining life style and status and is therefore more likely to vote Conservative as a means of differentiation from the working class.

Alford, in a comparative study on the effects of class voting in Britain, U.S.A., Canada and Australia holds variables other than class constant and comes to the conclusion that class has a more significant effect on voting in Britain than in any of the other countries.

Subjective Social Class

This provides very similar results, but all the studies find that people who call themselves 'middle class' are more likely to vote Conservative than those who call themselves 'working class'. Of course, in many of the cases there will be agreement between the objective and subjective ratings, but Young and Willmott have shown that, particularly among manual workers, there is a tendency to rate occupations in a somewhat different hierarchy. Admittedly there may be some mistaken self-ratings due entirely to ignorance of normal class definitions (e.g. the shopkeeper who calls himself 'working class' simply because he works) and the way the question is framed is vitally important: American studies, for instance, have found that when they ask a person to choose between 'middle class' and 'lower class' there is a much higher tendency for people to call themselves 'middle class' than when the term 'working class' is used. Milne and Mackenzie show the subjective class allegiances (in Bristol NE) as follows:

Self-Class	Upper Middle–Middle	Lower Middle	Working
Conservative	66·6	59·6	36·1
Labour	25·0	24·7	56·5
Liberal	8·4	15·7	7·4
number	108	89	271

This shows pretty much the same picture as objective class allegiances, with the lower middle class stepping into prominence once again. But if we can apply objective and subjective measures at the same time a much clearer picture emerges, and this is what was done in the Greenwich study. There they found that in four out of five cases the objective and subjective class ratings coincided, but the interesting case was the fifth.

Benney, Gray and Pear's figures are:

Actual Status	Average+		Average−	
Self-class % voting	'middle'	'working'	'middle'	'working'
Conservative	75	38	60	17
Labour	14	52	32	80
Liberal	11	50	8	3

From this, they conclude that subjective class seems to be more related to party choice than objective class. This in turn suggests that the way in which a person thinks of his place in the class structure has a stronger influence on the way he votes than economic interests bound up with his objective position. They propose a two way casual relationship: voting Conservative may be the cause as well as the effect of thinking oneself middle class.

Sex

In all the voting studies quoted above women consistently, in all classes and age groups, vote more conservatively than men. It is even possible on opinion poll statistics to argue that if women had been denied the vote in 1945 we should have had a Labour government in continual office since then! Two studies show the effects of sex on voting with the subdivisions of social class and age. First from the Greenwich survey (the 'average +' etc. ratings were made by trained interviewers while conducting interviews, and are based on several criteria):

Sex, Class and the Vote

Class Sex % voting	Average+		Average−	
	male	female	male	female
Conservative	61	68	21	30
Labour	28	19	75	66
Liberal	11	13	4	4

It is clear that sex outweighs even class as a voting factor. In the Bristol study, with the exception of the 50+ female voters voting Labour in excess of the male voters, the same trend is observable. Milne and Mackenzie's figures are:

Sex, Age and the Vote

Age Sex % voting	21–49 male	female	50+ male	female
Conservative	43·8	47·1	50·5	53·3
Labour	49·7	44·3	35·8	38·0
Liberal	6·5	8·6	13·7	8·7
number	153	140	95	92

In all voting studies done, age seems to have a conservatizing effect. There are tables to show this in all the books, but it is only with Benney, Gray and Pear that the reason for this emerges. They break down the age groups further by socio-economic status, with the following result:

Age, Class and the Vote

Class Age % voting	Average+ 21–49	50+	Average− 21–49	50+
Conservative	63	67	18	42
Labour	24	23	79	53
Liberal	13	10	3	5
number	93	49	359	186

The cause of the 'age effect' is obvious: it occurs almost entirely in the lower socio-economic groups. Various reasons can be tendered for this—the Labour party was still a relatively new force when the men who were 50 or more in 1950 were growing up, and anyway youth is popularly associated with radicalism—but it does seem that the working class swops the red flag for the blue carpet slippers.

It will be seen when we deal with 'changers' that very few people change in the period when propaganda is at its height, i.e. in the actual election campaign, and that those who do change are more likely to be influenced by other factors than party propaganda. From all the voting studies it seems that party meetings are fairly ineffectual as a means of spreading political propaganda, although this varies with the type of meeting, factory gate meetings and celebrity meetings being the best attended (presumably the factory gate meetings are not conducted when workers are on their way home).

The party image is often called the irrational element in voting behaviour, because people do not always look at a party in terms of a rational appraisal of various social, economic and international issues. Studies show that people do not even select the 'most important issues' in an election; by far the most important factor selected is the party image, which is in effect a mental set or impression of 'what a party stands for' gathered from impressions, propaganda and discussion. This factor is probably partly responsible for the tremendous stability in voting behaviour, because it has been found that images are extremely resistant to change; thus, even when the accepted image of a party is untrue (for instance, the image of the Conservative party as a party 'only for the rich') the image remains. This timelag enables a party to 'trade' on old issues while developing new ones; abrupt changes are suspect, so images allow change over time with the minimum of disturbance. The fact that politicians see the importance of images for their support can perhaps be illustrated by Morrison's wooing of the middle class in the postwar Labour government. The following examples from the 1955 Bristol survey bring out another feature:

Party Images

Images of the Labour Party % identifying with:	by Lab*	by Cons
for working class	68	32
for Welfare State	18	12
for the whole country	5	4
for full employment	4	2
for nationalization, controls	4	32
impractical extravagant	1	18

Images of the Conservative Party % *identifying with:*	*by Lab**	*by Cons*
for all classes	6	30
for free enterprise; business	7	26
for the rich, big business	85	8
for individual freedom	—	14
for denationalization	1	5
for full employment	—	9
capable, experienced leaders	1	8

* by Lab = by Labour supporters; by Cons = by Conservative supporters.

These tables suggest that Labour supporters are more likely to rely on a very few commonly held images than the Conservatives. This may be an indication of class solidarity; certainly, some studies suggest that party images are more important to the working class than to the middle class.

Further Reading: Power

V. L. ALLEN: *Power in Trade Unions*, London, Longmans, 1954.

W. L. GUTTSMAN: *The British Political Elite*, London, MacGibbon and Kee, 1963.

* D. LOCKWOOD, J. H. GOLDTHORPE, F. BECHOFER AND J. PLATT: *The Affluent Manual Worker, 2, Political Attitudes and Behaviour*, Cambridge, Cambridge University Press, 1968.

* R. T. MACKENZIE: *British Political Parties*, London, Heinemann, 1964.

*† W. J. M. MACKENZIE: *Politics and Social Science*, London, Penguin Books, 1967.

R. MILIBAND: *The State in Capitalist Society*, London, Weidenfeld and Nicholson, 1969.

* C. W. MILLS: *The Power Elite*, New York, Oxford University Press, 1959.

A. A. ROGOW AND P. SHORE: *The Labour Government and British Industry*, Oxford, Blackwell, 1955.

* R. PRESTHUS: *The Organizational Society*, New York, Random House, 1962.

R. ROSE (ED.): *Studies in British Politics*, London, Macmillan, 1966.

* W. H. WHYTE: *The Organization Man*, London, Penguin Books, 1961.

* Available in paperback
† Reference

Chapter Seven Values

Cultural values are part of the social structure. Like many of the terms used so far there is little consensus about the concept of values. It is most usefully seen as a standard against which things are compared and held to be, for example, desirable or undesirable, appropriate or inappropriate. Actions, individuals, groups, goals, ideas, beliefs and feelings may be evaluated in this way. Values provide the basis of emotional commitment. Culture is in part concerned with our ideas of the world around us and its properties and also with moral ideas involving judgments. It is more than this. Man becomes human as a member of society but the kind of human being depends largely on the culture. Our learning is always selective. It depends on group influences: our age, sex, where we live, social class, whether we are a member of an ethnic or religious minority, and many others. Within every culture there are subcultures distinguishable by such factors as language, clothing, occupation, gesture and behaviour.

Values extend to systems of belief of various kinds, including science and religion, but for the purposes of this chapter we shall be particularly concerned with values, current assumptions and versions of reality, which underwrite some of our social institutions. At any time there are sets of received ideas which continue to be influential long after the situations which caused them to gain acceptance have changed. In many respects we may remain prisoners of these systems of belief: two extreme examples might be those who believe that the earth is flat even now against all the evidence, and those who believe in the literal interpretation of the Bible and the acceptance of its chronology about, for instance, the creation.

There is in the interpretation of all social life, as Galbraith has pointed out in *The Affluent Society*, 'a persistent and never-ending competition between what is relevant and what is acceptable'. He suggests three reasons for the prevalence of the 'conventional wisdom': people associate truth with convenience; we find most acceptable what contributes to self-esteem; and people approve most of what they best understand. So we may explain the desire of some members of the middle classes to see strikes purely in terms of the irresponsibility of workers, or for people to explain the decline of Britain in terms, say, of the entry of outsiders (migrants from the Tropical Commonwealth). These simple explanations have the consequence often of removing responsibility for the state of affairs onto other groups. Sometimes they may reflect inflexible prejudgments or information which is not objective.

Our 'British culture' may be seen in relation to the norms of all sections or, as often in the image of our society abroad, in relation to the norms of the dominant group, with an emphasis on a 'public school ideal', team-spirit, playing the game, physical fitness, which has a direct relevance for only a small minority. (Norms are of two kinds: those which specify positive obligations (such as those between parent and child, worker and employer) and those which are permissive: they form a continuum, from what *must* be done, *may* or *may not* be done, to what *should* or *should not* be done).

Some of these themes appear in the Readings. There are many others for which there is not space which can be studied best by taking statements from those who believe such things and subjecting them to analysis. Three kinds of values are considered in what follows. First there are those beliefs on which our society is said to depend (social justice, or certain principles of social selection). Secondly there are the ideas about the structure of society, social processes and the place of the society in the world. Finally, there are the received ideas and the varied forms of the conventional wisdoms.

It has often been suggested that the family is declining and that the quality of the people of Britain, variously defined, is not what it used to be. McGregor examines some of these ideas in relation to the institution of marriage and contrasts what he calls 'theological

expectations' which demand in his view disintegrating
homes with what he sees as the reality of a remarkably
stable institution.

There are more recent statements about the balanced
community than the one by Orlans, which is the next
Reading, but he highlights in particular some of the
assumptions which have governed the provision of housing
in the kinds of settings in which many people now live.
The kinds of housing provided at Stevenage, and on large
numbers of the estates built by private building and local
authorities after 1919, reflect in their arrangements and
gardens, however inadequately executed the ambition of
Ebenezer Howard to put the best of town and country
together: 'Human society and the beauty of nature are meant
to be enjoyed together . . . The town is the symbol of society
. . . The country is the symbol of God's love and care for
man.' From their concern to provide for the town dweller
some of the benefits of the country stem many of the
planning conventions (about, for example, density of
housing) which have been adhered to for most of the past
fifty years. Orlans also raises points about leadership in the
community.

There follow three Readings on different aspects of the
educational system. In the first we have the view of an
American educator on certain of the assumptions which in
his view compose the core of our tradition. This provides
an interesting and controversial perspective especially in the
way that he suggests that educational thought has avoided
the recognition and resolution of conflicts between new
needs and idealized traditions. In the second Cotgrove
discusses some of the relationships between education and
occupation and points out the distinctions between the
ostensible aims of educational institutions which prepare
their students for certain occupations and the actual
consequences which follow from the training. There has
been a 'constellation of ideas and values' strongly opposed
to vocational secondary and university education. Moreover,
conflicting demands on education arise from the various
needs of industry and society.

Finally Halsey views the educational system in the light
of the pursuit of equality in our society. This provides one
statement and analysis against which others can be viewed.
The Reading links with others in Chapters III and V, by

Little and Westergaard and by Douglas respectively, but focuses upon the long-term philosophy underlying equality of opportunity.

The argument about the quality of our society is often carried on in relation to the Welfare State and its presumed effects. Three Readings on this theme are provided here. In the first Runciman looks at three theories of social justice which reflect, to a large extent, the political standpoints of those who hold them and poses questions about the place of ideas of social justice in our society. Titmuss considers the question of redistribution as an aspect of social policy and refers to the widely held misconceptions about how effective this has been in the Welfare State. Marshall examines the most important aspects of the Welfare State and then goes on to examine the way in which contradictory principles may be followed in different fields.

One of the most widely publicized areas of conflict in our society is that between the young and the old. The young may be held responsible for a rejection of authority and the traditions of British life. This provides a good example of the way in which stereotypes develop. The changed attitudes to parental authority also reflect changed attitudes towards 'authority' generally and Worsley has interesting points to make on criminality as a phase in the life cycle of the individual and the content of 'youth culture'.

Finally three other aspects of British society are examined. In the first, Lupton carries on some distinctive themes which have already emerged, such as lack of moral fibre, inadequate leadership, false ideologies, and the like. He looks at the social structure of Britain to explain some of our inadequacies but also contrasts what is commonly believed with what is the reality he has discovered. He takes up the question of economic efficiency and the consequences of technological change, and explains how, for example, more complex division of labour has posed threats to the working class and has evoked certain kinds of response.

A distinguished American observer, Shils, comes next with part of a general critique of British society he wrote under the title of 'Britain Awake!' He points out some of the aspects of British life which he considers to be worthwhile, as well as its disadvantages, notably what he calls a 'constrictedness' of imagination and aspiration. In his comments about the changes which have taken place, and how the apparent single-mindedness of the Victorians has given way to our self-deprecating image, he prepares the scene for the brief opinion, and historical perspective, from Tawney. However Tawney's view is received he makes a statement around which discussions about the nature and content of British society can proceed.

Family
O. R. McGregor

Reprinted with permission from 'The Stability of the Family in the Welfare State', *Political Quarterly*, Vol. 31, No. 2, 1960, pp. 132–7.

Those well-meaning persons and organizations who assume a right to tell other people how to behave now sustain a formidable indictment of the welfare state. It rests primarily on the assertion that the admitted and always approved benefits of greater material security have been purchased at the price of a steady weakening of 'the moral fibre of the people.'

At bottom, these gloomy assessments rest on three beliefs. First, that social security has made other people feel secure, thus exposing them to moral danger. Sir Keith Joseph has explained that 'it is harder for the rich or the relatively secure to be pure.' Secondly, that social provision has 'stripped the family of its functions.' This is customarily translated to mean 'they even expect the state to look after their children and aged relatives.' Thirdly, that the great rise in the number of divorces in the twentieth century measures a corresponding increase in broken homes and marital irresponsibility. This is 'the flight from stability in marriage.' The first belief reflects widespread anxiety for the relatively poor (relatively, of course, because poverty has now been abolished) in moral peril on the deep of statutory services that fail to discriminate between the deserving and undeserving. The second and third beliefs stem from historical ignorance of the social facts of life and from a simple misunderstanding of divorce statistics.

Nineteenth-century industrialism created an urban society in which only affluent families could self-helpfully discharge their functions and responsibilities. Working-class families could become going concerns only within the shelter of collective provision that came to supply the decent houses, the schools, and the substitutes for personal thrift that such folk could not afford for themselves. This is why liberal politicians justified their social legislation in the years before 1914 as a means of buttressing the homes of the people at a time when the upper classes were pioneering new freedoms made possible by a declining birth-rate and by women's growth into citizenship. The family today is the product, on the one hand, of the diffusion of democratic habit and the destruction of Victorian domestic tyrannies and, on the other, of the extension of social policy accompanied by death and birth control.

There have also been striking changes in the community's family-forming habits during this century. The sex-ratio has altered from 962 bachelors for every 1,000 spinsters in 1901 to 1,089 at the last census. In late-Victorian days some 140 women in every thousand would be unmarried on their fiftieth birthday; today their number has fallen to fifty-five. Moreover, people are now marrying at unprecedentedly low ages: half the men and almost three-quarters of the women are married before they reach the age of twenty-five. This enthusiasm for marriage has grown persistently throughout the course of a reproductive revolution which has established the pattern of small families as it has enabled women, relieved of the burden of successive pregnancies, to participate in the general rise in the expectation of life. There is no evidence here of a flight from marriage, and it is against this experience that the asserted 'flight from stability in marriage' must be examined.

The contrast between the reality of a remarkably stable institution of marriage and the sickness perceived by moralists, though at first sight puzzling is easily explicable. In the first place, theological expectations require disintegrating homes. All the Christian sects derive a set of rules for the regulation of the family from their interpretation of the will of God. Such rules have two characteristics. On the essential practical issues such as birth control or the permissibility of divorce, they differ irreconcilably; and they have been consistently ignored by the population for whose guidance they were promulgated. Indeed, in the last half-century, the inability of the Churches to influence behaviour has been as striking as the power of behaviour to alter theological doctrines. Thus, the Church of England was denouncing contraception in 1900 and demanding its statutory suppression: now its attitude is positively welcoming. Christians agree that God's law defines marriage as a monogamous relationship dissoluble only by the death of a spouse. This the Church of Rome asserts to be an invariable rule. The Reformed Churches, on the other hand, insist that it is an ideal standard to which earthly marriages should conform, and they all claim divine authority to permit divorce in certain circumstances which frustrate the integrity and purposes of marriage. Men equally pious, equally learned, and equally zealous for the public good have for centuries based differing conclusions about God's intentions on the same texts, and it is not to be supposed that agreement is now in sight. But there are clear signs of a marked shift of emphasis. Fifty years ago, all Churches justified their marriage disciplines in terms of distinctive theological principles. All are now prepared, like Archbishop Heenan, a contributor to a recently published and authoritative volume, Catholics and Divorce, to show that their teachings are 'not only true in principle but true also in social practice' and that their neglect has led to social disaster. 'Since few people now accept the Bible,' writes the Archbishop, 'either as the word of God or even as a code with binding authority . . . it will, therefore, be more useful to consider divorce as a social evil.' And he turns confidently, in company with his protestant colleagues, to the crude statistics of divorce that so conveniently measure the mounting wreckage of broken homes and social deterioration and so neatly confirm his theological expectations. Unwary ecclesiastics who venture to cross the great divide that separates the revelations of religion from the methods of the social sciences should be alive to the dangers of exposing their conclusions to the test of empirical verification.

The Balanced Community
H. Orlans

Reprinted with permission of Laurence Pollinger Ltd. from *Stevenage*, London, Routledge & Kegan Paul, 1952, pp. 218–23.

The social motives for the balanced community were ambiguous. Indeed, they sometimes seemed to represent opposing goals and forces—the classless and class societies, the Socialist and Conservative Parties and ideologies.

A high degree of class segregation in housing and social intercourse almost invariably characterizes contemporary urban society (the lower degree of segregation often prevailing in rural areas does not contradict this fact, but suggests something of the world and the century from which many planners drew inspiration). Different patterns of segregation obtain, however, in different urban areas, which influence the nature of community life and interclass relations. The middle-class suburbs and working-class slums of metropolitan areas exemplify the one-class neighbourhood which may extend over a large area, while in districts like London's Chelsea or Bloomsbury or almost any small town various social classes live together in closer proximity. A modern version of the latter type of environment was what Ministry and Corporation planners hoped to achieve in the New Towns, since they believed this induced social consequences—greater political and social stability and a broader range of social and cultural activity—preferable to those of one-class neighbourhoods.

Planners often try to repair with one hand what they have damaged with the other—that is, they try to remedy conditions which are themselves (in part) a consequence of previous remedies. And so, to a considerable extent, the 'mixed class' neighbourhood and town was advocated now as a reaction against the one-class neighbourhoods which had developed partly as a consequence of the zoning regulations of inter-war planning legislation, under which vast districts were 'developed at the scale of one house to the acre, eight to the acre, or twelve to the acre, thus inevitably segregating families according to their incomes', and partly as a consequence of previous (and continuing) housing policy which produced segregated working-class council estates in every urban area:

'Historically, large-scale class segregation . . . is a comparatively recent thing. It did not occur in the medieval city, and such segregation as there was in pre-Industrial Revolution towns was on a small scale. Even then it occurred only in the planned streets and squares of London, Bath and similar places: and it was a segregation by streets rather than by quarters or whole towns: there were streets of big houses and streets of little ones, but generally they were near to each other and closely associated. In the naturally growing towns larger houses and cottages stood . . . side by side in exactly the same way as they do in villages to-day. The split came with the rapid development of the new 19th-century industrial towns, and as the housing conditions of the workers became more and more debased the split widened, till the middle classes began to live in special places of their own . . .

'The recent and present segregation . . . has arisen . . . from activity by government itself . . . As a result of governmental activity in the housing of the working classes, we have now in every town or city in the country whole estates devoted entirely to the housing of one particular wage-earning group.'

The advantages of class segregation can readily be imagined and are, indeed, the social part and psychological parcel of a class system of society: in its relative isolation from others, each class can freely enjoy the material, social, and psychological rewards of their status much as do their opulent brethren who sprawl over the tables of fashionable clubs, although it is not customary for the two classes to enjoy themselves together. Custom implies general, not invariant, practice; what a man elects to do one way he can also elect to do another, and no sociological or psychological law prevents a rich man from associating with a poor man if he chooses to—of course, he often does. But more often he does not; indeed, one contemporary school of sociology both defines and determines social class by the frequency and intimacy with which individuals associate together, and, in this view, a degree of contact between members of different classes as high as that between members of the same class is anomalous. It does not follow that each—or any—social class need be content with its lot; if it were, there would be no revolutions or pressure for social change. But each class must live its own life and not that of another, and nature readily conspires to make that life liveable.

In favour of encouraging social intercourse between different classes is, of course, the tradition that all men are equal before God and the gravedigger in the quantum of humanity. The opposite proposition, however, that (through birth or chance) all men are unequal, can lead to the same conclusion: charity and effective social control both require the upper and middle classes to retain contact with the lower classes. It is interesting to recall that Ebenezer Howard adduced for his balanced garden cities the same arguments that were used against the early exclusively lower-class colonization of Australia:

'We send out colonies of the limbs, without the belly and the head, of needy persons, many of them mere paupers, or even criminals; colonies made up of a single class of persons in the community, and that the most helpless and the most unfit to perpetuate our national character . . . . The ancients began by nominating to the honourable office of captain or leader of the colony one of the chief men . . . of the State, like the queen bee leading the workers. Monarchies provided a prince of the royal blood; an aristocracy its choicest nobleman; a democracy its most influential citizen. These naturally carried along with them some of their own station in life—their companions and friends; some of their immediate dependants also—of those between themselves and the lowest class; and were encouraged in various ways to do so. The lowest class again followed with alacrity, because they found themselves moving with and not away from the state of society in which they had been living. . . . They carried with them their gods, their festivals, their games—all, in short, that held together and kept entire the fabric of society as it existed in the parent state.'

This was the opposite of a revolutionary creed, as a Stevenage Communist perceived when he dismissed the theory of a balanced community as 'not in line with the Socialist theory of a classless society', adding scornfully, 'I can't imagine people of the retired class settling down here among the working-class people of Stevenage. I'm afraid they will regard the working-class woman as very convenient labour for dinner parties and so forth'. That Ministry and Corporation officials conceived their task in benevolent and not repressive terms, and were as likely to suggest that the upper classes would benefit from contact with the lower classes as vice versa, did not contradict the conservative function of the concept. The chairman told the Press that the Corporation hoped to persuade 'some retired, fairly wealthy people' to come to the New Town 'because they are so invaluable at organizing clubs and activities'. In the same manner, the National Council of Social Service complained that because of workers' segregation on new council estates, little 'community activity' occurred there; residents had 'a large store of latent talent in the social and creative sense. This talent, however, needs some preliminary leadership to unlock it and make it available. . . .' Which class would provide, or design, the key to the strangely impounded and misdirected talents of the working classes was not difficult to imagine. 'Community activity', of course, was a euphemism (and none the less a euphemism for being sincerely espoused) for 'activity congenial to the middle classes'. Boumphrey has observed that

'The whole essence of Howard's idea was that by rehousing the working-class man in a garden city, he would be transported into a clean atmosphere and healthy surroundings . . . and instead of wasting his spare time in the gin palace, to the detriment of his health, pocket, and home life, he could spend it in the healthy and fascinating pursuit of gardening.'

We conclude, then, that many garden city and New Town planners merely translated into sociological terms and architectural forms middle and upper-class ideologies of a conservative or liberal-reformist nature, and that the 'balanced community' concept thus served the forces of law and order, middle-class morality, and the social and political status quo.

That, for other planners (and, formally, for the Socialist Government), the 'balanced community' concept was part of a utopian Socialist creed, is too evident to require emphasis. Indeed, this was often all that the Conservative Stevenage home-owner saw.

Education 1
M. B. Katz

Reprinted with permission from 'From Bryce to Newsom: Assumptions of British Educational Reports, 1895–1963', *International Review of Education*, 11, 1965, pp. 287–90.

Educational systems reflect the dominant values and assumptions of their cultural contexts. In England, this paper contends, there is a distinct educational tradition, which can be defined in terms of certain key assumptions. To isolate some of these assumptions and, hence, to make a start towards defining the British educational tradition is one purpose of this paper. Indirectly, then, the paper hopes to shed some light on a number of persistent and deeply rooted values of British society. The twentieth century, however, has been unkind to tradition; massive economic, social and political changes have dissolved the cultural context of old beliefs while new intellectual influences have directly challenged existing assumptions. The second purpose of this paper, therefore, is to examine aspects of the impact of modern history upon the British educational tradition and to suggest the intellectual operations through which educators attempted to come to terms with the twentieth century. British educators, this paper maintains, sought to preserve the traditional and respond to the modern by avoiding the resolution of uncomfortable dilemmas, and their evasions of the essential confrontations have left British education with a number of unresolved and potentially debilitating tensions.

I

Ten assumptions compose the core of the British educational tradition. This section of the paper first states and then describes in more depth these ten assumptions. The second part of the paper analyses the confrontation of tradition with the challenges of the twentieth century.

1. The duty of the school is to transmit a distinctive cultural ideal and intellectual style, which are the foundations of a genuine, or liberal education.

2. A crucial distinction exists between education and instruction; above all, the school must avoid narrowness of outlook in curriculum, teachers and students.

3. The school must provide training in 'character', defined as morality and religion and the 'Victorian' virtues.

4. The school's moral responsibility implies that the 'corporate' aspects of school life are fully as important as the intellectual.

5. The individual teacher is the most important factor in the educational process, and most of the successes of British education have been the result of inspired, individual effort.

6. To serve the needs of the economy and society is one of the two major purposes of education.

7. Education must also serve the needs of the individual not only by preparing him vocationally but also by affecting the 'quality' of his life. In fact, there is an identifiably superior style of life.

8. Education should perform its functions as efficiently as possible: waste of money and individual talent must be avoided.

9. Education reflects the values and stratification of society; schools may contribute to modifications within the existing social framework, but they cannot initiate fundamental change.

10. The essential passivity of the school as a social institution has two implications for educational reform. First, reform must not advance beyond the limits of public opinion. Second, educational reform must follow historical development; it must rationalize the outcome of institutional evolution while altering existing institutions as little as possible.

The history of modern British educational thought is not the placid development of persistent assumptions but, rather, the development of concepts and solutions which have evaded the confrontation of tradition with the challenges of the twentieth century. Instead of recognizing and resolving confrontations, educational thought, as represented by the reports, verbalized solutions which, in reality, left unresolved and debilitating tensions to undercut and delay urgently required educational reform. Educational thought is not unique in this respect; it reflects the wider, and far from entirely successful, effort of British society to come to terms with the modern world while preserving as much as possible of an idealized past.

One tension resulted from the potentially conflicting objectives of education. Committees increasingly have been aware that they have assumed two not entirely compatible goals for education: service to society and service to the individual. The tension between the two first became explicit in the 1926 Hadow Report, and, in 1958, the Crowther Committee still wrestled with the problem. Throughout most of British history, the committee argued, the individual goal was dominant, but because of the importance of economic growth to national survival, the emphasis recently has been reversed. The report, however, avoided the difficulties of trying to resolve the two objectives by claiming that both 'are worthy and compelling, and we accept them both', and they made 'no attempt to disentangle the two purposes of education'. The Crowther solution, education will serve both objectives simultaneously, is an evasion of the problems of resolution, and there are dangers in evasion. Britain requires many expensive educational reforms, and the necessity of choice will demand a realistic confrontation and resolution of the traditional goals of British education. In fact, the danger is that the desire to avoid theoretical conflict implies the delay and evasion of reform itself.

The oldest conflict within the educational tradition involves the tension between the cultural-intellectual ideal and the assumption that the school should serve the economic requirements of both society and the individual. This conflict between vocational and liberal education pervades virtually every report. The task was especially urgent since the economic necessity of increased technical education was more and more apparent. The solution was the concept of adaptability. Adaptable individuals were required by a rapidly changing technology, and adaptability, the antithesis of a strict and narrow vocationalism, became a key word in the reports.

Through the concept of adaptability British educators attempted to integrate the aim of serving the economy with the cultural-intellectual ideals. They identified the needs of industry with the goals of education, and the old tradition of the generalist or amateur, the man with the good liberal education who could manage any position, was extended from the Civil Servant to the manual worker. The concept of adaptability, it is clear, is based on the assumption of the inherent worth of the cultural-intellectual ideal and, as such, without empirical validation. The purpose of the concept, indeed, seems to be the evasion of the necessity for a painful evaluation of a deeply rooted assumption. The evasion, moreover, has had serious consequences; for one thing, technical education has developed with often infuriating lack of speed in Britain and has left the country with a shortage of technically skilled manpower.

The challenge to morality is a major tension that has emerged within the educational tradition since the Second World War. Earlier reports assumed a fairly stable set of moral values on which there was general consensus. But after the war the content and method of moral training in a world of rapidly altering standards emerged as a major dilemma. Men have been 'left without a generally accepted standard by which to test their own views and conduct', and, in this situation, 'men are apt to feel an undue strain'. Thus, it is 'urgent . . . that the individual should not be left indefinitely without the support he needs'. 'Everybody' is expected to have a code of morality or standards, which is partly an individual matter and partly the result of membership in society. Morals and standards, continued the report, are 'the foundations of our way of life . . . men must be able to judge for themselves what is good and what is evil, and be able to choose the good'.

The report [on 'School and Life', 1947] implies that the 'good' is capable of definition. In spite of the disintegration of morality and religion, the Committee, without rigorous consistency, implied that certain moral verities form the basis of the good life. The report identified three strands in the British moral heritage: the classical, the Christian, and the scientific. Children should be shown all three 'and absorb, as part of their moral inheritance, the virtues of each'. Yet, the children should choose their own set of values, and their choice should represent 'intellectual and moral freedom'. Here was the evasion. Children should emerge with a pre-conceived conception of the good life in an age when such a conception was being severely challenged. The school should provide moral training but preserve intellectual freedom. The essence of moral education was exposure. Expose children to the moral heritage, and, without coercion, the assumption appears to be, they will choose properly. Obviously, this solution is evasive. Intelligent people choose a wide variety of moral codes, some which would undoubtedly appear strange or deviant to the Committee. What guarantee, then, is there that the children will choose correctly? Intellectual freedom and moral standards surely will conflict often. Where, then, does educational authority stand? Thus, the solution is verbal only; it provides little guide for action and leaves unresolved another tension in the British educational tradition.

The tensions between the assumptions of the educational tradition were heightened by the challenge and acceptance of new intellectual assumptions. These were the assumptions of 'progressive education'. 'Progressive education' is a difficult term to define. Here, it means that body of educational theory developed in the late nineteenth and early twentieth centuries in opposition to the tradition-centred, formalistic education characteristic of most schools of the period. In particular, three key assumptions were influential in England. First, education should proceed from the interests, needs and stage of development of the child. The focus of education should be the present, not the past. Second, the most effective learning involves motor activity rather than merely passive drill and memorization, and motor activity implies the integration of subjects or disciplines. Third, education should be related to the environment of the child. Education, in other words, should be concerned with the experience of the students.

In Britain the assumptions of progressive education, restrained always by the cultural-intellectual ideal, never degenerated into anti-intellectualism. Yet, unwillingness to confront fundamental intellectual conflicts has prevented the formation of a viable and vital amalgam. Of course, no simple formulas for reform, let alone ones that are entirely intellectu-ally and socially satisfying, will be found. Nevertheless, the confrontation and analysis of assumptions remain possible, and in such painful processes lies the most solid basis for reform.

Education 2
S. F. Cotgrove

Reprinted with permission from 'Education and Occupation', *British Journal of Sociology*, Vol. 13, No. 1, 1962, pp. 33–42.

In many occupations, intellectual knowledge must be accompanied by the possession of various personal qualities and skills. Two broad alternatives are possible. Occupational choice and selection may take place first, followed by the appropriate education and examinations. Alternatively, occupational selection may occur after the examination hurdle has been passed. Rejection at this stage may be very costly where the educational investment has been substantial.

There is a variety of institutional arrangements to ensure that aspirants will have suitable personal qualities. Interviewing boards for the selection of social work students may be instanced. Emphasis may be placed on the social and educational background of applicants. Medicine may well illustrate this process. Although there is a high degree of self-recruitment in the major professions, a particularly large proportion of medical students are the sons of doctors. This cannot be accounted for solely by educational criteria. The recruitment of the higher echelons of business and political elites from public school alumni provides a further example of this method to ensure the possession of the necessary personal qualities.

Any discussion of the relations between education and occupation will quickly bring to light the existence of a constellation of ideas and values which are strongly opposed to any vocational element in secondary and university education. Such values are usually asserted as self-evident, and even as 'basic moral assumptions'. F. Clarke points out that 'Often in the most ingenuous way (English writers) give vigorous expression to quite English politico-socio ideals while believing themselves to be discussing pure educational theory'. Yet these ideals influence the functioning of the educational system and constitute what Malinowski calls the 'charter' of the institutions to which they are related.

The notion that the proper role of academic man is the disinterested pursuit of knowledge for its own sake is one such notion that deserves more detailed analysis. It functions to motivate and legitimize the activities of the intellectual and shields him from any questioning of the social relevance of his functions. But such a notion is by no means self-evident, though it operates powerfully to prevent the emergence of a more socially relevant curriculum. The real task of the university it is said is 'to teach people to think'. The university is the 'gateway to knowledge, not a preparation for commerce. What graduates do after leaving is of no immediate concern to us. Our own duty is to maintain high standards of scholarship . . . not to prostitute learning to modern requirements.'

The dominant English tradition to educate for culture lies at the root of many of our current problems. The traditional solution of the classical-humanist education combined education for culture with special education for rulers and administrators. No such synthesis has yet been achieved for the education of those who will perform a much wider variety of social roles. Indeed, the notion that many branches of knowledge are banausic has hindered the development of the universities as places of preparation for a variety of occupations. Thus it is possible to receive education and training for social work in the universities, but not (generally) as an architect.

One further example of the powerful influence of ideology on education can be seen in the development of technical education in Britain. The strongly held belief that only the workshops of industry could give practical training, while the colleges should confine themselves to teaching the principles underlying trades was a major factor in the development of a predominantly part-time system of technical education. Many of the present problems of apprenticeship can be traced to this source. Yet the belief was based on the most flimsy evidence, and many countries have in fact developed successfully college-based systems of craft training.

It is the task for the sociology of education to bring to light not only the social roots of the values and ideologies which shape the educational system, but also the social consequences of the resulting practices. The growing pressure on the university is from students seeking qualifications of vocational value, not only for the traditional functions of administration, but for a growing range of specialist functions in industry and commerce and the social services. Such students are confronted by dons, many of whom believe that the university should resist any pressure to give its activities greater social relevance. It is important to examine the resulting problems of adjustment facing the student, both as an undergraduate and after graduation.

One of the major conclusions which has emerged from the recent study of educational institutions which prepare for occupations is the important discrepancies which exist between their ostensible aims and purposes and the actual consequences which they achieve. Moreover, some of these consequences have not been intended by those responsible for educational policy, nor recognized until they were brought to light by sociological research.

Recent studies of apprenticeship provide excellent examples. The traditional and 'official' function of apprenticeship as the means for the transmission of skills has led the Ministries of Education and Labour to rely on industrial apprenticeship as the vehicle for the post-war expansion of technical education and training. Yet the researches of Lady Williams and Dr. Liepmann have documented the serious inadequacies of apprenticeship. Rigid age requirements, the absence of any test of competence, the meagre facilities for practical training in most firms provide little evidence of its training function. Dr. Liepmann's studies suggest that the main function of apprenticeship for the trade unions 'is that of maintaining exclusiveness of training as a means for protecting the privileges of their members'. The insistence on protracted apprenticeships is the basis for the craftsman's claim to differential wages, for job demarcation, and for regulating the supply of labour and thus providing a cushioning effect against insecurity of employment in slack times.

Apprenticeship is failing then to meet the needs of society for a trained labour force because administrators have looked only at some of its official functions. But apprenticeship is multi-functional, and in practice its regulating functions dominate its training functions. The consequences are in many respects dysfunctional for a society which relies on industrial apprenticeship as the main vehicle for increasing the supply of trained manpower. It is by bringing to light such unintended and unrecognized consequences of social action that sociology provides a basis for changes of policy.

Educational institutions perform a variety of functions. Preparation for occupational roles is only one of these, but an examination of the implications of this important function can bring to light many of the problems which will have to be taken into account in any radical examination of the future of higher education. In particular, there is need to resolve the problems which arise from the many and sometimes conflicting demands made on education by the various needs of industry and society. The traditional values of the university are in many ways in conflict with their changing role in society. It is no longer self-evident to many that the rewards of the life of scholarship are sufficient justification for the social support of educational institutions but the criterion of social utility raises fresh problems requiring the investigation of the social functions of educational ideologies and the empirical testing of many of the assumptions involved.

Education 3
A. H. Halsey

Reprinted with permission from 'Education and Equality', *New Society*, 17 June, 1965.

Some people, and I am one, want to use education as an instrument in pursuit of an egalitarian society. We tend to favour comprehensive schools, to be against public schools and to support the expansion of higher education. Our opponents want to use education for the preservation of old or the creation of new inequalities. They tend to be against comprehensives, for public schools and against expansion especially of universities.

The argument is complicated in many ways: education has other purposes than that of promoting equality. It enables us to become literate, patriotic, occupationally skilled and capable of using leisure constructively.

Above all, there are many definitions of equality and many variants of inequality, each with appropriately different educational implications, Ultimately the argument is one about values and their priorities. At this level we may never reach agreement: there is, as Tawney said, 'no agreement with the choice of a soul'. But in practice we may never need to face each other with these passionate abstractions. Certainly we can start with the facts.

The first unavoidable fact is that whatever else it does or could do, education is about equality. Education has always stood necessarily in close relation to class, status and power. In the past half century it has become part of the economic foundations of industrial society, a major avenue of social mobility and one of the principal agencies of social distribution. An advanced industrial society is inconceivable without means through which people are selected and trained for places in a highly diversified labour force. The educational system is accordingly used to establish claims and opportunities. If education is unavoidably an instrument for distributing life chances, we can only argue profitably about what kind of distribution is both desirable and possible. To recognize this is to accept that education is a proper object of political debate and a challenge to sociological analysis.

The facts of inequality have been documented by sociological research since the war. They can be summarized by considering how opportunities for education are socially distributed. This can be done by applying the concepts of 'class chances' and of 'ability' as indicated by measured intelligence.

In an enquiry into education and social selection in England in 1952, carried out by Jean Floud, F. M. Martin and myself, it was appropriate to take entry to grammar as opposed to secondary modern schools as the crucial point of educational opportunity. Using entry to grammar schools as the measure of opportunity in the early 1950s, class chances descended from nearly 1:1 for the children of the professional and business owning and managing classes, through 1:2 or 3 for the children of white collar workers, to 1:6 for skilled workers and 1:10 for unskilled workers. During the subsequent decade a slow modification of the English secondary system has taken place with slight increase in the provision of courses of a grammar school type, either in grammar schools or comprehensive schools, and through the extension of secondary modern school courses to enable children to take G.C.E. examinations. The proportion of 17 year old children at school rose from 6·6 per cent in 1950 to 7·9 per cent in 1954 and 12 per cent in 1962. The proportion attaining five or more 'O' level passes in G.C.E. rose from 10·7 per cent in 1954 to 15·3 per cent in 1961. There are no data on recent changes in class chances in British secondary education, but in discussing this issue the Robbins Report concluded that 'if there were data on the educational attainment of school children in each social class in, say, 1950 and in 1960, this would probably not show a great narrowing of social class differences'.

The trend in differential class chances of entry to full time higher education in the period 1928 to 1960 also shows a static picture. The proportion entering universities in the period 1928–47 was 3·7 per cent and this had risen to 5·8 per cent by 1960. The chances of entry for boys of all classes had roughly doubled, leaving the situation in 1960 as it was earlier, namely one in which the child of a non-manual worker was six and a half times more likely to go to a university than a boy from the manual working class.

These class inequalities are not simply a reflection of the social distribution of measured intelligence. The Robbins Report contains evidence that at descending levels of social class, children of equal ability have reduced chances of entering higher education. For children born in 1940–41 who entered maintained grammar schools and were classified by intelligence at the 11 plus examination, it has turned out that among those with IQs of 130 or more, children of non-manual workers had twice as much chance of entering a degree course as did children of manual workers. For the group whose intelligence fell between IQ 115 and 129, the differential chance was 2·12 and for those between IQ 100 and 114, the chances of the middle class child were three times as high as those for the working class child.

The present organization of schooling is less than just in that, at any given level of native ability, the social and economic status of a family determines access to educational facilities. Rich men can buy educational privilege in public schools and apart from this, by and large, the better off districts have the greater proportion of grammar school places. Wealth and residential segregation of the classes are translated into unequal educational opportunities. Clearly the abolition of purchased privilege, the integration of the private with the public sector and the alleviation of present geographical inequalities are possible roads to formal equality of educational opportunity.

Redistribution of formal opportunity is not, however, enough. The determinants of ability are also social and they are weighted in favour of the better off classes. Redistribution of educability as well as of education is also possible. There is clear evidence that social and educational conditions have a cumulative effect on measured ability. Slum children in slum schools, whether or not they are born stupid, certainly become stupefied by their experiences, as shown for example by J. W. B. Douglas's studies of the growth of IQ among children in different social and educational circumstances.

Attractive Strategy

Educational expansion is another attractive strategy for the egalitarian. It permits reduction of injustice by reducing, or at least deferring, selection and by offering more education to everyone. Studies of the development of secondary education in France and of higher education in America both bear out this point. In France in 1953 a national survey showed that chances of secondary education varied systematically with social status, from 87 per cent among children of professionals to 13 per cent among the children of agricultural labourers. The 1959 reform of the structure of secondary education included the development of long courses in collèges d'enseignement général from which children can transfer to the lycées at a later stage. If the C.E.G. courses are added to those at the traditional lycée, then it appears that between 1953 and 1962 the proportion of all children entering secondary courses (entrée en Sixieme) rose from 30 per cent to 55 per cent. This expansion was accompanied by marked reduction in differential class chances of secondary education. Thus, comparing the professional and unskilled groups, in 1953 the chances of children in the former group were four times better and in 1962 were reduced to twice as good.

Estimates by Professor Havighurst for United States higher education over the period from 1920 to 1960 indicate a similar trend to that which has shown itself in French secondary education in the 1950s. Havighurst distinguishes four strata; comparing boys in his upper middle and upper lower strata, the differential chances in 1920 were 20:1. For the upper and upper middle class they more than doubled in the case of boys by 1960, and the differential chances between this class and the upper lower class in the same year had been reduced to something over 3:1. These statistics indicate that only great educational expansion has the power to make inroads into long standing inequalities of educational opportunity and only where, as in America, secondary education is both universal and linked comprehensively to higher education can expansion make educational selection democratic.

The Welfare State 1
W. G. Runciman

Reprinted with permission from 'Social Justice', *The Listener*, 29 July, 1965.

There are, broadly speaking, three different and mutually incompatible theories of social justice: the conservative, the liberal, and the socialist. In the conservative theory, social justice consists in a social hierarchy, but a hierarchy governed by a stable system of interconnected rights and duties. Those at the top are the holders not merely of privilege but of responsibility for the welfare of those below; and through the recognition that different strata in society have different functions to fulfil, the hierarchy is accepted without dissension or envy as long as the responsibilities imposed on each class are in fact properly exercised.

In the liberal theory, by contrast, there is also a hierarchy; but this hierarchy is only legitimate if it has been arrived at from a position of initial equality. The liberal is not against inequality, but against privilege. He demands equality not of condition but of opportunity. He places a value not on an elite of caste, or inherited culture, but of individual attainment. The socialist theory, finally, is the strictly egalitarian theory. It may or may not require as a corollary that the state should play a predominant part in economic affairs. This is really only a means to an end—the maximum of social equality in any and all its aspects.

All three of these theories are persuasive, and internally consistent. How, therefore, can one adjudicate between them? How, having looked at the social structure of twentieth-century England, are we to judge it by the standard of social justice except by appealing to whichever one theory happens to suit our own interests or temperament? By what possible criterion can one be shown to be any more or less arbitrary than the other two? There is no one just distribution of the national income, no one just constitution, no one just mode of social relations. But what it is worth looking for is a principle. We may be able to find not a set of rules for the one just society but a criterion by which a set of rules as such may be assessed. We want to be able to say, not 'Is this particular inequality unjust?' but, 'Does this inequality derive from a rule which could not be defended by appeal to the notion of justice?'

The notion of justice which best enables us to assess a system of inequalities is not the conservative, or liberal, or socialist notion as such, but one which goes behind all three. It is a notion of justice which has been recently put forward by Professor John Rawls of Harvard, and which may be summarized as follows: the essence of justice is fairness, and for an understanding of the concept of fairness the most appropriate model is that of a contract between equal persons. This does not mean in any sense a reversion to the theory of a social contract which actually happened in the state of nature. It means only that when assessing particular inequalities which we find we must ask one simple question: is this an inequality defensible by a principle which we could have agreed before we had any idea which of the unequal positions we should eventually occupy?

A just system, therefore, is a system to which people would have agreed if they had had to decide on the principles by which social systems were to be regulated before they knew either what their own system would be or what would be their own place in it. Suppose I had to decide on the principles by which education was to be run in my eventual society before I knew either where I would be placed in the social hierarchy or what the abilities or temperaments of myself or my children would be. Would I agree that the best education should go to the children of the richest parents? I think there is no doubt that I would not; and by this token any educational system of such a kind is demonstrably unjust.

Should no Inequality be Justified?

It might seem that this line of argument leads directly to the socialist view of social justice. You may feel that we would all, in the state of nature, have agreed that no inequality should be justified—that all jobs should be equally rewarded, that everyone should treat everyone else as a social equal, and that nobody should have more power than anybody else. But one of the virtues of Rawls's model is that it shows that what would have been agreed is not a total egalitarianism. In Rawls's state of nature, we should only have agreed that no inequality could be justified in our eventual society unless it followed from a principle agreed in advance of vested interest. The contract model is, therefore, fundamentally egalitarian, but only in this special sense. It requires all inequalities to be justified. But among those which it justifies there may well be some which would be justified also by the conservative or liberal theories of social justice.

The suggestion that everyone should receive an equal reward breaks down at once. If, as far as I know, I may turn out to be a man doing a difficult and responsible job with long hours, and to have in addition many dependents to support, I will surely want to be able to claim a higher reward than will be allotted to a man who has no dependents and an easy half-time job. I will, conversely, be prepared to concede this even if I in fact turn out to be the second man (having had, as far as I knew, an equal chance of being either). In fact, I shall be prepared to agree on three principles by which I shall be willing, if it so turns out, to be the loser. These principles, which in their various forms are familiar throughout the history of political theory, are need, merit, and contribution to the common good. By merit I do not, of course, mean moral virtue, but things like danger money; and the criterion of merit must also be linked with the third criterion: contribution to the common good—it would be absurd to suggest that, say, an outstanding solver of crosswords should be paid an extravagant income unless the solving of crosswords contributed in some widely accepted sense to the national welfare. But these three principles, however difficult their application in practice, would surely be agreed by people in the state of nature who did not yet know what their position in the social structure would turn out to be.

No Acceptable Formula

This argument obviously is not enough to show whether a coalminer contributes more to the national welfare than an architect, whether a laboratory technician should be paid more than a policeman, or whether the state should provide a family allowance for the first as well as subsequent children. But there is never going to be a formula which will answer such questions as these. The concept of social justice can only be brought to bear at a different level—the level at which we can establish the principles by appeal to which any divergence from strict equality can be justified.

If we picture ourselves in a state of nature, we can agree for a start that jobs requiring a long training and a high degree of skill and fulfilling an essential need should be accorded higher reward than where this is not so. We can also agree that any unemployed person willing to work should have a claim on the communal resources on the grounds of need; if I know that I have as good a chance of finding myself in this position as in any other, I shall surely want to stipulate in advance that I should have a claim on the communal resources even at the price of conceding this claim if I should turn out to be among the employed. This much might be agreed on any theory of justice; even the more extreme versions of the conservative or liberal theories do not nowadays require the unemployed to starve. But there are three consequences which follow from Rawls's theory of justice which are rather more important. The first is the importance of needs. The second is the irrelevance of conventional comparisons. The third is the requirement of redistribution.

The most obvious provisions that follow from this are hardly at issue in contemporary Britain. We have freedom of speech, restrictions on theft or assault, and universal suffrage. But there is still a case to be made for saying that there is less equality of power in our social structure than would be consonant with what would have been agreed from the state of nature. Whatever position I turned out to occupy in twentieth-century Britain, I would surely want a maximum of say in the decisions by which my life was governed; and any inequality of power would have to be justified in the light of this injunction. Would it not therefore be just that workers should have a greater say in management? The reasons why such demands have not been more strongly pressed is largely —perhaps even entirely—because they are impracticable. But because justice is impracticable it does not cease to be justice; and if the ordinary worker has less say in the decisions by which his working life is governed than we should all have wished to stipulate before knowing what our own location would be in the economy of industrialized Britain, then this is a social injustice.

But—and it is a big but—to show that a social structure is unjust is not to show either how it ought to be changed or even that it ought to. Would more people be happier in a just society? Even if they would, might not more unhappiness than happiness be caused in the transition to justice? Inequalities are always least resented when expectations are low; and, conversely, deprivations are most strongly felt when a previous expectation has been disappointed. This much, indeed, is a truism. But it has the important consequence that the reformer, in attempting to make society just, may risk causing as much unhappiness as he will cure. Whether a system is just or not has nothing to do with people's attitudes towards it; even if slaves preferred to be slaves, this would not make slavery just, and even if everyone was miserable under a just regime, this would not make it unjust. In the same way, the efficiency or even the workability of a system has no necessary connection with its justice. It never follows, from the fact that a system is unjust, that is must be undone, and it is only by recognizing this that a clear and useful appeal to the notion of social justice can be made.

The Welfare State 2
R. M. Titmuss

Reprinted with permission from *Commitment to Welfare*, London, Allen & Unwin, 1968, pp, 195–8.

The major positive achievement which has resulted from the creation of direct, universalist, social services in kind has been the erosion of formal discriminatory barriers. One publicly approved standard of service, irrespective of income, class or race, replaced the double standard which invariably meant second-class services for second-class citizens. This has been most clearly seen in the National Health Service. Despite strict controls over expenditure on the Service by Conservative Governments for many years it has maintained the principle of equality of access by all citizens to all branches of medical care. Viewed solely in terms of the welfare objective of non-discriminatory, non-judgmental service this is the signal achievement of the National Health Service. In part this is due to the fact that the middle-classes, invited to enter the Service in 1948, did so and have since largely stayed with the Service. They have not contracted out of socialized medical care as they have done in other fields like secondary education and retirement pensions. Their continuing participation, and their more articulate demands for improvements, have been an important factor in a general rise in standards of service—particularly in hospital care.

But, as some students of social policy in Britain and the United States are beginning to learn, equality of access is not the same thing as equality of outcome. We have to ask statistical and sociological questions about the utilization of the high-cost quality sectors of social welfare and the low-cost sectors of social welfare. We have to ask similar questions about the ways in which professional people (doctors, teachers, social workers and many others) discharge their roles in diagnosing need and in selecting or rejecting patients, clients and students for this or that service. In the modern world, the professions are increasingly becoming the arbiters of our welfare fate; they are the key-holders to equality of outcome; they help to determine the pattern of redistribution in social policy.

These generalizations apply particularly when services in kind are organized on a universalist, free-on-demand basis. When this is so we substitute, in effect, the professional decision-maker for the crude decisions of the economic marketplace. And we also make much more explicit—an important gain in itself—the fact that the poor have great difficulties in manipulating the wider society, in managing change, in choosing between alternatives, in finding their way around a complex world of welfare.

We have learnt from 15 years' experience of the Health Service that the higher income groups know how to make better use of the Service; they tend to receive more specialist attention; occupy more of the beds in better equipped and staffed hospitals; receive more elective surgery; have better maternity care; and are more likely to get psychiatric help and psychotherapy than low income groups—particularly the unskilled.

These are all factors which are essential to an understanding of the redistributive role played by one of the major direct welfare services in kind. They are not arguments against a comprehensive free-on-demand service. But they do serve to underline one conclusion. Universalism in social welfare, though a needed prerequisite towards reducing and removing formal barriers of social and economic discrimination, does not by itself solve the problem of how to reach the more-difficult-to-reach with better medical care, especially preventive medical care.

Much the same kind of general conclusion can be drawn from Britain's experience in the field of education. Despite reforms and expansion during the past 15 years it is a fact that the proportion of male undergraduates who are the sons of manual workers is today about 1 per cent lower than it was between 1928 and 1947. Although we have doubled the number of University students the proportion coming from working-class homes has remained fairly constant at just over a quarter.

The major beneficiaries of the high-cost sectors of the educational system in 'The Welfare State' have been the higher income groups. They have been helped to so benefit by the continued existence of a prosperous private sector in secondary education (partly subsidized by the State in a variety of ways including tax deductibles), and by developments since 1948 in provisions for child dependency in the category of fiscal welfare. Take, for example, the case of two fathers each with two children, one earning $60,000 a year, the other $1,500 a year.* In combining the effect of direct social welfare expenditures for children and indirect fiscal welfare expenditures for children the result is that the rich father now gets thirteen times more from the State than the poor father in recognition of the dependent needs of childhood.

Housing is another field of social policy which merits analysis from the point of view of redistribution. Here we have to take account of the complex interlocking effects of local rate payments, public housing subsidies, interest rates, tax deductibles for mortgage interest and other factors. When we have done so we find that the subsidy paid by the State to many middle-class families buying their own homes is greater than that received by poor tenants of public housing (local government) schemes.

These are no more than illustrations of the need to study the redistributive effects of social policy in a wider frame of reference. Hitherto, our techniques of social diagnosis and our conceptual frameworks have been too narrow. We have compartmentalized social welfare as we have compartmentalized the poor. The analytic model of social policy that has been fashioned on only the phenomena that are clearly visible, direct and immediately measurable is an inadequate one. It

* Roughly £25,000 and £600 at current exchange rates. *Editor's note.*

fails to tell us about the realities of redistribution which are being generated by the processes of technological and social change and by the combined effects of social welfare, fiscal welfare and occupational welfare.

How far and to what extent should redistribution take place through welfare channels on the principle of achieved status, inherited status or need? This is the kind of question which, fundamentally, is being asked in Britain today. And it is being directed, in particular, at two major areas of social policy—social security and housing. Both these instruments of change and redistribution have been neglected for a decade or more. We have gone in search of new gods or no gods at all. It is time we returned to consider their roles afresh and with new vision. Perhaps we might then entitle our journey 'Ways of Extending the Welfare State to the Poor'.

The Welfare State 3
T. H. Marshall

Reprinted with permission from 'Social Selection in the Welfare State', *Eugenics Review*, Vol. XLV, No. 2, 1953.

It would be difficult to find any definition of the Welfare State acceptable to both its friends and to its enemies—or even to all its friends. Fortunately I needn't try to define it; I have only to explain what are the characteristics of the Welfare State which seem to me to provide a distinctive setting to the problem of social selection. I take the most relevant aspect of the Welfare State, in this context, to be the following.

First, its intense individualism. The claim of the individual to welfare is sacred and irrefutable and partakes of the character of a natural right. It would, no doubt, figure in the new Declaration of the Rights of Man if the supporters of the Welfare State were minded to issue anything so pithily dramatic. It would replace property in those early French and American testaments which speak of life, liberty and property; this trinity now becomes life, liberty and welfare. It is to be found among the Four Freedoms in the guise of 'Freedom from Want'—but that is too negative a version. The welfare of the Welfare State is more positive and has more substance.

It was lurking in the Declaration of Independence, which listed the inalienable rights of man as 'Life, Liberty and the Pursuit of Happiness.' Happiness is a positive concept closely related to welfare, but the citizen of the Welfare State does not merely have the right to pursue welfare, he has the right to receive it, even if the pursuit has not been particularly hot. And so we promise to each child an education suited to its individual qualities, we try to make the punishment (or treatment) fit the individual criminal rather than the crime, we hold that in all but the simplest of the social services individual case study and family case work should precede and accompany the giving of advice or assistance, and we uphold the principle of equal opportunity, which is perhaps the most completely individualistic of all.

But if we put individualism first, we must put collectivism second. The Welfare State is the responsible promoter and guardian of the welfare of the whole community, which is something more complex than the sum total of the welfare of all its individual members arrived at by simple addition. The claims of the individual must always be defined and limited so as to fit into the complex and balanced pattern of the welfare of the community, and that is why the right to welfare can never have the full stature of a natural right. The harmonizing of individual rights with the common good is a problem which faces all human societies.

In trying to solve it, the Welfare State must choose means which are in harmony with its principles. It believes in planning —not of everything but over a wide area. It must therefore clearly formulate its objectives and carefully select its methods with a full sense of its power and its responsibility. It believes in equality, and its plans must therefore start from the assumption that every person is potentially a candidate for every position in society. This complicates matters; it is easier to cope with things if society is divided into a number of noncompeting social classes. It believes in personal liberty because, as I choose to define it, it is a democratic form of society. So although, of course, like all States, it uses some compulsion, it must rely on individual choice and motivation for the fulfilment of its purposes in all their details.

How do these principles apply to selection through the educational system? The general social good, in this context, requires a balanced supply of persons with different skills and aptitudes who have been so trained as to maximize the contribution they can make to the common welfare. We have, in recent years, seen the Welfare State estimating the need for natural scientists, social scientists and technicians, for doctors, teachers and nurses, and then trying to stimulate the educational system to produce what is required. It must also be careful to see that the national resources are used economically and to the best advantage, that there is no waste of individual capacities, by denying them the chance of development and use, and no waste of money and effort, by giving education and training to those who cannot get enough out of them to justify the cost.

On the other side, the side of individualism, is the right of each child to receive an education suited to its character and abilities. It is peculiar, in that the child cannot exercise the right for itself, because it is not expected to know what its character and abilities are. Nor can its parents wholly represent its interests, because they cannot be certain of knowing either. But they have a rather ambiguous right at least to have their wishes considered, and in some circumstances to have them granted. The status of parental rights in the English educational system is somewhat obscure at the moment. There is no reason to assume that the independent operation of the two principles, of individual rights and general social needs, would lead to the same results. The State has the responsibility of harmonizing the one with the other.

So far I have merely been trying to explain the general meaning which I have discovered in the title of this lecture. As I have already said, I shall first limit this broad field by concentrating on selection through the educational system. I shall then limit it further to the two following aspects of the problem. I shall look first at the selection of children for secondary education and try to see what is involved in bringing it into harmony with the principles of the Welfare State. I choose this particular point in the selection process partly because of its intrinsic and often decisive importance, and partly because so much has recently been written about it. I shall look in the second place rather at the social structure and consider how far it is possible to achieve the aims of the Welfare State in this field—particularly the aim of equal opportunity—in a society in which there still exists considerable inequality of wealth and social status. In doing this I shall be able to draw on some of the still unpublished results of researches carried out at the London School of Economics over the past four years, chiefly with the aid of a generous grant from the Nuffield Foundation.

The Welfare State, as I see it, is in danger of tying itself in knots in an attempt to do things which are self-contradictory. One example, I submit, is the proposal to assign children to different schools, largely on the basis of general ability, and then to pretend that the schools are all of equal status. If this means that we shall take equal trouble to make all schools as good as possible, treat all the children with equal respect and try to make them all equally happy, I heartily endorse the idea. But the notion of parity of esteem does not always stop there; and I feel it really is necessary to assert that some children are more able than others, that some forms of education are higher than others, and that some occupations demand qualities that are rarer than others and need longer and more skilled training to come to full maturity, and that they will therefore probably continue to enjoy higher social prestige.

I conclude that competitive selection through the educational system must remain with us to a considerable extent. The Welfare State is bound to pick the children of high ability for higher education and for higher jobs, and to do this with the interests of the community as well as the rights of the children in mind. But the more use it can at the same time make of allocation to courses suited to special tastes and abilities the better. It further seems to be that, for the purpose of selection on grounds of general ability, the objective tests are already accurate enough to do all that we should ever ask them to do, while, so far as 'allocation' is concerned, they will never be able to give a decisive verdict in more than a minority of cases, although they can be of great value in helping to decide what advice to give.

The problem which now faces us is more administrative than psychological. There is less to be gained by trying to perfect the tests and examinations than by thinking how to shape the structure of our educational and employment systems. It is better to minimize the effects of our decisions in doubtful cases than to imagine that, if we only try hard enough, we can ensure that all our decisions in such cases are correct. The word 'correct' has no meaning in this context; it is a bureaucratic fiction borrowed from the office where there is a correct file for every document.

By 'minimize the effects of our decisions' I mean refrain from adding unnecessary and artificial consequences to acts whose real meaning and necessary consequences I have been urging that we should frankly recognize. A system of direction into distinct 'types of secondary school' rather than 'courses of secondary education' (to use the titles I quoted earlier) must, I think, intensify rather than minimize the consequences. I am aware of the educational arguments on the other side, but do not intend to enter into a controversy for which I have no equipment. The other point at which artificial consequences may be added is the point of passage from education to employment. The snobbery of the educational label, certificate or degree when, as often, the prestige of the title bears little or no relation to the value of the content, is a pernicious thing against which I should like to wage a major war.

There is another matter on which the Welfare State can easily try to follow contradictory principles. It relates to occupational prestige, social class and the distribution of power in society.

Although the Welfare State must, I believe, recognize some measure of economic inequality as legitimate and acceptable, its principles are opposed to rigid class divisions, and to anything which favours the preservation or formation of sharply distinguished culture patterns at different social levels. The segregation when at school of those destined for different social levels is bound to have some effect of this kind and is acceptable only if there are irrefutable arguments on the other side. Further, a system which sorts children by general ability and then passes them through appropriate schools to appropriate grades of employment will intensify the homogeneity within each occupational status group and the differences between groups. And, in so far as intelligence is hereditary and as educational chances are influenced by family background (and I have produced evidence to show that they are), the correlation between social class and type of school will become closer among the children.

Finally, the Welfare State, more than most forms of democracy, cannot tolerate a governing class. Leadership and power are exercised from many stations in life, by politicians, judges, ecclesiastics, business men, trade unionists, intellectuals and others. If these were all selected in childhood and groomed in the same stable, we should have what

Raymond Aron calls the characteristic feature of a totalitarian society—a unified elite. These leaders must really belong to and represent in a distinctive way the circles in and through which their power is exercised. We need politicians from all classes and occupational levels, and it is good that some captains of industry should have started life at the bench, and that trade unions should be led by genuine members, men of outstanding general ability who have climbed a ladder other than the educational one. It is important to preserve these other ladders, and it is fortunate that the selection net has some pretty big holes in it. It is fortunate too, perhaps, that human affairs cannot be handled with perfect mechanical precision, even in the Welfare State.

Authority
P. M. Worsley

Reprinted with permission from 'Authority and the Young', *New Society*, 22 July, 1965.

It seems universally agreed among publicists and guardians of public morality that we are in the midst of a crisis, in which traditional values and institutional controls have been rejected, and that nothing has emerged to replace them. This decay of authority is believed to be most visible among young people, not only in Britain, but in all developed countries, whatever their cultural and ideological differences. T. R. Fyvel, for example, has described the 'Teddy boy international': Soviet stilyagi, Swedish skinnknuttar, French blousons noirs, Australian 'bodgies' and 'widgies', Japanese taiyozoku, West German Halbstarken, and so on—a new generation (of vipers) whose language is jazz, who dress alike, who share the same style of non-work life, and who though not radical ideologically, are detached from official society to the point of constituting a delinquent international sub-culture.

Impressionistic as this may be, it is not without some foundation in reality. Yet we lack adequate studies of inter-war youth against which we might more accurately assess just how different post-1945 youth is in fact. The quite limited literature on contemporary youth, too, by no means supports the thesis that the end of World War II inaugurated an era of social disorganization.

Barbara Wooton, in her study of criminality published in 1959, for example, pointed out that the U.K. statistics of indictable offences of all kinds (with all their acknowledged limitations) exhibited a remarkable stability: 787,482 in 1938; 753,012 in 1952; and 735,288 in 1955. Taking youthful crime separately, young people were responsible for 36 per cent of all indictable offences in 1938, and in 1955—33 per cent. Subsequently there has been a distinct rise, the significance of which is still being debated. What is of particular interest to us in all this, however, is that when the figures are looked at within the processual analytical framework of age, rather than globally, they suggest that criminality is a phase in the life cycle of the individual rather than a phase in the 'life' of the whole society.

Changed attitudes to parental authority go hand in hand with changed attitudes to 'the authorities' in general. But it was the parents themselves who started the rot (if 'rot' it is): they overthrew the old Victorian paterfamilias; they urged youth to be free, experimented with bottle feeding, struggled so that 'the kids' could have better homes, more rewarding (in every sense) jobs, better education than themselves. And now, confusingly, 'the kids' are biting the hands that fed them. The 'scholarship boys', absorbed into middle-class ways, can't even find anything to talk to their parents about. On all sides, the laments rise up.

If they are radical, however, this is scarcely a radicalism of ideas and beliefs, it is a radicalism of personal independence: a manifestation of the normal structural phenomenon of inter-generational separation of experience, exacerbated in an era in which the Depression and the War are only historical events to the children of parents for whom these were crucial experiences.

The fact that youthful criminality exhibits a marked sexual division of labour alone suggests that we are dealing with patterns of behaviour that cannot be explained merely as the adding together of thousands of idiosyncratic cases, each one unique. There are very distinctive styles of crime, too. Crime, here, is not a mode of production, or a career: it is more commonly a mode of expression, or a phase during which personality needs are satisfied in precisely the ways held out as desirable by respectable society in other contexts. It is frequently opportunity-crime, or by rationalistic standards, purely destructive. It yields microscopic returns. And, classically, it is often oriented towards the acquisition or use of consumption goods, such as clothes and cars. Its values are the values of a consumption-oriented society, not those generated by basic poverty.

The emergence of a specialized 'youth industry', engaged in selling goods to young people, obviously reflects the fact, as we are always being reminded, that youth can now afford to buy what it wants, or is led to want. Teenagers' real earnings have risen faster than those of adults (though as Mark Abrams has noted, their share of the national wealth is 'very modest . . . (and) . . . scarcely sustains a picture of an extremely prosperous body of young people'). It becomes profitable to exploit this market. This is indeed a necessary departure point in analysis, but it does not tell us why these kinds of goods are produced and consumed and not others. Clothes, for example, are important because they make the man: they express a personality, buttress a personality if it needs it, provide an artificial one if a real one is effectively lacking. So young people are interested in what they look like, how they project an image of themselves (for they are not too sure of themselves yet), particularly to the opposite sex they have so marvellously discovered. They are so insecure, in exchanging the controlled and hierarchical regularities of school for what is, for so many, visibly a dead-end job at the bottom of the ladder, in changing their status within the family (and soon in leaving it altogether), that they cling together and create a new world which quickly becomes powerfully normative.

Nothing is more striking than the way in which the very revolt of youth is so standardized. 'Deviance', indeed, has its quite prescriptive uniform and regalia, and fashion exercises as authoritative a sway over the beatniks as it does over the readers of Vogue. Hence the dictatorship of the 'Top Twenty' reflects and responds to far deeper wants than could ever be artificially induced by the most ingenious or unscrupulous public relations teams. Yet the media do command very considerable power, and the values they purvey are importantly internalized: when the young audience says that they'll buy it 'because it'll be a hit', they are at once internalizing commercial values (it will sell), and the social values of identification and solidarity with the culture of the peer-group: their friends will be playing it, dancing to it, and talking about it.

If youth is 'materialistic', this is precisely the path pioneered for them by their parents, and in particular by those who run the world in which their parents are pretty powerless and confused, too. . . . The inculcation of dispositions and values starts very early—and the parents start it. The middle-class striver, for example, has his 'deferred gratification' pattern well built into his psyche during that brief period between potty and primary school: his life is a career-pattern—and he sees it as such—long before he enters the world of work.

For him, the phase of independent 'youth culture' is less defined. He can never be as 'free' as the young worker, anyhow, since he is still financially dependent on the state or parents, and socially is pressurized to remain sexually immature: he is not supposed to have an adult sex life, and is highly discouraged from marrying (particularly if he is attracted to a girl of the wrong class). At a time when the age of puberty begins earlier, and in a society in which working class youth are marrying ever younger, the conflicts and contrasts are immense and full of tensions.

Those at the top pass from the private sector of the educational system through to the universities, scooping up the Oxbridge open scholarships with the confidence that has characterized the modern public schoolboy since he was invented in the mid-nineteenth century. At the other end, the doors are closed: 2 per cent of the children of semi- and unskilled manual workers reach the universities. Even so, every fourth students in the provincial universities comes from quite modest origins. They often identify powerfully with the 'Opportunity State': after all, they themselves have 'made it', so they know it to be true. They do not need to internalize an ideology of social mobility: it is the story of their success by referring to 'intelligence', 'personality', 'hard work', or 'ambition'. Those who didn't, 'explain' their failure as due to lack of 'influence', or 'contacts', or lack of education.

The 'failures' adapt, not necessarily by challenging society's criteria of what 'failure' or 'success' consists in, but by 'explaining' their 'failure' within the 'rules of the game'—they weren't taught to play properly, or other people cheated, but the game is, in principle, a fair one. Equality of opportunity is accepted as equality. Even so, since they know that money can 'buy' brains, and thereby re-engender wealth, status, and power, there is a chronic bitterness. They also adapt by lowering their threshold of aspirations.

British Society 1
T. Lupton

Reprinted with permission from 'The Culture is Wrong', *New Society*, 22 September, 1966.

Economic explanations of Britain's inability to maintain even a moderate rate of economic growth are nowadays frequently accompanied by reference to lack of moral fibre, absence of positive leadership, false ideologies, petty sectional interests, and latterday Luddism. Politicans refer nostalgically to the 'Dunkirk spirit.' We hear of 'wreckers' who promote class warfare and spread false economic doctrines. Managers are urged to show more initiative and to learn imported skills from Harvard professors at summer schools. Even a sympathetic observer like Edward Shils can write of a 'constriction of imagination and aspiration' in contemporary Britain.

All this shows a growing awareness that some obstacles to growth are non-economic. It would be wrong to conclude, however, in an excess of George-Brownism, that mass conversion to the doctrine of national salvation through individual effort is possible, or a solution. Since economic nostrums also have limited effect, it might be of use to attempt to identify socio-cultural obstacles to higher productivity and healthy growth.

British social structure is demonstrably highly resistant to shifts towards greater equality of wealth, power, and educational and career opportunity. Yet it is commonly thought that educational and career opportunities have greatly improved in the last 50 years. This gap between fact and belief could well be at the root of much of the dissatisfaction, frustration and cynicism which can be found in the 'lower' strata of British society, and which affect responses to appeals for greater effort, and attitudes to new machinery and administrative methods.

At the top of British society, access to key positions is based too much on family connection and type of school and university, and not enough on intrinsic merit and educational and economic achievement, irrespective of social background. This has often been stated and as often challenged. My own inquiries show there is more hard evidence to back it up than to contradict it. Its effect could be a plethora of polished duffers in seats of power, or of able men ill-equipped to run the institutions of a technically complex siege economy, or both. Traditional values perpetuated by educational exclusiveness, inherited leadership, amateur 'all-roundism', continuity, cultured leisure and leisured inquiry and what Tawney once referred to as 'the sentimental aroma of an aristocratic legend'—all these may be thought to suffocate the urge for radical reform and the growth of specialized professional competences.

The importance for economic development of having the right kind of elites has often been emphasized. Perhaps we have inherited the wrong kind. It is true that our traditional elites are highly absorbent, but so pervasive is the 'sentimental aroma' that it mellows the absorbed, and sours the rejected. The extent to which our economic performance has been inhibited by these factors merits closer inquiry.

The increasing traffic between Whitehall and the business world is usually thought of either as an example of pressure group activity, or as evidence of growing consensus—both healthy symptoms. In a persuasive article J. P. Nettl has thrown serious doubts on these interpretations. The facts he adduces, and the logic of the situations he describes, suggest rather that big business is infected by bureaucratic values and procedures and that businessmen are weaned from their proper concerns. They, too, play the Whitehall game and become amateur all-rounders. Another example, it would appear, of the propensity of our institutions, and the values which suffuse them, to blunt the qualities needed for highly specialized performance, and to misuse talent.

Again, it would be difficult, on present evidence, to prove a direct causal connection in the wrong direction between the processes of economic decision-making in Whitehall and business efficiency, productivity and growth; but the idea is worth following up.

From a different perspective McLelland provides theoretical backing for the general line of argument pursued so far.

Careful psychological experiments and thorough international comparisons together lead him to the view that economic development depends upon individuals with 'high achievement need'—which is, put crudely, a mental state which induces vigorous pursuit of self-generated standards of excellence, a kind of lay Puritan ethic.

Traditional values stifle it. McLelland's remedy is to arrange the primary socialization of children and subsequent social experience to increase the supply of persons with high achievement need, and to alter social arrangements to create opportunities for its full expression. It might be that Britain produces too many who complacently accept traditional standards, and discourages those who do not.

The sociological evidence about top people is thin, perhaps because sociologists, whose nosing around is an implied threat to the status quo, are unwelcome among them. Much more is known about the lesser folk. Little and Westergaard have recently reviewed the state of knowledge. They conclude that, though inequalities of access to secondary education have been (expectably) reduced in the last half century, the reduction has been small. Increased opportunity has been given to working class children, but many of them, for class-cultural and economic reasons, have been unable to benefit fully. For the same reasons many bright ones fail even to gain entrance. The significant increase in university places has been taken up mainly by middle class children.

Over the same period, rates of social mobility have altered hardly at all. This indicates perhaps that what we have gained by a limited increase in educational opportunity has been lost by the closing up of extra-educational channels of mobility as some sectors of economic life have become increasingly bureaucratic and professional.

Plainly, at all levels, despite the movement of some individuals, the structure of our class system has remained so far impervious to radical reform. This is more than just a matter of occupational inertia. Class differences are also differences in life chances and styles of living. The classes are separated by social and geographical distance, by barriers of communication, by differences of speech idiom and techniques of culture transmission, of intellectual climate, in patterns of consumption, and in leisure pursuits. It is a moot point whether the mass media, reflecting and emphasizing as they do distinctions in the social structure, make a desirable impact.

A favourite theme of after-dinner speakers is the need in the interests of economic efficiency to end once and for all the talk of 'two sides' in industry. We are all in the same boat now, they say, and in a rough sea we ought not to rock it. A more refined version of the same theme says that the separation of industrial ownership and control has given rise to a new breed of professional managers, efficient and dedicated to the public weal. Entry to the new technocracy is open, it is said, to the humblest if the talent is there. No one wants to grind the faces of the poor any more for the sake of profit. So Marx was wrong, and Burnham was right, and trade unions are an anachronism and declarations by businessmen about industrial relations make sense.

It sound good. Unfortunately, the facts do not point in that direction. In the first place, technological advance and increases in scale of business operation have emphasized career discontinuities between managers and non-managers—which are already implicit in the social structure, as Lloyd Warner showed long ago. The professionalization of the middling ranks of management, and the growth of large-scale national and international organizations has now produced what Watson has called the 'spiralist,' a mobile man with no firm social roots, a very different animal from the working man tied by kin, occupation and life style to the local community. There are few, if any, crosscutting ties between the two groups to moderate the conflicts between them which arise from division of function and cultural incongruence, and the quarrels over access to scarce power, cash and satisfaction at work.

The working class has not escaped the consequence of technical change. A more complex and minute division of labour has threatened many traditional occupational interests and allegiances, and hallowed working practices. For this reason, among others, the increased power and security brought by full employment has seen a tightening, rather than a relaxation of protective practices, and increasing conflicts of interest between occupational groups. It is misleading to consider that these processes, when taken together with the growth of technical and white collar occupations, are evidence of the break-up of the working class and its cultures and institutions. Common patterns of residence and style of life, an oral tradition of culture transmission, and common experience of relative deprivation and the expectation of deference to one's 'betters' preserve solidarity and an equalitarian ethos. All this is in sharp contrast to the competitive culture of the career professional, and the ways of the traditional 'cultured' elite.

This analysis helps to explain the persistence of restrictive practices, and the alienation of union leaders from rank and file difficulties of geographical redeployment of the labour force and retraining.

It might be comforting if, in the middle ranks of society, the managerial revolutionaries were on the march—dedicated technocrats and super-organizers moving into the seats of power. But some evidence from a recent study reveals that if the separation of ownership and control has produced a new breed of trained salaried managers, they are strangely absent from the boardrooms of British industry, where the cult of the amateur still persists. It is not difficult to see why education for management is so difficult to get off the ground.

If our social class structure, with its fairly distinct and discrepant subcultures, stifles movement and change, and produces conflict, there is at least one positive goal the politicians and the advertisers have got us all to agree about —that to accumulate material possessions is good, and that a man is judged and socially categorized as much by these as by his intrinsic worth or proven achievement. This being so, barriers to accumulation arising from doubtfully legitimated social inequalities, may well channel energies into doubtfully legitimated means of accumulation in attempts to buy intangible signs of social prestige. This is a partial explanation of the increase in crime. Taken together with the boring and uninteresting work which technical progress brings for working men and women, it serves also as a partial explanation of fiddles, restrictive practices, 'instrumental' attitudes to work, and a resentment of technical and administrative pushes to higher effort and efficiency.

We seem, in short, to be suffering from severe cultural 'lag.' Our social structure and institutions and their values on the one hand, and our economic goals on the other, are strangely but perhaps understandably incongruent. We have no social regulators to prevent cultural hangovers, to compare with the post-Keynesian economic regulators we now confidently and hopefully deploy. Perhaps, as some suggest, drastic wage freezes and stiff central controls will force a change of attitudes and set off the required social changes. Experience does not bear this out.

Patient research, enlightened administration, better (or more appropriate) education and training, improved occupational selection, the encouragement of talent, and a campaign against snobbery, privilege and incompetence—all these combined might help. But one sometimes wonders whether we have been irrevocably entranced by the fatal charms of social continuity, tolerant and civilized incompetence, and a moderately growing material affluence.

British Society 2
E. Shils

Reprinted with permission from P. Hall (Editor): *Labour's New Frontiers*, London, André Deutsch, 1964, pp. 6–16.

British society today certainly is no paradise. Yet as human societies go, its attainments, in recent decades, are very considerable. It has made great progress in the present century towards the moral equality which is a sine qua non of a good society. The level of material well-being of previously horribly, impoverished strata has been greatly improved. The weak, the defenceless, the young, the failures are better cared for than ever before, and even where the actual care remains markedly insufficient, solicitous concern exists and promises real improvement in the future. Educational opportunity is diffusing more widely than ever before the capacity to share in the cultural inheritance, to broaden the range of intellectual and aesthetic experience and to acquire the skills and qualifications necessary for occupational and professional achievement. It has continued to remain in the front ranks of the pioneers of scientific research. It has renounced with relatively good grace its empire which was until quite recently, among its greatest glories, and among the greatest creations of world history. The country has had stable government and the government has remained democratic. The institutional machinery for the public conduct of conflict and for the peaceful adjudication of contention is likewise fairly good by any realistic standard. Civility remains high. The manners of public life are relatively gentle and considerate. The political system, although far from meeting ideal standards, has at least not collapsed as it has in France. Public liberties have remained more or less intact. There are no large parties which are so alienated from the rest of the political system that they are committed to the subversion of the existing constitution, as in Italy and France. Its immunity from ideological fevers has not had to be acquired, as in contemporary Germany, by recuperation from a long bout of murderous madness.

Yet the situation in Britain today distresses many who contemplate it. They are, quite reasonably, not content that there should be no growth in virtues already acquired. Sometimes distress over present shortcomings blinds critics to the accomplishments, persisting and recent, of British society, but our awareness of their blindness does not invalidate their criticisms. There still remain, despite the transformation of the public appearance of the ancient regime, very deep strata of 'darkest England', of hierarchical harshness, of contemptuous hostility towards the weak and unsuccessful. There are still pockets of misery particularly among the aged. A 'race problem' is beginning to emerge in and at the edges of the Negro and Indian ghettoes in some of the larger cities. The educational system at nearly every level is unable to cope with the increased numbers who should be educated, and it is contorted by its inegalitarian inheritance. The inter-university hierarchy and the inferior dignity of technological studies, both of which are related to the class system of this country, are still alive and injurious to the fruitfulness in life and in society of whose who suffer at the lower strata of these hierarchies. Much of the urban physical environment—especially housing accommodation and amenities—is inconvenient far past the point necessitated by modern technology, and it is hideously ugly. The major provincial centres are dreary and boring. Political and economical leadership, although generally virtuous and mild mannered, is unimaginative and inspires little confidence; it is lacking in initiative and self-confidence. The British economy, which must provide the wherewithal for the next necessary improvements, is encumbered by archaic practices and arrangements, and both at its top and at its bottom it shows the constraints and distortions of its hierarchical traditions. The enormous progress that has been made in the movement towards moral equality only makes more evident the crippling inequality and the powerful snobbery which still exist. The power of the aristocracy and gentry has been largely broken, but the aura of deference which attended that power still persists. This manifests itself in many ways, the most important of which is the inhibition of individuality and initiative.

One of the features of British society which impresses a foreign observer is its constrictedness of imagination and aspiration. There is a lack of vigour and daring in the conception of new possibilities of life and a too narrow radius of aspiration. In its older industries, there is an anxious adherence to past practices. Foreign models dominate the vision of those who would leave the British past behind. Those who try to break away into some new sphere seem to lack self-confidence and innovators are distrusted. Too little is expected of life and too little is expected from oneself and from others in the discovery of new ways of doing things. The demand for pleasure is too restricted; curiosity too confined to conventional paths.

It is true that there are variations in this picture of the situation. Certain industries do attempt to find better techniques through research; there are great scientists at the height of their power, at work in the country. Some new universities are trying out new syllabi; certain local education authorities introduce innovations. But on the whole, they stand out by their rarity. It is in the younger generation throughout British society that the compression of desire which the traditions of Biritish society demand is less willingly accepted. The 'youth culture' which includes pop music, sartorial elegance, early sexual intercourse, motor-bikes and juvenile delinquency, is part of this refusal. These all express a new aesthetic sensitivity, a greater appreciation of more diverse experiences and a livelier contact with other human beings. Yet there too, in this most notable manifestation of spirit, one perceives a readiness to retract under the pressure of adulthood, into a more confined 'life-space', more like that in which the elders have been living.

The class system which took form in the 19th and early 20th centuries in this country demanded a lot both from those who were its obvious beneficiaries and those who were its obvious victims. From those at the bottom, it demanded more than obedience, it demanded respectability. There were many who did not conform but they were outcasts; they were expected neither to 'get on' nor even to hold their own before the universal dangers of unemployment, dependence on charity and base impulse. An iron discipline which looked straight ahead and not very far and a steady attendance to obligation did not leave much room for the opening of imagination or sensibility. The religion of respectability and the religious beliefs of the respectable reinforced what was necessitated by private property, scarcity and the police. Respectability entailed not only self-restraint, it entailed deference to one's betters, which involved self-derogation.

The obvious beneficiaries had their own religion of respectability too. It was a respectability which was less confining but it was acquired by a discipline in institutions which restricted the range of experience and narrowed the imagination. It had the great advantages that those who survived it felt themselves qualified for anything. It was a discipline which was integral to ruling. Those who passed through it went on to the Civil Service, the Indian Civil Service, the Colonial Service, politics, the law, and the Anglican clergy which in those days was much closer to the atmosphere of ruling than it is today when it lives in miasmal depression. Those who followed none of these paths still inhaled the air which is breathed by rulers.

Had Britain been a rather rich, hierarchical society without an empire, like Sweden, those at the top might not have felt so ascendant. But having an empire meant that India and Africa, and parts of the Middle and Far East were also in a sense the lower strata of British society, the peak of which was the destined inheritance of the successful survivors of institutional discipline. The 'effortless superiority of the Balliol man' or of any man who had successfully passed other parts of the institutional system was the product of a sense of confidence. Their mere 'being' qualified them to do what had to be done—to administer, to do research, to understand the essentials of any problem and to take the action called for.

The great changes within national societies and between them in the present century have eroded the ascendancy of the beneficiaries of the British system of stratification. Within Britain the continuous growth of democracy has almost obliterated the power of the aristocracy and it has especially diminished its symbolic grandeur; and the growth of trade union power and the nationalization of major industries has restricted the power of the plutocracy. The dissolution of the Empire and increasing real independence of the English-speaking dominions have contracted the size of the society over which the British elite—and British society as a whole—were superordinated.

These two simultaneous diminutions of the power of the British elite have had tremendous consequences for the life of present day Britain. The elite have lost that sense of effortless superiority which came from 'being' what they were. Their diminution has laid them open to self-criticism and to criticism by those who shared in their glory. Those over whom they ruled at home are now no longer so impressed by the standard which they represented or by the ideal of respectability which was its immediate derivative. Humiliated pride and once repressed resentment both come forward now.

British society is no longer regarded by those who live in it as a repository of a charismatic quality which exalted its members and imposed itself on the world. Pride in being British is no longer what it was. There is little confidence that one's inherited pattern of institutions and culture or one's own party has the answers to important questions. There is a critical spirit abroad. Much of it is a nagging criticism and offers only archaic solutions to real problems.

British Society 3
R. H. Tawney

Reprinted with permission from R. H. Tawney: *The Acquisitive Society*, London, Victor Gollancz, 1937, pp. 9–10.

It is a commonplace that the characteristic virtue of Englishmen is their power of sustained practical activity, and their characteristic vice a reluctance to test the quality of that activity by reference to principles. They are incurious as to theory, take fundamentals for granted, and are more interested in the state of the roads than their place on the map. And it might fairly be argued that in ordinary times that combination of intellectual tameness with practical energy is sufficiently serviceable to explain, if not to justify, the equanimity with which its possessors bear the criticism of more mentally adventurous nations. It is the mood of those who have made their bargain with fate and are content to take what it offers without re-opening the deal. It leaves the mind free to concentrate undisturbed upon profitable activities, because it is not distracted by a taste for unprofitable speculations. Most generations, it might be said, walk in a path which they neither make nor discover, but accept; the main thing is that they should march. The blinkers worn by Englishmen enable them to trot all the more steadily along the beaten road, without being disturbed by curiosity as to their destination.

But if the medicine of the constitution ought not to be made its daily food, neither can its daily food be made medicine. There are times which are not ordinary, and in such times it is not enough to follow the road. It is necessary to know where it leads, and, if it leads nowhere, to follow another. The search for another involves reflection, which is uncongenial to the bustling people who describe themselves as practical, because they take things as they are and leave them as they are. But the practical thing for a traveller who is uncertain of his path is not to proceed with the utmost rapidity in the wrong direction: it is to consider how to find the right one. And the practical thing for a nation which has stumbled upon one of the turning points of history is not to behave as though nothing very important were involved, as if it did not matter whether it turned to the right or to the left, went up hill or down dale, provided that it continued doing with a little more energy what it has done hitherto; but to consider whether what it has done hitherto is wise, and, if it is not wise, to alter it.

When the broken ends of its industry, its politics, its social organization, have to be pieced together after a catastrophe, it must make a decision; for it makes a decision even if it refuses to decide. If it is to make a decision which will wear, it must travel beyond the philosophy momentarily in favour with the proprietors of its newspapers. Unless it is to move with the energetic futility of a squirrel in a revolving cage, it must have a clear apprehension both of the deficiency of what is, and of the character of what ought to be. And to obtain this apprehension it must appeal to some standard more stable than the momentary exigencies of its commerce or industry or social life, and judge them by it. It must, in short, have recourse to Principles.

Further Reading: **Values**

† R. K. MERTON: *Social Theory and Social Structure*, New York, Free Press, 1957.

T. BRENNAN, E. W. COONEY, AND H. POLLINS: *Social Changes in South West Wales*, London, Watts & Co., 1954.

* J. FAWCETT (AND OTHERS): *Human Rights*, London, Heinemann, 1967.

* J. C. FLUGEL: *Man, Morals and Society*, London, Penguin Books, 1955.

S. M. LIPSET: *Political Man*, London, Heinemann, 1960.

K. MANNHEIM: *Ideology and Utopia*, New York, Harcourt Brace & Co., (First pub.: 1936).

* W. E. MOORE: *Social Change*, New York, Prentice Hall, 1963.

* E. J. B. ROSE & associates: *Colour & Citizenship*, London, Institute of Race Relations & Oxford University Press, 1969.

* M. SHANKS: *The Stagnant Society*, London, Penguin Books, 1965.

* H. STREET: *Freedom, Society and the Individual*, London, Penguin Books, 2nd edition, 1968.

B. WILSON: *Religion in Secular Society*, London, Watts & Co., 1966.

* Available in paperback
† Reference

Textbook Reference

As we pointed out in the Introduction, this book of Readings is not intended as a substitute for conventional textbooks, any more than it is hoped to supplant the reading of original material.

The aims and intentions are that the easy availability of original material in the form of a Reader will increase the value of courses organized round one or other of the major textbooks in the field, or a basic lecture course in 'Modern Britain'.

Accordingly we compiled a list of the textbooks which seemed to be in most common use in teaching courses of this type, and in introductory sociology generally. We then traced out the major themes which seemed to be important within the institutional areas which form the framework of this book of Readings, whether we had been able to select readings in these areas or not. Although there are doubtless many other texts which could be included and many more will be on the market within a short time, there seem to be advantages for the student in having a readily accessible summary of the *comparative* coverage of the major textbooks, and of the areas within which one is substitutable for another. In our experience, a good deal of disillusion and disappointment on the part of students can be associated with inappropriate advice about textbooks, and a lack of guidance about which texts are relevant for particular sections of a course.

It would be wrong to consider Josephine Klein's *Samples from English Cultures* as a textbook but it is included because it contains material relevant to most of our chapters.

The annotations are derived from a systematic and comprehensive survey of the contents of each chapter. No references are given for the chapter on values because of the special nature of that selection.

BOTTOMORE, T. B. *Sociology: A Guide to Problems and Literature*, London, George Allen and Unwin, 1962.

BREDEMEIER, H. C. AND STEPHENSON, R. M. *The Analysis of Social Systems*, New York, Holt Rinehart and Winston, 1962.

BROOM, L. AND SELZNICK, P. *Sociology, A Text with Adapted Readings*, London, Harper and Row, 1965 (International Student Reprint, 1968, page numbering different).

CHINOY, ELY. *Society: An Introduction to Sociology*, New York, Random House, 1961.

COTGROVE, S. F. *The Science of Society* (An Introduction to Sociology), London, George Allen and Unwin, 1967, Hardback and paperback (Minerva Series No. 19).

JOHNSON, H. M. *Sociology: A Systematic Introduction*, London, Routledge & Kegan Paul, 1961

KLEIN, J. *Samples from English Cultures*, London, Routledge & Kegan Paul, 1965

MCIVER, R. M. AND PAGE, C. H. *Society: An Introductory Analysis*, London, Macmillan, 1964.

MITCHELL, G. D. *Sociology: The Study of Social Systems*, London, University Tutorial Press Ltd., 1959

OGBURN, W. F. AND NIMKOFF, M. F. *A Handbook of Sociology*, London, Routledge & Kegan Paul, 1960, 4th edition

SMELSER, N. J. (ED.). *Sociology: An Introduction*, New York, London, Sydney, John Wiley & Sons Inc., 1967.

1. Family

DIVORCE: Bottomore, 170–2; Bredemeier & Stephenson, 208–12; Broom & Selznick, 358–9, 419; Chinoy, 128, 156; Cotgrove, 62–4; Johnson, 171–5; Klein, 155–219, 283–302, 331–51; McIver & Page, 258–63; Ogburn & Nimkoff, 457–60.

SEX BEHAVIOUR: Bredemeier & Stephenson, 178–85, 201–3; Broom & Selznick, 365–8, 385; Chinoy, 115–17; Cotgrove, 47–9, 57–8; Johnson, 147–9; Klein, 146–55, 524–30, 567, 569, 576, 584–6; Mitchell, 67–70; Ogburn & Nimkoff, 228–9; Smelser, 373–4.

KINSHIP SYSTEM: Bottomore, 172–4; Bredemeier & Stephenson, 190–3, 208; Broom & Selznick, 39, 355–6; Chinoy, 110–13; Cotgrove, 43–5; Johnson, 177–200; Klein, 131–42, 185–93; McIver & Page, 591–6; Mitchell, 53–76; Ogburn & Nimkoff, 444–5; Smelser, 508–16, 535–43, 720–2.

EXTENDED FAMILY: Bottomore, 165–6; Bredemeier & Stephenson, 194, 205; Broom & Selznick, 355, 358–60; Cotgrove, 59–62; Johnson, 155–60; Klein, 54–7, 160–1; Smelser, 517.

2. Community

TYPES OF COMMUNITY: Bottomore, 94–5; Broom & Selznick, 31–2; Klein, 74–90, 94–6; Ogburn & Nimkoff, 267–9; Smelser, 96–102, 144–50, 674–85.

3. Socialization

4. Work

5. Class

Fontana Modern Masters

A series edited by Frank Kermode, who writes as follows:

'By Modern Masters we mean the men who have changed and are changing the life and thought of our age. Everybody wants to know who they are and what they say, but hitherto it has often been very difficult to find out. This series makes it easy. Each volume is clear, concise and authoritative. Nothing else can offer in such an acceptable form, an assured grasp of these revolutionary thinkers.'

Published:

CAMUS	*Conor Cruise O'Brien*
CHOMSKY	*John Lyons*
FANON	*David Caute*
GUEVARA	*Andrew Sinclair*
LÉVI-STRAUSS	*Edmund Leach*
LUKÁCS	*George Lichtheim*
MARCUSE	*Alasdair MacIntyre*

In preparation:

FREUD	*Richard Wollheim*
JOYCE	*John Lyons*
MAILER	*Richard Poirier*
MCLUHAN	*Jonathan Miller*
ORWELL	*Raymond Williams*
REICH	*Charles Rycroft*
WITTGENSTEIN	*David Pears*

And many more to follow

Fontana Philosophy Classics

Texts and anthologies, with substantial introductions

Fontana Classics of History and Thought

Fontana Books about the Study of History

Debates with Historians
Pieter Geyl
'If I were asked to name the historian whom I have most venerated in my lifetime, I should not hesitate for an answer. I should name: Pieter Geyl.' A. J. P. TAYLOR, *Observer*

To the Finland Station
Edmund Wilson
This classic analysis of the intellectual origins of communism is subtitled 'A Study in the Writing and Acting of History'. It is, in the words of Philip Toynbee in the *Observer*, 'a marvel of industrious scholarship and narrative power'.

Lectures on Modern History
Lord Acton
Introduced by Hugh Trevor-Roper, who discusses some of the reasons why Acton's greatness is more apparent in our times than it was in his.

The Practice of History
G. R. Elton
'An important book', HUGH TREVOR-ROPER, *Sunday Times*. 'An admirable manifesto . . . lucidity and forcefulness, two qualities he demands of the historian as writer, are here in good measure'. C. B. MACPHERSON, *Listener*

Christianity and History
Herbert Butterfield
'At once simple and profound . . . if Acton gave the classic statement of the one side, Butterfield has now given the classic statement of the other . . .' *Observer*

Fontana Philosophy and Theology

Bertrand Russell and the British
Tradition in Philosophy
D. F. Pears
'One can say with confidence that everyone seriously inter-
ested in philosophy should read this book. It is very good
indeed.' MARY WARNOCK, *Listener*

Sartre
Iris Murdoch
'Really constructive criticism, wide-ranging, faithful to its
subject.' STUART HAMPSHIRE, *New Statesman*

Symbolism and Belief
Edwyn Bevan
In the Gifford lectures a famous scholar discusses the truth
of the symbols employed in the expression of religious beliefs.

The Tragic Sense of Life
Miguel de Unamuno
The masterpiece of Spain's greatest writer since Cervantes—
the last of the great Romantic protests and the one that opened
the way for Existentialism.

Ethics
Dietrich Bonhoeffer
The author's most important single work.

The Humanity of God
Karl Barth
'Theology has had many talents in our time, but no other
genius.' ALASDAIR MACINTYRE, *The Guardian*